# THE POLITICAL THOUGHT OF SAINT-SIMON

# THE POLITICAL THOUGHT OF SAINT-SIMON

Edited by
GHIȚA IONESCU



OXFORD UNIVERSITY PRESS
1976

*Oxford University Press, Ely House, London W. 1*
GLASGOW NEW YORK TORONTO MELBOURNE WELLINGTON
CAPE TOWN IBADAN NAIROBI DAR ES SALAAM LUSAKA ADDIS ABABA
DELHI BOMBAY CALCUTTA MADRAS KARACHI LAHORE DACCA
KUALA LUMPUR SINGAPORE HONG KONG TOKYO

CASEBOUND ISBN 0 19 874018 2
PAPERBACK ISBN 0 19 874019 0



Printed in Great Britain by
Richard Clay (The Chaucer Press), Ltd.
Bungay, Suffolk

# Contents

# Introduction

This collection is presented to the public on the double assumption that there is a general interest in the work of Claude-Henri de Saint-Simon and a more special interest in his *political* thought. The distinction between these two types of interest requires some further explanation.

As far as general interest is concerned, it should be noted here that for the last five years or so anyone wishing to read this classic work of the social sciences in English could do so only in borrowed copies. All previous editions, including F. H. Markham's particularly useful selection, published in 1952, have long been out of print. Though there have been French, German, Spanish and Russian editions, the complete works of Saint-Simon have never been available in English. This circumstance has increased the demand for anthologies and collections in English; the supply of these has already proved to be inadequate.

But a reservation should be made at the start on the subject of the general interest that Saint-Simon's work might have for contemporary readers. From the general point of view Saint-Simon, like most social or political philosophers, can be read either literally or in its perspectives. If read literally, the works of Aristotle, Bodin or Hobbes are difficult, and frequently unpalatable because they contain assumptions or attitudes no longer consonant with our own as, for instance, Aristotle's shocking attitudes towards slavery and women. Saint-Simon's work is perhaps one of the most vulnerable to this charge of archaism. Read literally now, it strikes us by its characteristic naïvety, even utopianism. This quality may seem to condemn it to take its place among the 'great designs' which flourished in the decades of the end of the eighteenth and the beginning of the nineteenth centuries. Saint-Simon's work could be called the 'great social design'. Moreover his work, when read literally, is often tedious because of his repetitive, homiletic and seemingly inconsequential approaches to his subject. But this is not how we read social and political philosophers. We read them in order to distil from them the conceptual essence valid at all times and in all situations. We also reinterpret them with every generation, adjusting them to our own views, as I shall show at greater length. But this raises the problem of anachronism, the trap open under the feet of all interpreters of classical political thought. Whether this presentation of Saint-Simon is anachronistic, will be discussed in these pages and in the conclusions reached here.

## I. THE POLITICS OF THE INDUSTRIAL-TECHNOLOGICAL SOCIETY

The lack of English versions of Saint-Simon's work has been all the more noticeable since the advent of the industrial-technological society has encouraged the circulation of his ideas once more. The number of new studies of Saint-Simon published since, say, the mid-fifties shows a disproportionate increase when compared with the figures for other decades (although public interest in Saint-Simon's work has always been, both in his life time and since his death, capricious and intermittent). But another and more substantial proof of this renewal of interest is to be found in the general accolade which all the philosophers of the 'post-industrial' or 'industrial-technological' society, like Daniel Bell or François Perroux, have given him.

Does this mean that, seen in the light of our incipient knowledge and understanding of the industrial-technological society, Saint-Simon's work now appears to us to contain a general theory of the industrial-technological society? This depends on how one defines the industrial-technological society and on how one characterizes Saint-Simon's work.

This is not the place to expound a general theory of the industrial-technological society[1] (I have tried to do this in my book *Centripetal Politics*). But a working definition can be proposed as follows. The advent of the industrial-technological society produces at least two specific features: the rapid transition

1. The reasons for which the name 'industrial-technological society' is used here in preference to 'industrial society' (Aron), 'post-capitalist society' (Dahrendorf), and 'post-industrial society' (Daniel Bell), will be shown later in this Introduction (see *infra*, p. 30f.). But the concept of 'industrial-technological society' is founded on the three above-named theories which can be seen as different versions—even stages—of a similar interpretation of the industrial society which has been developed since the Second World War. Raymond Aron's theory of the industrial society asserted the concept of 'industrial' as against 'developed', 'modern' or 'capitalist' society, with all the implications in political theory and in comparative politics which this entails. Ralf Dahrendorf's theory of the post-capitalist society developed the principle of the separation of the power of decision-making in society from the economic power of ownership. Daniel Bell's theory of the post-industrial society emphasizes especially the major changes produced in the industrial society by the post-Second World War technological revolution: the prevalence of science and of knowledge, the change from a goods-producing to a service economy, etc.

from manufacturing to service industry and the application of theoretical knowledge to all phenomena of industrial life. It then becomes a new type of society, different from the industrial society from which it emerged, and which it has been in the process of transforming ever since the end of the Second World War.

Also by way of a working definition, let us propose that Saint-Simon's central theory can broadly be described as the prediction that the industrial society of the future will be 'administered, as against governed' by a condominium of the 'industrialists', i.e. both the employers and organized labour, and by the 'scientists' and 'technologists'. (Saint-Simon's theory will unfold itself as this Introduction progresses, and there will be ample opportunity to discuss all his concepts.)

If one takes the definitions of the industrial-technological society and of Saint-Simon's theory as proposed, they clearly fit together. Nevertheless, we must admit at once that for the sake of achieving this essential link-up, we have to oversimplify rather ruthlessly, and to overlook the vast differences between the dramatic realities of the industrial society as it has emerged today, and the allegories which Saint-Simon used to describe it, long before it could be discerned clearly. In particular Saint-Simon failed to foresee the terrible scars and deformations which capitalism and the class struggle which it engendered have inflicted on the industrial society. This is the Achilles' heel of his discourse.

But this is a good point from which to continue because this cross-fertilization of his old theory with the new reality, is produced by the changes in the historical perspective of capitalism. Industrial societies can develop without being capitalistic. More undeniably still they can continue to exist after capitalism has been abolished. We have today, under our eyes, the living proof that formidable as it is, the course of capitalism is historically and geographically more limited than the course of the industrial society. We see this currently in the very fact of the existence of the industrial communist societies. But at the same time sociologists and economists have found so many structural differences between the 'old' and the 'modern' capitalism, that they have put forward the new concept of the post-capitalist society—Ralf Dahrendorf's work is the *locus classicus* of this approach.

Saint-Simon's theory was criticized by Marx, and many others, as 'utopian' because, among other reasons, his model of the future industrial society took practically no account of capitalism and of the struggle of the economic classes formed by capitalism. But among the new features of the industrial-technological society there are three which can be seen as basic trends of change in the capitalist system. One is that the importance of the private owner of capital and of the role of private capital in production have become relative (many major industries are nationalized, and the individual owner/entrepreneur of the Rockefeller, Nuffield or Thyssen type is now gradually being replaced by impersonal boards as well as by charismatic managers of the Mattei type). The second is that the functional differentiation of roles, status and control between the technical and managerial élites and the bulk of organized labour has become a characteristic feature of the industrial-technological society. In spite of intensive social mobility and constant broadening of the decision-making circles by virtue of the diversification of specialized technical know-how, it is this dichotomy between the technical, managerial and political élites on one side and the mass of workers, on the other, which is common to both communist and capitalist-industrial societies. This is why, and this is the third trait, the modern industrial decision-making processes, or what Galbraith perceptively called the 'group-decision-making', are essentially participatory. What is now sought is a way to achieve this intensive participation in decision-making.

These three major social changes or trends form the background to the current revival of interest in Saint-Simon's theory. His search for what seems to him the best organization for the future industrial(-technological) society is based on his contention that the future societies, free though they may be of economic constraints, will need new *political* organizations within which they can function.

To be sure, the presupposition that capitalism is being transformed, modernized, or indeed ushered out, is the subject of one of the principal controversies of our time. But it is also one of the working hypotheses of modern political economy, and this is where Saint-Simon comes back. Whereas Marx remains the economic and social critic of the *capitalist* society, Saint-Simon comes into his own as the political theoretician of the functioning of the *industrial* society. If one could overlook in Saint-Simon's theory the grave faults of omission, and if one were to deny Marxism the ability to adapt to new situations, one could say that once industrial societies, capitalist or communist, have revealed their functional basic similarities, Saint-Simon and his model of the functional organization of the industrial society offer a firmer conceptual grasp and a vaster comprehensiveness than does Marxism.

Can we go further and conclude that what is now being revealed as the new relevance of Saint-Simon's work eluded previous interpreters, most of whom did not have 'factual evidence available to them'? This is indeed a matter of *Zeitgeist*. Interpretations of works of social philosophy depend on the perception of the interpreter in his own environment, and are therefore open to suspicion as anachronistic. There are, according to a recent critic, nine basic Machiavellis.[2] The Marx of the fifties is the Marx of alienation; the Marx of the seventies is the Marx of anti-humanism. Rousseau of 1848 is libertarian; Rousseau of 1948 is totalitarian. Who reads Comte nowadays for information? Oakeshott's Hobbes and MacPherson's Hobbes can hardly be the same philosopher. Clashes of interpretation like these happen only too frequently.

But then there are some authors who, mostly because their works have never been fully explored or reconstituted, remain identified only with one particular approach, a flash-in-the-pan idea, a *leit-motiv* or even a system. Suarez, Vico, Benjamin Constant, Michels or Sorel are in the history of political thought such 'peaks', seen in their full light only by some zealots. But they remain clouded for the great majority of historians of political thought, the official custodians of reputations. The zealots claim that such authors are insufficiently acknowledged as representing turning-points in the history of ideas. The historians, on the other hand, are inclined to treat the ideas of such authors as early intuitions which were only later to find their proper formulators. But these intellectual St. John the Baptists haunt the official pantheons, and they are 'rediscovered' generation after generation and new, albeit contradictory, interpretations are put forward on their behalf. Saint-Simon is one of the most typical of these cases.

Gouhier's Saint-Simon or Durkheim's Saint-Simon, Proudhon's Saint-Simon or Hajek's Saint-Simon, to mention a very small proportion of this writer's interpreters, cannot be contained within one personality alone. Revolutionary, anti-Jacobin, anarchist, socialist, positivist, technocratic, proto-totalitarian, Christian-radical, these are only the principal ways in which disciples or critics have tried again and again, in different contexts, to identify him, '*tel qu'en lui-même enfin*'. Yet his work has continued to smile as inscrutably as Mona Lisa.

2. Claude Lefort, *Le Travail de l'œuvre Machiavel*, Paris, 1972. Sir Isaiah Berlin counted twenty-seven ways of interpreting *The Prince* only.

This should make us all aware of the danger of claiming one more—in our case because of the plausible relation between his predictions and the emerging realities of the industrial-technological society—that it was given to our *Zeitgeist* to see Saint-Simon in his full authenticity. The history of social thought is after all, like Stendhal's definition of a novel, only a mirror taken along a winding road, and whether from the long bend which our generation has happened to round, we have caught the most penetrating view yet of Saint-Simon will be for other generations to decide.

These provisos are an introductory caveat to the second question, asked at the beginning of this book: why Saint-Simon's *political* work? The collection presented here tries to contribute in a modest way to the current effort, undertaken simultaneously by French, Italian and American scholars, to get at Saint-Simon's *original* work, which has been so terribly scribbled-over by the grafitti of disciples or critics. One way of achieving this is to try to keep as closely as possible to Saint-Simon's own vocabulary. One of Saint-Simon's characteristic gifts was precisely to find the right and striking expression for what he actually wanted to say, even if this meant coining an expression, for instance the celebrated *positivism*. Nearer to our subject, he transformed the French adjective *industriel* into a noun: *l'industriel* or *les industriels*, (what we shall call 'industrialists') and he coined the expression '*industrialism*' as the name under which he wanted his doctrine to be known. Last but not least he was one of the first to speak of 'political science'.

It is therefore rather surprising that it was Durkheim, his most faithful, penetrating and generous interpreter, who committed the mistake of defining his work, first as an ideology or doctrine to be known as 'socialism', and then as a science to be known as 'sociology'—both anachronistic and extraneous expressions. What is worse, these were expressions which Saint-Simon had certainly heard, for they were already in use in his time, and which he could easily have adopted, since he never felt any inhibitions in using a name or an idea which suited the trend of his thought. Both 'socialism' and 'sociology' had already started their successful runs. They were ringing with novelty and Saint-Simon was in constant pursuit of novelty. Yet he deliberately ignored them and clung most resolutely to the, to him, value-free expression of 'system' for the first concept and of 'political science' for the second.

Like Marx, Saint-Simon did not want to be known as an ideologue, and here he succeeded in spite of the fact that, in circumstances to be explained later, the Saint-Simonians appropriated his work for a while. What he genuinely thought was that he was proposing a neutral, value-free, system, one might even say—by playing in turn anachronistically with words—a systems analysis, based on scientific conceptualization and empirical research, and through which he could predict what kind of institutions and processes the emerging industrial society would require. This is why, for instance, he indulged in the otherwise doubtful practice of offering his 'system' to everybody who exercized power in France after the fall of the Jacobins and of their heir Napoleon, both of whom, in his view, had usurped and deflected the industrial revolution. He offered it to the Congress of Vienna; he offered it to Charles X, he offered it to Louis XVIII. He offered it in particular to the 'industrialists', the new producers whom he thought should form their own party. Later in this Introduction it will be proved that because his functional approaches to the concepts of class, equality or ownership were so different from those of mainstream socialism he could not, *pace* Durkheim, fully qualify as a socialist. (And whether, as it is currently argued, functionalism itself is yet another normative approach, indeed another ideology, is a matter which goes beyond the limits of this discussion.)

In two respects Saint-Simon gave priority to the *political* content of his doctrine. First, Saint-Simon thought that his principal task was to find the political organization to suit the transformed society. Second, the conceptual centre of Saint-Simon's discourse is to be found in the political sphere, in his general (economic, sociological and political) theory of the industrial society.

To take the first point first. The aim of Saint-Simon's exhortations remains always the same: to change the institutional framework of feudal society so as to accommodate the forces and processes of the new, industrial society. Behind this continuity of purpose lies Saint-Simon's belief that the changes had already taken place functionally and that to delay the adjustment they required would only be to obstruct and suffocate the entire process. But the ways in which, according to him, this adjustment could be effected, gradually changed as his view itself was altered by age and by an increasing sense of hopelessness.

At first, in a period which lasted roughly from 1803 to 1817, he seems to have believed that all men of goodwill, from all classes and regardless of whether they were governors or governed, would see with their own eyes (helped by the new political science) the obvious changes taking place in the society. They would reasonably prepare themselves to occupy the new functions and roles assigned to them in the future meritocracy. This was the period when, as I have already mentioned, he offered his 'system' to anyone who had eyes to see, regardless of their different social and political positions. In fact he offered it first to those who were in or near the seat of power.

From 1817 to 1825 he was disappointed with and embittered by the crass resistance of the upper classes, and sensed the rapid split opening between the bourgeois leaders of industry and the mass or proletariat—the two wings of the large societal group of 'industrialists' which he had previously seen as functionally homogeneous. He then exhorted the latter to take themselves the lead in the action of deliverance, and to achieve this by force if necessary.

But this orientation towards voluntarism, or revolutionarism, was soon overshadowed by his concern with the ultimate values of the individuals who would be engaged in the great historical action; with what was later to be called, albeit with a different connotation, their consciousness. The collective *Bewusstsein* was not for him the perception by individuals of their relation with (participation in and commitment to) their social environment. It was the individual's own dialogue with God, conducted in terms of Christian ethics and of the Christian social principle of love of one's neighbour. The *New Christianity*, his last work, in many respects as sombre as the last Beethoven Quartets, in addition to the harsh attacks which it delivers against the Christian Churches and atheists alike, poses the fundamental question of the moral education and transformation of men themselves. Incidentally, this question is often asked, after the dizziness of triumph, by leaders of socialist revolutions, like Lenin, Mao and Tito, as they become increasingly concerned with the importance of the education of the new or socialist men without whom the new society will not materialize.

But even more important for the understanding of this selection of Saint-Simon's works is the realization of the way in which politics is situated at the centre of Saint-Simon's thought. It is the avowed contention of the present interpretation that the originality of Saint-Simon's work can best be grasped by focusing principally on his politics, i.e. on his interest in the processes of public decision-making,[3] and thus, to a certain

3. See, for a discussion of political science as the study of decision-making 'rather than power, legitimate authority or political system', W. J. McKenzie, 'The Study of Political Science Today', *Studies in Comparative Politics*, 1972, pp. 85–7.

extent, ignoring his study of economic and social structures. This is not the place nor the time to re-open the quarrel about the epistemological boundaries between, and relative priorities of, sociology and politics, and their buffer zone of political sociology. Durkheim, and after him Georges Gurvitch, claimed Saint-Simon for sociology.[4] But E. Vidal in his penetrating *Saint-Simon e la scienza politica*[5] for the first time made the point that, from a disciplinary angle, Saint-Simon belongs to political science. There is, of course, ample textual evidence that Saint-Simon himself described his ultimate 'scientific' competence and interest as lying in the realm of politics. 'We ought to acknowledge,' he says in *Le Politique*, '1. that politics has been until now a conjectural science; 2. that in the present state of knowledge politics can perhaps be raised to the level of the positive sicences; . . . and 3. that the social crisis in which the most advanced peoples of today are now engaged will not be totally terminated until the time when politics will be treated, cultivated and taught in the same way as physics, chemistry and physiology are taught today.'[6] Furthermore, in the proposed synopsis of *Le Politique* it is announced that the first part will deal with *la politique pure*, an ambitious purpose only emulated since by Bertrand de Jouvenel.[7]

There is also ample textual evidence that what Saint-Simon called political science, or the new science of politics, was the scientific observation, based on empirical research, as well as the conceptualization of observed phenomena which would enable the new science, like most other sciences, to predict the recurrence, or change, of these phenomena. 'A scientist, my friend, is one who can predict,' he boasted at the very beginning of his new career.[8]

The main principles of this new science were presented thus: 'Until now the methods of the sciences of observation were not introduced into the political question: everybody brought his or her own way of seeing, of reasoning. . . . The time has now come where this infancy of science must stop . . .: for it is from the obscurities of politics that the social trouble originates.'[9] This problem is pursued throughout his work, and was always described in the same words. Thus an entire chapter of

4. E. Durkheim, *Socialisme*, op. cit., p. 147. Georges Gurvitch, *Les fondateurs français de la Sociologie contemporaine*, I, *Saint-Simon Sociologue*, Paris, 1951.

5. E. Vidal, *Saint-Simon e la scienza politica*, Milan, 1959.

6. *Le Politique*, pp. 189–90.

7. Bertrand de Jouvenel, *De la politique pure*, Paris, 1960.

8. *Lettres d'un habitant de Genève à ses contemporains*, p. 36.

9. *De la Réorganisation de la Société Européenne*, p. 183.

*L'Industrie* was called the 'Political progress of industry', and interpreted as 'the knowledge of the ways in which industry could use power—and which is nothing else than a political plan'.[10] Later still, the problem comes to the fore again, as for instance in *Du Système Industriel*, where Saint-Simon states that 'politics is going through a great change, the change from the conjectured to the positive, from metaphysics to physics';[11] and in the *Catéchisme des Industriels* the same idea reappears in the more positive statement that 'our examination . . . will give to politics an entirely new character, it will change the nature of this branch of our knowledge.'[12] Saint-Simon's conception of 'political science' is thus very clear.

What is much less clear, however, is what exactly Saint-Simon means in principle by 'politics'. This raises again the inter-disciplinary question. First, Saint-Simon seems to attribute different objects to practical politics and political science. Further, there is a semantic nuance in the sense in which he uses the expression 'political science' which enables Vidal to assimilate it with contemporary political science or indeed, more specifically, with political sociology.[13] This seems to blur once more the differences between the two sciences and leave us with no clear-cut answer to the question of where to place Saint-Simon's work between them.

To be sure, Saint-Simon's contribution to sociology is enormous, both directly through his own work, and indirectly through the work of the founder of the science of sociology, Auguste Comte. The umbilical cord linking the work of the latter with that of Saint-Simon has never been properly severed. Should we, in the light of this close association, believe that the disciple went further in epistemological revelation and conceptual formulation than the master was able to go, given the limitations of his own personal and historical age? Or, on the contrary, should we believe that for Saint-Simon—as up to a point for the young Comte—the general study of society was only a preliminary exercise, the socio-economic background for

10. *L'Industrie*, pp. 141–50.

11. *Du Système Industriel*, p. 6.  12. *Catéchisme*, p. 15.

13. Which only begs the question of whether politics, and in particular political sociology, is part of, and subordinated to, sociology. Recently opposing views have been clearly expressed, among others by Raymond Aron in his *Études politiques*, Paris, 1972 (especially the essays on 'Science et conscience de la société' and 'De la théorie politique') and by Giovanni Sartori, in 'From the sociology of politics to Political Sociology' in *Government and Opposition*, Spring 1969. But see also W. J. McKenzie, op. cit., pp. 20–1 and Daniel Bell, *The Coming of Post-Industrial Society*, London, 1974, pp. 9–12.

the ultimate study of the political processes and institutions with which political science is concerned? The fact that Saint-Simon never changed his terminology might confirm the latter interpretation.

The real compatibility of purpose between Saint-Simon's work and classical sociology is of the greatest relevance to the entire problem of the political significance of this writer's *œuvre*. There is a conceptual junction at which the classic sociological approach and the basic political approach have to take their separate ways. This occurs when one poses the essential question whether politics is a perennial or a historical activity. Raymond Aron drew attention more than ten years ago to the pronounced bias of classic sociology, from the work of Comte and Marx onwards, against representative institutions, against representative politics in general, and ultimately against politics as a whole. Marx's antipathy towards politics and political institutions was an inevitable consequence of his theory of a future harmonious society of unfettered men of good will. This ideological escapism, inherent in classical sociology, leads, in the case of Marx, to the argument that if the future society is to be a conflictless society then politics, which according to Marx is an activity generated by conflict, and political organization, which according to Marx is based on coercion, will wither away because they are dispensable. Decisions will be made by mutual trust and social co-operation, without the need of institutions, which can only obstruct this new self-generating process.

It is on this question that conceptually Saint-Simon's position is opposed to that of classic sociology. To be sure, one of his basic theories (and one which Marx so clearly misappropriated) is that in the industrial society government will be replaced by the 'administration of things'. But read carefully, in the correct semantic and conceptual context of Saint-Simon's work, this never amounts to, and indeed is the contrary of, proclaiming the abolition of politics and the withering away of institutions. Saint-Simon believed that politics, which in an Aristotelian way he saw as the dialectics of decision-making, were perennial. But precisely because they were perennial, Saint-Simon believed that at the great turning-points of social history, politics (or at least what, for the want of a better word, one could call the *style* or the *technique* of politics) must be changed. He considered the one great turning-point in history to be the passage from the feudal to the industrial society. At this point he saw the need for a fundamental change in politics: from the decision-making processes of what he called the 'politics of power', to the decision-making processes of what he called '*la politique des abilités*', the 'politics of abilities'.[14]

Should this proposition be taken literally, to mean a denial of the concept of power itself, which would engage Saint-Simon in a battle royal with Machiavelli and Hobbes? Or, as I am more inclined to believe, should it be understood as the political corollary of the diffusion of power, effected directly by the coming of the participatory industrial-technological society? This is the question which is discussed in the fourth part of this Introduction. What is not in doubt, however, is that Saint-Simon believed that the perennial functioning of politics will continue in a new and appropriate framework of transformed political institutions and organization. It is here that the test of examining the terminology he employs and the vocabulary he imposes gives such positive results. For throughout the course of his fragmented and disjointed work not once does he abandon or change his key expressions: politics, political economy, political science and political organization. These expressions are the very pillars of his theoretical construction.

There are two further reasons for thinking that the key to the basic interpretation of Saint-Simon's entire theory of the industrial society is linked with his theory of politics. The first is that once the entire argument of his discourse is re-organized around the *political* nexus, most of the contradictions which mar his theory when it is seen from any other perspective, and which have had to be interpreted away in other presentations, are now reconciled. The new meaning incorporates what otherwise seem like the disjointed limbs of the body of his doctrine. The other reason is that once his inquiry is projected on to the value-free mechanics of decision-making, the discourse loses most of its normative, utopian ballast, and reduces itself to a scheme, or a method. We can then be much less hesitant in weeding out the extravagant allegoric examples, and in delineating the hard core of the analytical method. The entire work regains more of its original clarity and coherence.

## 2. THE ORIGINALITY OF SAINT-SIMON

Claude-Henri de Rouvroy, Comte de Saint-Simon had an extraordinary life. It was extraordinary, first, because of the period (1760–1825) over which it extended. It started with the American and French Revolutions, in both of which Saint-Simon was personally involved. It ended within sight of the Revolution of 1830, and the reforms which it brought about, in

14. See *infra*, p. 37 and p. 60, for an explanation of the translation.

the preparation of which he was also involved. Thus his journey in life took him from the feudal age, through political revolution, to the industrial society: from the age of absolute monarchy to the Napoleonic Empire and then the parliamentary régimes: from the age of metaphysics to the age of the social sciences.

Moreover, his life was extraordinary because of its pace, quickened (like that of a man running in a fast train) by his own metamorphoses, made as the world around him transformed itself under his far-seeing eyes. Born into the French aristocracy, a nephew of the Duke of Saint-Simon, the chronicler, member of a family descending from Charlemagne, he became at seventeen an officer in the battalions of the French army which fought in America. Then before, during and after the Revolution he was a successful entrepreneur, as behove a young gentleman in the new age of industry. This activity came to a stop at the very end of the eighteenth century: the nineteenth found him determined to be the founder of the new science of the industrial society. This resolve was made in spite of the fact that in the meantime he had been reduced to mendicity. To achieve his purpose he had to read and write all that mattered in a bare quarter of a century.

Finally, his life was extraordinary for the reputation he left behind him. This became a matter of bitter controversy between those who worshipped him and those who detested him. It is perhaps convenient at this point to give a selected bibliography of the principal studies, for and against him.

*For:* C. H. de Saint-Simon, *Sa vie écrite par lui-même*, Paris, 1808 [outstanding in its lucidity]; G. Hubbard, *Saint-Simon, sa vie et ses travaux*, Paris, 1857; Georges Weill, *Un précurseur du socialisme*, Paris, 1844; Dr. George Dumas, *Psychologie de deux messies positivistes, Saint-Simon et Auguste Comte*, Paris, 1905; Maxime Leroy, *La vie véritable du comte de Saint-Simon*, Paris, 1924; C. Bouglé and Elie Halévy, *Doctrine de Saint-Simon* [meaning the Saint-Simonians] Paris, 1924; Emile Durkheim, *Le Socialisme: la doctrine Saint-Simonienne*, edited by Marcel Mauss, Paris, 1928 [but in spite of the title, this is concerned exclusively with the work of Saint-Simon]; Werner Leendentz, *Die industrielle Gesellschaft als Feld und Grundlage der Sozial-reform*, Lechte, 1938 [relevant to this study]; Jean Dautry, 'Preface' and 'commentaries' to *Saint-Simon, textes choisis*, Paris, 1951; F. K. Markham, 'Introduction' to *Saint-Simon, Selected Writings*, Oxford, 1952; Mathurin Dondo, *The French Faust, Henri de Saint-Simon*, New York, 1955; E. Vidal, *Saint-Simon e la scienza politica*,

Milan, 1959 [particularly relevant to this study]; Georges Gurvitch, *Saint-Simon Sociologue*, Paris, 1961; Frank Manuel, *The New World of Henri Saint-Simon*, Harvard, 1962 [the best biography in English]; François Perroux, *Industrie et création collective: I: Saint-Simonisme du XX-eme siecle et création collective*, Paris, 1964 [also particularly relevant to this study] and Pierre Ansart, 'Saint-Simon' in *Marx et l'anarchisme*, Paris, 1969 [an outstanding study of Saint-Simon's influence on Marx].
*Against:* Lucien Lévy-Bruhl, *La philosophie d'Auguste Comte*, Paris, 1900; Henri Gouhier, Vol. I, *La jeunesse d'Auguste Comte et la formation du positivisme*, Vol. 2, *Saint-Simon jusqu'à la Restauration*, Paris, 1936, Vol. 3, *Saint-Simon de 1814 à 1825*, Paris, 1941 [the most complete and erudite work, indispensable to all students of Saint-Simon, but successfully intended to be Comte's witness for the prosecution in the trial of Saint-Simon]. For all other references, see Jean Walch, *Bibliographie du Saint-Simonisme*, Paris, 1963.

Briefly, his biography is as follows: He was born on 17 October 1760 in Paris. There were also family estates in Picardy. In 1777, he became an officer in the Touraine regiment and from 1779 to 1783 he was in America, whence he returned with the rank of colonel. In 1785 he was in Holland; in 1787 in Madrid, proposing to finance and construct a canal across Spain. In Spain he met Count de Redern, later Prussian ambassador in London, who put funds at his disposal for investments. From 1789 to 1793 he lived principally in Peronne, Picardy, where he relinquished his title and name and invested massively in the lands confiscated from the church (especially abbeys) and the nobility (*biens nationaux*). On 19 November 1793 he was arrested in Paris, but he was released in August 1794, at the end of the Terror, thanks to the unflinching support of the people of Peronne. From 1794 to 1798, he acted as entrepreneur, Maecenas and dandy, host of one of the most high-powered and high-brow salons in the Paris of the Directoire. In 1799 he parted with Redern who bought him out for £144,000. In 1801, he married Sophie de Champgrand and divorced her in June 1802. He then went to Geneva to visit Madame de Staël, widowed in May 1802.

In 1803, he published *Lettres d'un habitant de Genève à ses contemporains.* In 1804, he was totally ruined, and published *Essai sur l'organisation sociale*: from 1805 to 1810, he was given shelter by his valet Diard. In 1807–8 he published *Introduction aux Travaux Scientifiques du XIXe siècle*, followed by *Lettres de*

*C. H. Saint-Simon, Nouvelle Encyclopédie* (1809–10). In 1810, he was very ill. In 1813, *Mémoire sur la Science de l'Homme* appeared. In 1813, Augustin Thierry became his secretary; *De la Réorganisation de la Société Européenne* appeared in 1814, *Sur l'établissement du parti de l'opposition* in 1815, and *L'Industrie* (four volumes) in 1816–18. In 1817, Auguste Comte became his secretary. *Le Politique* appeared in 1819; *L'Organisateur*, which contains the *parable*, in 1819–20. Prosecuted for this text, he was acquitted in 1820. *Du Système Industriel*, appeared in three parts in 1820–2 and *Catéchisme des Industriels* in 1823–4. In 1823, he attempted to commit suicide. In 1824 he separated from Comte. His 'disciples', Olinde Rodrigues, Elie Halévy, Bazard, Enfantin surrounded him with their care. In 1825, *Opinions littéraires, philosophiques et industrielles* and *Nouveau Christianisme* were published. He died in Paris on 17 May 1825.

Saint-Simon had a fertile mind, which proceeded by flashes or prophetic intuition. But unlike Comte or Marx he did not have a proper academic training. His writing was more often than not, ad-hoc, hurried and thus careless (most of his works were published first in instalments for private subscribers). His style, which sometimes is of the highest quality is usually halting and repetitive. He was a much better speaker than writer. He needed the help of 'secretaries' (Thierry), 'sons' (Auguste Comte), or the entire 'Saint-Simonian' company of disciples (Enfantin, Bazard, Rouen, Olinde Rodrigues, Michel Chevalier). His ideas became inextricably tied up with some of theirs. But attempts at disentanglement led to acrimonious mutual complaints of plagiarism—especially in the case of Comte.

Comte's misappropriations and calumnies were bad enough but on the eve of the Second World War, Comte's own disciple, Henri Gouhier, attempted to destroy Saint-Simon once again in the second and third volumes of his three volume *La jeunesse d'Auguste Comte et la formation du positivisme*. This is an extraordinary work which reads more like the report of a private-detective agency than a work of history, let alone the history of ideas. In his effort to extricate, as in a Caesarian operation, the infant work of Comte from the womb of Saint-Simon's work, Gouhier seems to have been more interested in killing the mother than in saving the child—he never wrote the full and independent history of Auguste Comte or positivism. Yet if questions of intellectual paternity could be solved simply by means of recorded evidence there is no doubt that the concepts of positivism, social science and of the scientific (or positive) approach to politics—considered to be Comte's central ideas—were first formulated by Saint-Simon. Durkheim has proved this.

From Saint-Simon's symbiotic relationships with secretaries and disciples, the philosopher's need for close, human relations can be traced also in the less well-known realm of his sentimental life. His only marriage, which he described cynically as 'taking a graceful hostess for his salon', lasted only one year. Its initiation and its end can be explained by two dramatic circumstances. According to Gouhier,[15] Alexandrine-Sophie Goury de Champgrand had a child by her lover, the Prince Jules-Armand Camille Rohan de Rochefort, who was arrested one night in her room and then guillotined. On his deathbed, her father, a friend of Saint-Simon, asked him to protect her. Saint-Simon proposed marriage to her, which she accepted on condition that she should remain faithful to her dead fiancé. After a year they divorced, she being aware of his impending ruin, he for many obvious reasons, but perhaps for a secret one as well. Yet he cried so much during the divorce proceedings that the judge, thinking that it was his wife who wanted the divorce, appealed to her to take pity on him.

The secret reason might be—and here this essay sides with Gouhier[16]—that Madame de Staël lost her husband in May 1802. In June 1802, Saint-Simon divorced and went to live in Geneva, near where she lived; and in Geneva he published his very first work. Her books, but especially *De la litérature considérée dans ses rapports avec les institutions sociales*, published in 1800, made an indelible impression on him. Her statement, 'the study of history, it seems to me leads to the conviction that all important events tend towards the same end—the civilization of mankind', and the conclusion she drew that politics must become a science: 'why should it not be possible some day to compile tables that would contain the answers to all questions of a political nature based on statistical knowledge, on positive facts gathered for every country?' expressed his own two main ideas, which were beginning to form at this stage of his life. Knowing his buoyant and confident nature, as well as his need for communion with what Plato called the Other Half, it is not inconceivable that he should have entertained the dream of marrying her. This might have been the very moment when his life and personality changed entirely. From then onwards he was to dedicate himself entirely to his work. Unfulfilled, for ever

15. Op. cit., Vol. 2, pp. 112–25.
16. Ibid., pp. 123–5.

separated from the Other Half, he then had merely fatherly feelings for his young and devoted mistress–secretary–housekeeper, Julie Juliand. Although he took great care to send her away in 1823, when he wanted to take his life, she was there with the other disciples when he died in 1825.

Be that as it may, these peculiar aspects of his personal life, added to the facts of his intellectual biography—this particular need for symbiosis with other souls, combined with his carefree way of trading and sharing ideas with predecessors and followers, masters and disciples—make the unravelling of his own authentic contribution somewhat arduous. One of the reasons why Saint-Simon's work is still so controversial lies in the fact that it is so tangled with that of others, disciples like the Saint-Simonians, or disciples turned critics like Comte and Marx. An attempt has been made in the following two tables to show Saint-Simon's position among his contemporaries and to indicate where Saint-Simon's own theory of the politics of the industrial (-technological) society should be placed.

*Saint-Simon's contemporaries**

| Direct | | Indirect | |
|---|---|---|---|
| Jean-Jacques Rousseau | 1712–1778 | Adam Fergusson | 1723–1816 |
| Washington | 1732–1799 | Bentham | 1748–1832 |
| Condorcet | 1743–1794 | Madison | 1751–1836 |
| Siéyès | 1748–1836 | Robespierre | 1758–1794 |
| de Bonald | 1754–1840 | | |
| Lafayette | 1757–1834 | | |
| Pitt the Younger | 1759–1806 | | |
| Babeuf | 1760–1797 | | |
| | Saint-Simon 1760–1825 | | |
| Madame de Staël | 1766–1817 | St. Just | 1767–1794 |
| J.-B. Say | 1767–1832 | Napoleon | 1769–1821 |
| Benjamin Constant | 1767–1830 | Hegel | 1770–1831 |
| Chateaubriand | 1768–1848 | Fourier | 1772–1837 |
| Sismondi | 1773–1842 | Carlyle | 1795–1881 |
| Comte | 1798–1857 | Proudhon | 1809–1865 |
| John Stuart Mill | 1806–1873 | Herzen | 1812–1870 |
| Tocqueville | 1805–1859 | Marx | 1818–1883 |

* This table attempts only to indicate the coincidence of Saint-Simon's span of life with that of contemporaries who, during that span, were shaping the course of history either by their deeds or by their thought. With some of them he had direct contact, as for instance with Rousseau, whom he visited as a young man, Lafayette, under whom he served in America, Babeuf, whom he met as a young man in their native Picardy, Madame de Staël, whom he wanted to marry, Napoleon to whom he proposed his idea of political organization, Jean-Baptiste Say and Sismondi whom he frequented and admired, John Stuart Mill, who describes how he met Saint-Simon, etc. With the others the incidence is indirect.

*Genealogical Tree of Saint-Simon's Theory*

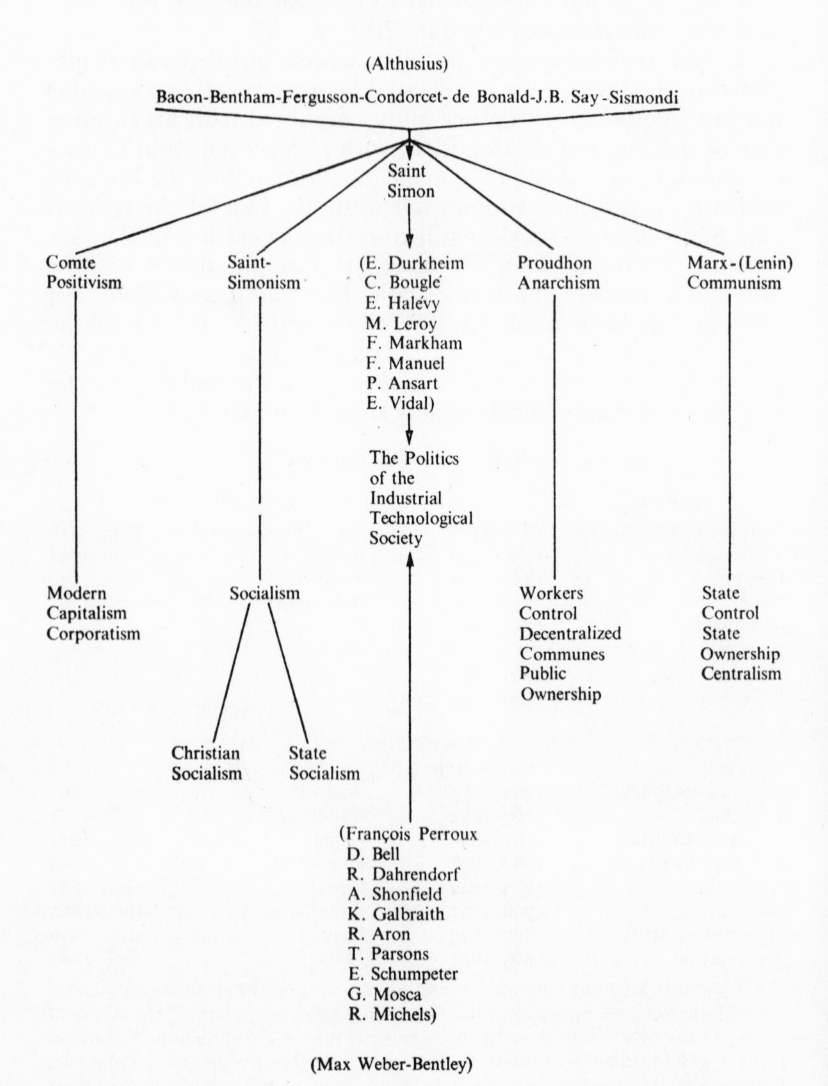

If one takes a closer look at the lines in the second table, the following explanations might amplify the table's significance. The first two lines show Saint-Simon's antecedents. Althusius is an antecedent—even though, to my knowledge, there is no direct trace or reference in Saint-Simon's work to the sixteenth-century Dutch political philosopher (unless he absorbed some of Althusius's idea through D'Alembert and the Encyclopaedia; and perhaps, as he was very careless with his sources, he merely failed to acknowledge his debt to Althusius). But in at least two essential respects the coincidence of approach between the two, across almost two centuries, is surprising. The first lies in their joint insistence on dealing with politics as the principal subject. *Politica methodica digesta* is Althusius's title; Saint-Simon's avowed intention is to found *La science politique*. Moreover Althusius, like Saint-Simon, tries to deal with it in the *new* politics (*opus politicum novum*). Their second resemblance lies in the fact that the substance of their thinking is essentially organicist. Althusius' idea of '*consociatio symbiotica*' (or *communio* or *communicatio* or indeed *mutua communicatio*) is that of an organic system in which the interdependent '*communes*', or *corporations* (*politeuma* or *universitas*) form a community. It is true to say that the *Genossenschaftdörfe*, the village communities in Germany, had in the Middle Ages a more characteristic and a clearer communal organization than in France; and it is also true that the sixteenth-century German *Bürgen* bore a more direct resemblance to Saint-Simon's idea of organized communes. Be that as it may, the fact is that the entire idea of the emancipated communes of producers forming self-administered communities is in Althusius. Yet Saint-Simon, whose theory is founded on this idea, does not mention this remote predecessor.

The second line consists of the openly acknowledged 'masters' of Saint-Simon's thinking: Bacon, to whom he attributed the origin of scientific thinking; Bentham, and the utilitarians from whom he drew his social positivism; Adam Fergusson, whom he credited with the separation of societies into military and civilian (although, at the same time, Benjamin Constant, one of the rivals he seldom mentioned, was publishing his *Esprit de Conquête* in which the theory of military power and its consequences is better expressed than in Saint-Simon); the Marquis of Condorcet whom he called 'the last of the philosophers', his dearest master and who, in retrospect, appears to have been his tragic *alter ego*—a man who devoted all his enthusiasm to the success of the Revolution and, when it turned against him, wrote with 'a lay-saintly' fervour his *Du progrès de l'esprit humain* (from which Saint-Simon drew a great deal of his inspiration) and finally died in jail; de Bonald, the Catholic political philosopher, from whom Saint-Simon derived the idea of 'system unity', and with whom he crossed swords all his life on the role of religion; Jean-Baptiste Say, from whom he borrowed the idea of the functional distinction between the capitalist and the entrepreneur (or manager or industrialist) and the sense of the social use of capital; Sismondi, with his early theories of economic planning and of the 'regulation of wealth'; and last but not least, Madame de Staël, who influenced his early thinking.

Of the influence of Saint-Simon's work on those who followed, the table shows that five great schools of thought—positivist, socialist, corporatist, anarchist and communist—irreconcilable among themselves, have acknowledged through their respective founders an original debt to Saint-Simon's system. This can also be seen today in the fact that many of the features of his model of the politics of the new industrial society can be found in governments as diverse as those of Franco's Spain and Tito's Yugoslavia, socialist Sweden and Brezhnev's U.S.S.R., not to mention organizations like the European Economic Community.

This, then, brings us back to the question of unravelling Saint-Simon's original thought from the misappropriations of it by others.

The relationship between Saint-Simon and Auguste Comte has been so exhaustively studied (and is still being explored—the recent publication of Comte's early correspondence, for instance, is of the first importance) that no justice can be done here to the controversial question of which of the two men introduced which new concept or approach in their common philosophy. Yet the fact that Saint-Simon laid the foundations of that philosophy is not denied even by Comte himself.

The separation of Saint-Simon from the doctrine of the Saint-Simonians has now become more obvious. In 1924, Bouglé and Halévy decided to take the text of the *Exposition* of the Saint-Simonian doctrine[17] as issued in 1829, four years after the death of the master, by the disciples Bazard, Enfantin and Michel Chevalier, as the summary of a series of lectures. In a most scholarly manner they explained the circumstances under which the text was compiled. Taking into account the exceptional disorder of Saint-Simon's published works and manuscripts, they tried also to differentiate between Saint-Simon's own views and what Walch called, 'the very free interpretation

17. C. Bouglé and Elie Halévy, *Doctrine de Saint-Simon*, Paris, 1924.

of the thought of the Master' by these disciples. But Bouglé and Halévy chose to give to this collection the title of *The Doctrine of Saint-Simon*. A title like *The Doctrine of the Saint-Simonians* would have saved much trouble. For the confusion created by this title led to serious misunderstandings. Many authors attributed to Saint-Simon himself theories and trends of thought which had been added to his 'doctrine' by his disciples. The Bouglé–Halévy collection is, in part, one of the sources cited by those who see in Saint-Simon's work the origins of fascist corporatism or totalitarianism. This is, as we shall see, in any case a misinterpretation of Saint-Simon's fundamental theory of politics. But such a view is also based on a failure to discriminate between the ideas of Saint-Simon and the ideas of the Saint-Simonians. Take, for instance, the case of Mr. Iggers. Mr. Georg J. Iggers is an American author who has persevered until recently in the mistake initially made by Bouglé and Halévy of calling 'Doctrine of Saint-Simon'[18] what is actually the 'Doctrine of the Saint-Simonians'; he has also followed the Hajek[19] interpretation of the 'Doctrine' as a proto-totalitarianism. But now he recognizes that this is wrong. On both counts, 'The doctrine of Saint-Simon', he says is 'the most decisive influence in the crystallization of the social philosophy of the Saint-Simonians (*as distinct from that of their Master, Henri de Saint-Simon*'[20]) [my italics]; and later, 'The basic concepts of Saint-Simon's philosophy found their way into the Saint-Simonian literature. Yet basic elements of Saint-Simonian theory . . . were not found in the master's work'.[21] Then Mr. Iggers absolves Saint-Simon *personally* of the terrible crime of authoritarianism, or totalitarianism, thus: 'The introduction in my opinion is correct in stressing the strongly authoritarian note in Saint-Simonian thought after 1828, a note which is for the most part absent in the writings of their Master, Henri de Saint-Simon, who had died in 1825 . . .'[22] 'I would be much more careful today in using the term "totalitarianism" to describe the Saint-Simonian doctrine than I was in the original introduction.'[23]

In theory there is no logical relation between the functioning

18. Georg J. Iggers, *The Doctrine of Saint-Simon*, 1972, Schocken Books, New York.
19. F. A. Hayek, *The Counter-Revolution of Science, Studies on the Abuse of Reason*, 1952.
20. Iggers, op. cit., p. ix.
21. Iggers, op. cit., p. xxii.
22. Iggers, op. cit., p. v.
23. Iggers, op. cit., p. vi. Mr. Iggers's first book was called *The Cult of Authority: the Political Philosophy of the Saint-Simonians*, The Hague, 1958.

of a *dirigiste* or collectivist society in which plural, social and political organizations share, by competition, in the policy-making processes, and the functioning of a total state machine which results in the total loss of freedom of its subjects. Socialist Sweden and Schumpeter's political theories represent opposites to respectively Nazi Germany and Vishinsky's political theories. Hayek's analysis overlooked the fact that the presence of the arch-centralistic *state*, abhorred by Saint-Simon, is *the* prerequisite of corporatist fascism and totalitarianism alike.

Further, it is necessary to disentangle Saint-Simon's conceptions from those of Proudhon and Marx and, generally speaking, from his association with anarchism and Marxist or Marxist–Leninist socialism. Durkheim was partly responsible for the identification of Saint-Simon's doctrine with both anarchism and socialism. This dual association can to a certain extent be explained by the fact that Durkheim's own brand of 'socialism', which was midway between socialism and anarchism, came very close to, and is indeed very faithful to, the essence of Saint-Simon's conception of the future industrial society. Durkheim's socialism was described by him as 'workers' socialism'; he contrasted it with Marx's 'state socialism', which in his view was the complete opposite of the decentralization and mutuality essential to genuine socialism. Furthermore, precisely because Durkheim conceived of socialism as 'workers' socialism', he extended it to embrace anarchism, or anarcho-syndicalism, as well. He explained clearly, in syllogistic form, why he believed this to be right. 'If therefore, following usage,' he says (oddly shielding himself with the invocation of common usage), 'every social theory in which governmental forms are more or less completely suppressed is called "anarchistic", one must also give this name to the doctrine of Saint-Simon.'[24] This is a very far-fetched piece of reasoning. Neither anarchism nor the doctrine of Saint-Simon is correctly defined.

But Durkheim's logical short-cut rests on a much better case. It rests on his equation of socialism with anarchism, through the logical link of producer self-management. 'Socialism,' Durkheim argues,[25] 'far from being authoritarian—as is often said—far from demanding a stronger organization of governmental powers, was on the contrary, in one sense, essentially anarchistic. We find the same attitude even more pronounced in Fourier than in Saint-Simon, in Proudhon than in Fourier, in Marx than in Proudhon.' This, in a nutshell, is Durkheim's own

24. *Socialism*, English translation, New York, 1962, p. 153.
25. Ibid.

view of decentralized socialism, so successfully presented in his important preface to the *Social Division of Labour*. But nevertheless this does not fully and really apply to Saint-Simon—or, for different reasons, to Marx.

What is even more surprising is that serious modern interpreters of Saint-Simon, like Pierre Ansart, continue to include him among the anarchists; Ansart does so even in the title of his excellent *Marx et l'anarchisme*. It is true that Ansart includes Saint-Simon and not just Proudhon, among anarchists, primarily to differentiate them from Marx—and stresses the political differences between Marx's socialism, controlled by the state, and the anti-state ideologies of the two Frenchmen. It is also true that he qualifies this inclusion by showing that in doing so, he only follows Proudhon. Proudhon, says Ansart, 'concluded that the theory of the withering away of the state was explicitly contained in Saint-Simon's works and that the latter must be considered as a precursor of anarchism'.[26] But Ansart adds that the validity of Proudhon's interpretation of Saint-Simon is doubtful. He also says that the influence of Saint-Simon's work on Proudhon was much more complex than Proudhon believed or realized.

It is surprising to see a man's views defined in terms which he explicitly rejects and abhors. 'Anarchy' is an expression which Saint-Simon particularly abhorred from the time of his very first work in 1802: 'anarchy, the greatest of all plagues, produces havoc unchecked until the nation which it afflicts reaches that point of misery which revives in even its most ignorant members the wish to re-establish order';[27] and from later work, *Des Bourbons et des Stuarts* (1822): 'all powers having been handed over to the most ignorant, were ill-administered; anarchy established itself, civil war and famine completed this public disaster.'[28] On all the occasions when Saint-Simon uses the word it is always and exclusively with the most pejorative meaning. Long after Saint-Simon's time, it is true that Proudhon succeeded in giving to the word 'anarchy' a new respectability, and in changing its meaning from that of destructive individualism to constructive solidarity. But it is still hard to believe that this would have been acceptable to Saint-Simon, who had used the word exclusively in its original sense, and whose main concern was for the organization of the industrial society, its effective functioning, its adequate institutionalization.

26. Ansart, op. cit., p. 40.
27. *Lettres d'un habitant de Genève*, op. cit., p. 33.
28. In *Works*, Vol. vi, p. 503.

For, coming now to a more substantive difference in conceptions: the difference between Proudhon's *anarchy*, which consists of the most complete decentralization, communism, and federation, and Saint-Simon's administration, is to be found precisely in the latter's conviction that the industrial society must be provided with a public management, drawn from its most honest, most disinterested and best qualified members: industrialists and members of the professions, sciences and arts. It is certainly true that both Saint-Simon and Proudhon were opposed to the Jacobins and to their ideas of the state and government and that, consequently, Proudhon opposed Marx on the question of the state continuing to exist, even if it were in the form of the dictatorship of the proletariat. But the difference between Saint-Simon and Proudhon still turns on the ultimate, *political*, question. The former starts from the principle of the political organization of society; a principle which the latter rejects. The former believes that organization needs and requires elites; the latter refuses to acknowledge any kind of hierarchy, including meritocracy. The former thinks of the rationality of production; the latter of the equality of consumption and distribution.

And so to Marx. We know of Marx's respect for Saint-Simon and of the fact that, while he criticized his utopianism, he never turned against him as he did against Proudhon, whom he had also admired during his early formative period in France. (It was in this period that Marx acquired what Lenin called the 'French Socialism' element in the original mixture of Marxism.) A sentence in the *Anti-Dühring* expresses the constant attitude of Marx and Engels towards Saint-Simon: 'In Saint-Simon we find the breadth of view of a genius, thanks to which almost all the ideas of later socialism which are not strictly economic are contained in his works in embryo.'

Marx's greatest debt to Saint-Simon is for his theory of the separation of civil society from the state—and subsequently of government from administration—for this led Marx to the first serious criticism he ever made of the German philosophers. It is against Hegel's conception of the state that *The Critique of Hegel's Philosophy of the State* (1843) is directed. Marx's initial 'realistic' objection to Hegel's abstract, floating concept of the state, is the almost subconscious reaction provoked by his deeply grounded belief in the reality of the people, as opposed to the state: 'The state is an abstraction,' he exclaims, 'only the people is a concrete fact!'

This quest by the young Marx for the human reality which

he felt Hegel had failed to grasp is generally attributed to the influence of Feuerbach. A second glance, however, reveals the hidden, almost subliminal, influence of Saint-Simon. Pierre Ansart, in his important work, *Marx et l'anarchisme*, perceived this. He rightly observed:

In the manuscripts of 1843, Marx, when he detects deep in Hegel's work the conceptualizations which distort the empirical reality, does not qualify his conclusion with regard to the empirical plane. He acknowledges, as a most obvious fact that the reality of German society is the division, the separation, that the State is not the state of the civil society, but he does not demonstrate these overwhelmingly important propositions. It is this kind of allusion which is so revealing: it suggests that Marx took it for granted that these commonplaces were so obvious, had become common knowledge for such a long time, that there was no reason to treat them as novelties. Yet this common background belongs to the Saint-Simonian methodology: it is in Saint-Simon's work that 'reality' is first situated in the social organization: and that the state is the relic which must be destroyed and whose destruction will allow the civil society, the society of producers, to develop freely.[29]

Biographical details confirm Ansart's interpretation of Saint-Simon's deep-seated influence on Marx. Both Marx's father, during his youth in Trier, and his teacher, Edward Jans, in Berlin, were followers of Saint-Simon. Saint-Simon also influenced the works of G. Nevissen and especially Moses Hess, which Marx read extensively during these years and through which he continued to absorb Saint-Simon's political and social philosophy. Then there followed the period of his unbounded admiration for 'the French Socialist'—his formative years from this point of view—the period of the Paris manuscripts and of his sojourns in Paris.

From Saint-Simon, Marx derived his early vision of the state as intrinsically opposed to society. This opposition leads to the domination of society by the bureaucracy, as a result of centralization. In 1842, he attacked Moses Hess for having thought that the ' "Centralization Question" would be solved on the abstract philosophical plane'. 'Whether one point is to govern or whether every province, etc., is to govern itself . . . the centralization question cannot possibly be grasped in this way!' However, the argument was not concluded, since Marx's manuscript remained unfinished and unpublished. Then, like Saint-Simon, Marx divided human societies into three great historical

29. Op. cit., p. 338.

phases: the feudal, the modern and the future society. Like Saint-Simon, he considered the French Revolution as the moment in history when civil, or what Saint-Simon called 'industrial' society, achieved its own self-sufficiency and ceased to be dependent on the state, or the government. Like Saint-Simon, Marx criticized the French Revolution (especially in *On the Jewish Question*) as having proclaimed the emancipation of civil society only on the political plane, and thus having ignored the social reality, the *new reality of society*. Society has become self-sufficient; it no longer needs the state; it 'subalternizes' the state.

Thus the young Marx was influenced by Saint-Simon. As he himself acknowledged, his ideas, other than his economic ones—i.e. his historical, social and political ideas—were already to be found in embryo in Saint-Simon's work. Now it was precisely on the economic plane, where the self-taught, late developer, Saint-Simon, had 'caught-up' less successfully with the academics, that the genius of the mature Marx was to triumph. Only his ignorance of, and probable lack of predisposition towards, economics can explain why Saint-Simon had failed to discern (even from Sismondi's work!) the importance of the problem on which, a generation later, Marx, the scholar, was to centre his work: the growth of capitalism and of the consequent class struggle. In this sense, it can be said that Marx continued Saint-Simon's study of the industrial society from the point where Saint-Simon had left off and on another plane. It might well be that it was this feeling of continuity of thought in different contexts which made Marx preserve his respect for Saint-Simon intact, and spared the latter from the sarcasm which Marx more often than not reserved for those from whose ideas he had once drawn his inspiration.

This is not the place to make an exhaustive comparison of the validity of Saint-Simon's and Marx's respective judgements on the future course of the industrial society. The whole Introduction is bound to fall back again and again into this comparative exercise, for it is only by evaluating Saint-Simon's judgements in the light of those who came after him that his originality can be clearly seen. But it is necessary at least to get down here the principal differences between them.

The first difference lies in the fact that, whereas Marx is the analyst of the *capitalist* society, Saint-Simon is the analyst of the *industrial* society.

The second is that, whereas Saint-Simon is principally concerned with the problem of the political organization of the *post-revolutionary* society, Marx is principally concerned with the historical inevitability of the socialist revolution. Once successful, the socialist revolution will so extinguish all conflicts in society that politics, the fruit of class conflict, will cease, and organization will be reduced to a minimum.

The third difference derives from the second. Even in the case of transitional politics, or of the transitional state—that state of the dictatorship of the proletariat which Marx had envisaged as having the object of ending all politics and all states—Marx saw the means of the achievement of this object as power, the change of the exercise of power from and against one class to and against the other class. As will be shown in part four of this Introduction, Saint-Simon on the other hand, considering the politics of the future industrial society, asked: What will be the nature and the form of political organization once power has become so diffused that it destroys itself?

Fourthly, both philosophers ultimately acknowledge that the transformation of society into more perfect forms will be achieved only when the men who form society will themselves have been transformed from within. But while Marx relies on human reason to achieve this transformation, Saint-Simon relies essentially on faith, that is on the Christian faith, which alone, in his view, can give reason sufficient strength to make men break with their historical condition.

Apart from the difference between the philosophies of Marx and Saint-Simon, what differences can we note between the theories of Saint-Simon and theories of socialism in general? Saint-Simon was undoubtedly one of the original inspirations of socialism, if only of 'utopian' socialism; but this fact should not conceal the differences between his views and the theory of socialism as it has evolved since his time, and as it is generally defined even today. On at least four concepts of socialism—class, ownership, equality and the role of the state—his views are difficult to reconcile with those of any kind of contemporary socialism.

Saint-Simon's views on class often changed and were always vague. He spoke of the opposition between the feudal class or classes, and the industrial class or classes. Then he spoke of the productive classes and of the idle classes. At one time he divided the productive classes into scientists, proprietors and the third class—presumably the rest. Later, he distinguished between the scientists, the proprietors and the industrialists. But the latter were not merely the toilers, or workers, let alone the industrial workers. They comprised 'all those who are useful in society', from bankers and investors to craftsmen and farmers and workers (later, however, he concentrated more on the latter, whom he described as '*Messieurs les ouvriers*' or even, later still, as '*le prolétariat*'). Class, therefore, was not a concept of major importance in his analysis of the industrial society. And, in any case, class struggle was not for him the motor of history, and the idea of one class replacing by power another class in power was for him, as we shall see, a somewhat irrelevant answer to what he considered to be the deeper question of the transformation of power itself.

Saint-Simon's theory of ownership is closer to the socialist idea in so far as he, too, believed that the system of ownership determines the character of the society. He also maintained that in a society of producers, ownership should be public. But the functionalism which pervaded his philosophy led him to the view that the problem of ownership was losing some of its relevance, as the functional separation between the rights and duties of owners and those of managers and producers was gradually accentuated, to the disadvantage of the owner. Gouhier effectively summed up Saint-Simon's view on this subject when he said that 'if production is the aim of the government, the very notion of ownership has from that moment only a relative significance dependent on its aim'.[30]

Saint-Simon's idea of egalitarianism is fundamentally opposed to that of the levellers. He called levelling down '*l'égalité turque*' or 'a sanguinary imbecility'. True, industrial equality is the freedom of each one to draw benefits from society in exact proportion to his social investment and his positive 'ability'. As A. Giddens points out, Saint-Simon's 'new society is to be a differentiated one in terms of the distribution of material rewards'.[31] In the *Catechism*, Saint-Simon explained clearly that 'each receives a rank of importance and benefits proportionate to his ability and position—which amounts to the largest degree of equality possible and desirable.' This tallies with his general conception of the natural hierarchy of the 'abilities'.[32] It tallies also with experience in the contemporary communist industrial societies where *uravnilovka*, the levellers' equality, has inevitably been superseded by social stratification, 'industrial inequality', and sharp cleavages and differentials between various kinds of labour.

But the greatest divergence between the thought of Saint-

30. Gouhier, op. cit., p. 193.
31. A. Giddens, *The Class Structure of the Advanced Societies*, London, 1974, p. 25.
32. *The Catechism of the Industrialists*, see *infra*, p. 61.

Simon and that of the classic exponents of socialism arises from the different views they take of the role of the state (and generally speaking of politics) in society. While socialism situates the state and the government in the centre of the industrial society, Saint-Simon's political organization starts from the abolition of the state and the central government. But it is to his theory of politics that we now turn.

## 3. POLITICS WITHOUT POWER

We have tried to see what Saint-Simon's work is *not*. It is not anarchism, fascism, communism or even socialism; indeed, it is not an ideology at all. But, on the other hand, it is not a science: neither sociology nor political science.[33] We should try to see now what Saint-Simon's work is. In order to do so, the following definition is put forward: Saint-Simon's work is a theory of the *system of the industrial-technological society, with special regard to its political organization.* But, like all working definitions, the present one begs the question of all the terms which compose it. We shall have to look at each of them, and defend each one separately, before re-assembling them into a coherent whole.

*System.* Saint-Simon studied the emerging industrial-technological society as a functionally interdependent and interrelated whole, or as a system of social organization. This is how he saw it, and this is how he maintained that it should be examined. '*On ne crée point un systéme d'organisation sociale*', he exclaimed in *L'Organisateur* in 1819; '*on aperçoit le nouvel enchainement d'idées et d'intérêts qui s'est formé et on le montre, voilà tout*'. The new amalgam of values and interests which he discerned, at the moment in history when the feudal society was passing away, was a new

33. The cause is obvious: although, as we have seen, Saint-Simon wanted his work to be called 'political science', and although he had rightly visualized the conceptual framework of the social *sciences*, he could not possibly practise them. The means for scientific analysis and empirical research were not available to him—and, what is more, the society which he wanted to study had not yet fully emerged. But perhaps in the case of Saint-Simon, one should follow Bernard Crick's advice in the case of Machiavelli, namely that 'it is perhaps not very important in what sense, if any, he deserves to be called a political scientist' (Bernard Crick, *Machiavelli: The Discourses*, London, 1972, p. 49). Regardless of the relative merits and importance of their work, what Machiavelli and Saint-Simon have in common is that they both projected political models of future societies by anticipation, e.g. Machiavelli presaged the politics of the era of the nation state and Saint-Simon those of the post-nation state era, or of the industrial-technological society. Machiavelli taught how to use power in the new politics; Saint-Simon taught how to use politics once power becomes less relevant. But for this see further in this whole section which is centred around this crucial argument.

and self-contained 'system' of an industrial-technological society. One system replaced another system, '*et voilà tout*', hey presto!

This organicist view is natural to Saint-Simon. He was, as an organicist, particularly interested in the biology of societies, in the way in which they function, in the way their limbs and bloodstream, nerves, etc., form and animate a common body, or a system, from which they are inseparable and to which they are indispensable. His subjective predisposition to studies of organization was enhanced by the strikingly system-like features of his object of study, the new society. The industrial society is more closely interdependent and enmeshed than all previous societies, certainly more so than the scattered and fragmented feudal society. Interdependence and organization were and are the essential qualities of the industrial-technological society. Even if one did not favour the systemic approach, one could not study the industrial-technological society if one did not see it as an enmeshed complex.

*Industrial-technological society.* Saint-Simon spoke only of the industrial society, and not of the industrial-technological society. In order to explain why we have added the word technological to his concept of the industrial society, we must take a closer look at the latter and at its ramifications.

Saint-Simon created the concepts of *industry*, *industrial society* and *the industrial* and *the industrialist* (which in French are both nouns: *l'industriel* and *l'industrialiste*).[34] Saint-Simon's avowed aim was to provide the *scientific analysis* of the interrelation and the functioning of the entire *industrial system*; indeed, to form a 'science of mankind' and to grasp the ultimate reality of modern and future mankind as transformed by industry. Industry transforms human production by allowing it to devote itself exclusively to nature and its resources—what Sartre has described as 'the dream of anti-nature'.[35] This new relation between man and nature, in turn, completely alters the relation between man and man; it should end the relations of exploitation and obedience and should lead, logically, to a relation of general co-operation, replacing rule over men by the 'administration of things'. The *industrial system* is the new phase of this interrelation, this new pattern of interactions.

34. 'The fact that he was the first to use "industrial" as a noun was never denied and therefore seems to have to be accepted.' Gouhier, op. cit., p. 35 n. As for industrialism, 'the word has been coined by Saint-Simon', ibid., p. 49n. Moreover, Gouhier recognizes that Saint-Simon himself has traced some of the origins of his philosophy of the *système industriel* in Montesquieu and Condorcet; ibid., p. 147.

35. Jean-Paul Sartre, *Baudelaire*, Paris, 1947.

But Saint-Simon discerned within the enmeshed complex of the industrial system two realms and three classes.

The two realms, the *spiritual* and the *temporal*, are according to him, to be found in all societies, from the most primitive ones of antiquity to the most sophisticated ones of the future. Moreover, the separation between these spheres is consonant with the duality inherent in the human condition itself, torn between the concern with immediate realities and the longing for eternity. At every turning-point in history, the nature of the occupations or professions, which dominate each of the two realms at a given point in time, changes. Thus, at the turning-point in history when European feudal society was replaced by European industrial society, what really happened was that science, learning and art replaced religion, metaphysics and law[36] as the dominant occupations in the spiritual sphere, and the industrialists (or producers or communes) replaced the military in the temporal sphere.

As we have seen previously, Saint-Simon's ideas on classes changed. In his early works, he discerned three classes: (1) the scientists, writers and artists; (2) the proprietors; and (3) the people or toilers. In his later work, and indeed in most of his work, he discerned two productive classes: the scientists and the industrialists (among whom were included the proprietors of industry, investors, bankers) and one non-productive class, the idlers (the military, the lawyers, the private proprietors, the nobility, etc.). At the very end he distinguished, within the previously homogeneous bulk of the industrialists, between the owners of the means of production, who drew the profits without working and thus rejoined the idlers, and the workers or the proletariat, who were exploited by the owners, but who remained both in industry and in agriculture the true representatives of the producers of the future industrial society.[37]

It is important to notice at this point that, although the two realms and the three classes are different concepts altogether, yet as the future industrial society crystallizes into its ultimate shape, so the two realms are more closely identified with the two productive classes: scientists with the spiritual sphere and

36. One of Saint-Simon's favourite examples of the way in which the availability of scientific knowledge brings about change in occupational qualification is the replacement of the astrologer by the astronomer.

37. This theory appears in endless variations throughout the entire work of Saint-Simon, and the reader might benefit from following it in the chronological order in which the extracts are presented in this collection. But perhaps the most substantial exposition of it is to be found in the first section of *Industry*, p. 99f., and in *The Organizer*, *infra*, p. 138f.

industrialists with the temporal sphere. Does this mean that the basic division of labour between manual and non-manual work, or between what we now call blue-collar workers and white-collar workers, perpetuates itself in the industrial society as well? In principle, and to a certain degree, the answer is undoubtedly in the affirmative; moreover, this concept of the division of labour is basic to the understanding of Saint-Simon's philosophy—precisely to what degree is a matter of interpretation.

In the 'socialist' interpretations of Saint-Simon—made by Marx, Durkheim, Leroy, etc.—the division of labour between the two orders is seen to melt in the process of the unification of all kinds of labour in the all-embracing category of producers, workers or industrialists. This interpretation is based on ample textual evidence and, moreover, it tallies with Saint-Simon's tendency to include under the definition of productive forces all those who are useful to society, regardless of the kind of work they do.

In the 'technocratic' interpretation of Saint-Simon—made by the Saint-Simonians, Hajek and, surprisingly, Daniel Bell—this division of labour goes beyond the professional or vocational aptitudes and actually constitutes the fundamental difference between those who rule by virtue of their position, and those who, also by virtue of their position, will always be ruled. This interpretation is founded mainly on Saint-Simon's early works,[38] and it corresponds with his unshakeable belief in the principle that science and scientific knowledge are the basic elements of leadership. But it would be a complete misinterpretation of Saint-Simon's thought to generalize further and to transform his vision of the leadership of knowledge into a theory of a permanent political class, or of a ready-made stratum of rulers. More of this later, when we come to the expositions of Saint-Simon's political theory, which yokes all his other theories together.

What matters now is to see how these two contradictory interpretations can actually be reconciled in Saint-Simon's work. As in the 'socialist' interpretation quoted above, Saint-Simon did actually argue that the producers dominate the society because they possess the physical power (they are the overwhelming majority, 24/25ths of the population); the financial power (they produce the entire wealth of the nation); and the best judgement (because those who possess the physical and financial power are much better informed and better able to

38. See, especially, in this collection, *Letters from an inhabitant of Geneva*, p. 65f.

make decisions than others).[39] But, and this is not in the 'socialist' interpretation of his work, Saint-Simon's 'producers' include not only the industrial workers, the craftsmen and the agriculturalists, but also the future corporations: trade unions, enterprises (complex terms with their own corporate existence), co-operatives, banks and credit institutions, and other complexes. This may seem utopian—and is fundamentally unlike the straightforward dialogue between capital and labour on which classic socialism thrives. But it does foreshadow the segmentation of decision-making caused in the modern economy by the action of corporations, associations, groups, companies, national, regional and supranational interests, trade unions and workers' councils, and other corporate interests which cut across class conflict.

Thus while Saint-Simon acknowledges the growing importance of labour and its organizations, he also asserts that of the 'scientists, artists and writers', and assigns to them a leading position in society. His vision of both these factors coming to the fore has been confirmed. The few hundred 'scientists, artists and writers' he could call to mind in Europe, at the dawn of the nineteenth century, have now multiplied and form distinct social groups numbered in millions. In capitalist industrial societies they are called scientific and cultural elites, and in communist industrial societies they are called the technical and creative intelligentsia. Their numbers are already large and are constantly expanding, for universities and special schools turn them out in ever-increasing numbers each year, and the variety of highly specialized skills practised by these people grows greater with the spread of technology. Yet the influence they exert on society is even greater than their numbers might seem to justify. This is, as Saint-Simon foresaw, because of their power to control the scientific and technological activities of society, and to influence world public opinion—as communicators they can manipulate the media which can now be used to convey information rapidly on a world-wide scale.

The elites or intelligentsias may come to form an 'Estate' in contemporary industrial society. It may well be that if the 'scientists', the planners, the artists, the academics and the communicators should continue to develop their growing '*esprit de corps*', the political circles, which have been the reputed centres of decision-making until now, will be squeezed more than they already are between the 'Estate' of industry and the 'Estate' of knowledge.

39. See, especially, *The Industrial System*, *infra*, p. 153f.

It is this kind of society, which I described in contemporary terms, that Saint-Simon visualized some 150 years ago. It is surprising therefore that he called it only 'the industrial society' or 'the industrial system', for it was he more than anyone else who stressed its dual *industrial* and *scientific* aspects. It is this omission which I have tried to correct in the working definition offered here. I have preferred, for two reasons, to use the formula 'industrial-technological', not 'industrial-scientific'. First, because the word 'technological' currently stands for those interwoven trends in modern society of highly technical specialization (most noticeable since the advent of cybernetics) and the widespread and inevitable application of science to production. Secondly, as I have shown elewhere,[40] the hyphen in the expression 'industrial-technological' signifies the transition (the phase we are in now) between the industrial society of the past and the technological society of the future, which may or may not take the shape which we forecast for it today.

*With special regard to political organization.* Here we enter the relatively unexplored part of Saint-Simon's political theory. This is surprising because not only is it one of the most fertile and original parts of his work, but also because it gives substance and coherence to his entire conception. There is therefore a lot of ground to cover in considering this side of his work. We shall try to do this by examining Saint-Simon's idea of 'political organisation' in its three main applications:

(*a*) as the technique of politics in a society with diffused power;

(*b*) as an institutional blue-print designed to replace the old nation state and two of its representative institutions, the central government and the political party; and, deriving from these first two aspects:

(*c*) as a modern doctrine which opposes Jacobinism in all the latter's historical manifestations from the French Revolution onwards.

(*a*)

The crux of Saint-Simon's political theory is the principle that with the coming of the industrial-technological society, an entirely different kind of politics will be needed. This he defined first in a negative way as the opposite of the 'politics of power'—in other words, as politics without power; then, he defined it positively as 'the politics of abilities'. Although this is obviously a dual concept, and the negative definition is inseparable from

40. *Centripetal Politics*, London, 1975.

the positive one, let us take first the idea of politics without power.

What Saint-Simon actually envisages is the situation in which political power neutralizes itself by its own diffusion—a situation which political anthropologists sometimes describe, in a different context, as *acephaly*. But Saint-Simon sees this political acephaly or—to coin a word—this political *a-potency*, as characteristic of, and inevitable in, the industrial society. This is so because, for the first time in history, the very functioning of society is conditioned by the participation in that functioning of all those who now have exclusive knowledge and skills. So interdependent are the elements of society and yet, on the contrary, all those who produce goods and deliver services have become so independent in that society, through their own expertise, that the withholding of services or of production by any of these innumerable groups of industrialists can immediately stop the functioning of the entire society. Power is nowhere, because power is everywhere.

To be sure, in all societies those who deliver goods and services have implicit power. But in all societies, prior to the industrial-technological society, political power was in the first place centralized in the political institutions, which were fed by the mechanisms of feudal allegiances; and, secondly, the political institutions could make their power felt by means of coercion. Neither of these premisses remains valid, according to Saint-Simon, in the industrial-technological society. In that society, each of the diffused groups of production or of service generates its own political power by virtue of its participation or non-participation in the functioning of the society. The power-generating groups as such can, if they so wish, dispense with their political representations or extensions, which in earlier societies linked them with the political centre of the sovereign nation-state. Nowadays, the power-generating groups can, if they so wish, dispense also with representative political institutions as a whole, because they know the power of their direct action and direct control in their own sectional spheres. Above all, the central political institutions (state and government) whose *raison d'être* in earlier societies was to exert power, if need be by coercion, in all sections of the society so as to keep them working together, can no longer do so. Although skilled technicians can be jailed or shot they can neither be coerced into producing nor be replaced at their work. To strike against the strikers in such a society is literally *counter-productive*, for it only further delays and disorganizes production.

But, further, does this mean that the possession of power changes hands, that power is transferred from the feudal-military class to the industrial class? Does political power, both as a concept and as a reality, still exist in the new society? Saint-Simon's answer to these questions is that whereas it is true that the feudal class, which lived by power alone, has lost its precarious power to the industrialists, who now exert the real and durable power—it is equally true to say that in the new society of the industrialists, the industrial-technological society, power dissipates itself. Power, which was palpably concentrated and centralized in the old society, is so widely shared in the new society that it nullifies itself. In other words, Saint-Simon was prepared to accept that politics can be separated from power, and that it can survive in this condition.

This position leaves Saint-Simon more than ever open to the familiar charge of political utopianism. Indeed who can dissociate politics from power without losing the sense of reality? Yet it is platitudinous to recall that historically the two concepts were not always identical. Aristotle's long meditations on the differences between rule, authority and power ('the members of a political association aim by their very nature at being equal and differing in nothing . . . [but] . . . when one body of citizens is ruling and the other is being ruled the former desires to establish a difference'[41]) are at the very heart of his conception of politics as association. During the Middle Ages power was only exercised locally and therefore it was precariously segmented. Moreover it was divided between the temporal and the spiritual authorities. The church and the king ruled differently, and had different politics, not to speak of policies. It is only after, and because of secularization, that politics were identified exclusively with power. This was the process which Machiavelli witnessed in the birth of the nation state and which made him combine these two concepts.

But Saint-Simon is speaking, in our view, of politics after the decline of the nation state, after the nation state and its central government lose their power and it passes into the—decentralized—hands of what he calls 'the abilities' (*les capacités*). It is of this dissociation of power from politics that he is speaking. And it is this diffusion of power among the abilities which makes him try to discover what kind of politics, what kind of political process, these abilities will produce. We turn now to

41. Aristotle, *Politics*, I, XII, 1259 b, 2, Oxford, 1948, p. 40.

the politics of abilities.[42] Saint-Simon's own words, quoted in chronological order in the following passages as the idea matured, will illustrate what he meant by this.

What is required is to find a new system of political organization.[43]

We have felt the need to break this lethargy of the political writers, and especially the duty to redirect the emphasis of attention and to show to philosophy the new task which is imposed on it by a new century, the industrial century.[44]

The change which I wish to see effected in the social organization is undoubtedly very vast; but the change is even vaster in politics because it consists of the passage from one system to another, based on absolutely opposed principles . . .

The old system . . . has lost the major part of its control over social action in general.

It still has possession of the power to form the general political plan and this situation will not be changed until a new system has been completely organized.[45]

Having thus stated that the purpose of his inquiry was to find out what changes in politics are brought about by changes in society as a whole, Saint-Simon continued the idea in

42. I had two problems in relation to the use of this expression. The first concerned the choice of an English word for the French '*capacité*': 'capacities', 'competences', or 'elites' or 'intelligentsias' offered themselves but in the end I preferred 'abilities'.

Secondly, the expressions 'the politics of abilities' or 'the politics of elites' had to be distinguished from 'the *policies* of abilities' or 'the *policies* of elites'. Saint-Simon's concern is not with the defence of the sectional interests of the elites or the intelligentsias through their policies, but with the kind of politics, in the sense of *political process and institutions,* which will be engendered in the age of abilities. How will politics work when the politics of power will no longer suffice? Of late several theories have tried to conceptualize the salient aspects of the political process: Dahl has produced the politics of *bargaining*; Rokkan the politics of *corporate pluralism*; Deutsch the politics of *integration.* Although of non-academic origin, the politics of *concertation* has much to commend it as a definition. In the original French, the term conveys etymologically the meanings of consultation, orchestration and harmonization. Indeed if the metaphor could be stretched further, almost to a pun, the concertation, orchestration or harmonization should include all those who are *instrumental* in the execution of a work. Thus the politics of abilities could also be defined as the *politics of instrumentality* (David Apter sporadically used this expression), or the *politics of an instrumental society.* The expressions 'instrument', 'concert' and 'concertation' would fit in with Saint-Simon's vision of the harmonious co-operation of all those whose skills, services or capital are indispensable to the functioning of the economy.

43. *L'Industrie, Works,* Vol. I, p. 182.

44. *L'Industrie, Works,* Vol. II, op. cit., p. 214.

45. *L'Organisateur, Works,* Vol. II, p. 77 and pp. 163–4.

*L'Organisateur*, where for the first time, he connected the difference between ability and power with two different political systems. The passage is crucial, and indeed Saint-Simon himself gives it a particular importance. He says,

> The emancipation of the communes gave birth to industrial property or ownership, based on labour, property distinct and independent and soon to rival landed wealth which was purely military in origin and nature.
>
> By this memorable change, industrial ability was able to develop, to be perfected, to expand, and nations were able to organize themselves on all fronts on an industrial basis, only the top ranks of society remaining military, as well as the general leadership which continued in power.
>
> Let us make for the spiritual power analogous observations to those made for temporal power.
>
> Positive scientific ability must in the same way have replaced the old spiritual power. . . .
>
> . . . a positive temporal power . . . reached the final stages of its development; and a positive spiritual ability, i.e. scientific ability, arose in the wake of the old spiritual power.[46]

But in order to make it clear to his readers that the terminology used here had a new and deeper meaning, Saint-Simon first drew attention to it in a footnote: 'The division of society between the temporal and the spiritual . . . provided the basis of the possibility of making a science from politics, and of distinguishing between theory and practice. But in the new system the division is no longer between two powers but between two abilities'[47] (an expression which can be translated also as 'capacities', 'competences', or even 'elites').[48]

In the text itself, Saint-Simon further stressed the importance of the distinction he had made:

> Before going on to the examination of ulterior forces, I beg you, dear compatriots, to consider this remarkable difference between the two systems, which has appeared since the birth of the new one, and which I have tried to express by the opposition of the words: power and ability. By this I am not saying: a new power is growing side by side with each of the two former powers . . . but an ability is appearing side by side with a power.[49]

46. Ibid., pp. 2–3 and p. 85.
47. Ibid., p. 85.
48. See *supra*, p. 10, a longer discussion on the expression 'politics of abilities', as well as 'Note on the selection of texts', p. 60.
49. Ibid., p. 85 (Italics in the text).

Saint-Simon's theory of the appearance in history of the two estates which had taken over or were in the process of taking over the role previously held by the military and the clergy—namely the industrialists in the sphere of temporal power, and the scientists in the sphere of spiritual power—combined with his theory of the inevitable participation in the processes of decision-making of all those engaged in the processes of production, form the groundwork of his theory of the change from power to abilities. Sheer power would no longer suffice as it could no longer be sufficiently *concentrated*. Everyone who had an ability necessary to the functioning of society would have power. The time had now come when *powers* would have to be replaced by *abilities* and, 'it is in this way that society, taken as a whole, can really exert sovereignty, which consists now of a principle deriving from the very nature of things'.

The temporal power, continued Saint-Simon, demanded by its very nature the highest degree of passive obedience on the part of the nation. But, in the realm of industrial ability, which from now on would be directing the temporal affairs of society, arbitrariness would be reduced to a minimum. There would be a very limited and very weak degree of power or command. Similarly, the spiritual realm, which by its nature was always conjectural, required in the feudal society the highest degree of confidence and of mystical submission. But positive scientific ability in the industrial society does not require either blind faith or confidence—not, at any rate, from those who can follow the arguments. Thus, argues Saint-Simon, if one so wishes, one can consider positive scientific ability as producing yet another power, in so far as it produces strength; but it is the strength of demonstration rather than the strength of revelation.[50] Thus the political process of command-obedience, which had proved increasingly unworkable in the new conditions, is replaced by the process of persuasion-understanding.

In this connection, the concept of corporate participation is crucial to the Saint-Simonian interpretation of the new politics of the industrial society. Saint-Simon believed that by the very act of their societal involvement in production, through their skills, crafts and knowledge, all producers should join directly in the processes of decision- and policy-making, because they were now inevitably at the very centre of things. He saw democracy based on implicit and intrinsic participation. Producers organize themselves into corporations, enterprises, trade unions or communes, which collectively can offer or withhold their

50. Ibid., pp. 86–7.

participation in production. As a result of the dependence characteristic of industrial society itself, as well as of the interdependence of the corporations among themselves and within themselves, the new processes of decision-making require consultation with all those participating in production. Lack of consultation becomes in a literal sense dysfunctional and leads to break down.

Incidentally, it must be noted that everything that Saint-Simon wrote about participation sounds particularly utopian because of the literary style of the epoch, and because of his own pompous style. (But then Marx and even Lenin were also pompous when they wrote on this subject, not to speak of Proudhon.) The rule of power will cease and a new era will start in the history of mankind, bringing harmony and gaiety. People will work with each other in love and joy, once they no longer exploit each other; collectively they will exploit the resources of nature; the latter will be inexhaustible when the new sciences and techniques are brought into play. The relations among men working in this new process will be those of spontaneously renewed consensus and of mutual generosity. All the overtones of utopianism are thickly laid on in these passages.

Yet, if one is to interpret his thoughts in their general context, one must continue to connect these allegories with his basic theory of and concern for organization, which is central to his philosophy. His main contention, in opposition to Proudhon's ideas, is that organization, with its corollaries of discipline and hierarchy, is indispensable. The need for rationalization and efficiency in production and for selective leadership, which is an idea compatible with Saint-Simon's qualified egalitarianism, is always at the very basis of his thinking. 'The works of the industrialists have different degrees of generality. This basic fact produces a kind of hierarchy between the different classes which form this enormous mass of citizens "useful in production",' he often repeats. Even Durkheim, in his socialist interpretation of Saint-Simon's work, sees a possible contradiction here. He reminds us that Saint-Simon's authoritarianism shows in his demand that a national catechism be established and that all contrary instruction should be prohibited.[51] Bertrand de Jouvenel has wondered why Saint-Simon did not foresee that a kind of military organization for production would replace the organization of the military for destruction, a feature of the

51. *Socialism*, op. cit., p. 155.

past which he so abhorred.[52] This aspect of Saint-Simon's thought is responsible for his, perhaps justified, reputation in the history of ideas as an 'elitist', a 'technocrat' or a 'meritocrat'. It has led also to the exaggerated allegation, mentioned earlier, that he could be considered as a proto-totalitarian. But the fact is that at first glance there seems to be a contradiction between his belief in participation and his belief in selectivity and hierarchy.

The necessary bridge between his participatory utopianism and his elitist rationality is to be found precisely in his theory of the passage from the politics of power to the politics of ability.[53] Because of the increasing spread of knowledge to ever wider circles of qualified producers, there take place simultaneously a diffusion and also a concentration of power on the new lines of a hierarchy of specialization of knowledge and of industrial leadership. To take diffusion first; because of the inevitable transfer of power in society from the power rooted in the ownership of wealth, based on coercion and typical of the military-feudal society, to the power rooted in the production of wealth, based on skill and inventiveness, the power to command the industrial society is diffused. Authority is transferred from the instruments and methods of coercion to the instruments and methods of participation in creation—what François Perroux describes, in the context of Saint-Simon's work, as *collective creation*. But the power is diffused throughout the internal organizations or organized groups. Saint-Simon attaches great importance to the formation and functioning of corporate organizations: trade unions as well as enterprises. The welfare of the industrial body can be ensured only if and when 'individuals in their overwhelming majority, will be grouped in industrial associations, more or less numerous, but interconnected . . . so as to form a general system of organization directed towards a great common industrial goal.'[54] The corporations must co-operate among themselves in the organization of the industrial society as a whole if anarchy, 'the worst evil of all', is to be avoided.

But, on the other hand, power spreads also towards those who possess the new, scientific knowledge among the leaders of the groups and their councils, necessary for co-ordination and planning, consultation and interdependence. This is where, in Saint-Simon's conception and terminology, government in the

52. 'Histoire des idées politiques', 'Les cours de droit', (roneotyped lectures, published for students) Paris, 1967, p. 170 ff.

53. See note on p. 60.

54. *Du Système Industriel*, II, p. 185.

old sense ends and administration in the new sense begins. The theory now comes fully into its own.

*There must be a new art for conducting public affairs. In the past the main political skill consisted in knowing how to govern, that is to say how to make oneself feared and obeyed: The science of administration was still in its infancy and had only a secondary importance.*[55]

*It is an entirely new doctrine which we must organize. The old doctrine has entrusted the governors with the task of commanding: the new doctrine must confer on them, as their principal function, to administer well.*[56]

These last passages and especially the ringing first sentence 'there must be a new art for conducting public affairs', seem to me the most enlightening in the entire argument. For it is at this junction that Saint-Simon's theory of politics distinguishes itself from the other trends of thinking with which up to a point it runs parallel: Marxism, and especially Marxism–Leninism on one side, anarchism, on the other.

(*b*)

In contrast with Proudhon's anarchism, Saint-Simon believed that society needs political organization. In contrast with Lenin's Marxism, Saint-Simon believed that such an organization should not be based on centralized power. (Marx and Engels, as we know, oscillated between anarchism and statism.)

In Saint-Simon's scheme for the political organization of the industrial-technological society, some old political institutions would disappear so that new political institutions could develop. The first institution to disappear would be the nation state, which, in his context, meant the nation states of Europe as they were in his time. The nation state would dissolve both from within and from without. From within it would dissolve among all the internal groups of abilities which disregard the mechanism of controls of and by the state and prefer self-administration, and which can no longer be coerced lest the industrial (-technological) society should grind to a halt. From without, the nation state would melt into a European confederative association,[57] because the economy of such a society can prosper only in large territorial units. It cannot survive within areas and with resources of the size of those of England,

55. Ibid., III, p. 91.
56. Ibid., I, p. 177.
57. See *infra*, *On the Reorganization of European Society*, p. 83f.

France, Germany, etc. All the new institutions and the new political processes will be European or nothing.

With the nation state, the central government would go too. The central government had been increasingly isolated at the apex of a network of more or less representative institutions which were gradually being emptied of real power. It was also proving unable to maintain its idea of 'order' in the 'disorder' provoked by the corporate, or sectional interests of the producers. The producers had acquired new national and international positions of strength and could deny the national interest and push the central government off the stage. According to Saint-Simon, there will still be some central institutions but they will be (1) European and (2) deliberative and administrative—'administrative' is used in the sense that there will be a need for functional administration (to administer 'things') but no need for government ('to govern men'). Government is what disappears. In so far as government was the organ of power by means of centralization, when centralized power goes, so does government.

A cluster of institutions connected with the representation of the national interest, and serving the central government, will disappear together with it. According to Saint-Simon, some of these institutions will go down with the former centres of national power, and some of them will die a natural death of obsolescence. Internationalization of the previously national centres of power and organs of representation is implicitly and explicitly contained in Saint-Simon's description of the birth of the European supranational Parliament and Executive of which we shall speak presently. But other institutions will simply lose their *raison d'être* in the new functional organization of the society. As direct administration will replace 'representative government', the organs of political representation will necessarily fade away.

In Saint-Simon's logic, the end of the nation state and the subsequent internationalization are caused by the advent of the industrial-technological society with its distinctively functional organization. In that context political representative institutions are bound gradually to lose their importance. As far as the political parties are concerned—to Saint-Simon the most typical intermediary political institution—the logic of the evolution of the industrial-technological society should bring about their subordination to the corporate bodies which they respectively claim to 'represent': trade unions, regions, enterprises. The contact between these bodies and the functional bodies of 'administration' (which would replace the representative government) could not be other than direct—and both could dispense with intermediaries such as political parties. Saint-Simon himself imagined and proposed at one time a party of the industrialists and indeed a 'national party'.[58] But this was to be an all-embracing association of all those 'useful in production', and was meant only to speed up the big changes needed by society in order to effect its reform and transform its structures.

A description of the political institutions which Saint-Simon visualized for the coming European industrial society can be made only by extracting the institutional common denominators from the many and contradictory projects he presented. These projects were drafted at different times, in different circumstances and even with different audiences in mind. But leaving aside these intermittent changes for the moment, an attempt, like the one made here, to present a simple model based on these projects must be preceded by some remarks on the gradual change of orientation in his thought which took place between Saint-Simon's earlier works and his later writings. In the earlier works he was particularly eager to propose institutional and indeed constitutional reforms; and he showed greater confidence in the effects of the setting up of new national and European corporate parliaments. In the later works, which in any case, reflect a more sombre mood, he concentrated much more on the changes he thought should be brought about in social and economic structures; and at the very end he dwelt on the changes which should take place in human ethics as a whole.

An institution which Saint-Simon considered to be indispensable to the industrial-technological society was a Plan.[59] The Plan should embrace all the activities of the society—that is both the wealth-producing activities (the exploitation of nature by industry, making use of the new scientific and technological means) and activities designed to achieve justice and happiness in the society itself. (It is interesting to note that he paid great attention to the organization of common holidays and celebrations; hymns and songs are written in advance for those occasions.) The Plan is the symbol of the scientific rationality of the society. It is also an instrument of co-ordination, and the fruit of the consultation of scientists and industrialists jointly engaged in running the society. The Plan should be yearly. It could not but be consultative. It was intended to lay down long-term

58. See *infra*, *Le Politique*, p. 129.
59. See *infra*, p. 147–52.

projects of public works, destined to bring greater prosperity to the society and to ensure that it advances further along the avenues which science is constantly opening up for it.

The drafting, discussion, preparation and execution of the Plan form the principal and continuous duties of parliament, that is to say of the 'local' or 'national' parliament, which is then subordinated to the European Parliament. Local or national parliament should consist of a house of commons with corporate representation of the most 'able' men of all sciences, arts, industries and crafts. Saint-Simon remarks that the inadequacy of the English House of Commons was evident in the contradiction between its name and its composition: instead of being composed by the leaders of industry and science, the genuine men of the commons, it was composed of lawyers, gentlemen and amateurs. Saint-Simon's house of commons approves the budget which, in his view, is the highest form of administrative control over society.

The parliament should be multi-cameral. The house of commons should consist of three chambers. The first chamber is a Chamber of Invention, which should be formed of technicians and artists. The task of this chamber is to prepare the yearly plan of public works. The second chamber is the Chamber of Examination or Scrutiny. It should be composed of three hundred members, scientists and experts, should examine the projects presented by the other chamber, and produce a programme of general public education. The third chamber is the Executive Chamber, which is formed by the other two chambers of the house of commons assembled in plenary session.

The work of the house of commons, and of the 'executive'—which is not separated from it, but is in fact the house of commons in plenary session—is therefore limited and mostly consultative: with the exception of its function of the approval of the budget. This is as it should be, for two obvious reasons connected with Saint-Simon's general theory of the organization of the new society. The first reason is that, in the society of the industrialists, in the society self-managed by the producers themselves, there is no need for governmental interference with the running of the society and its economy—indeed such interference would be inconceivable. The industrialists have an interest in the yearly consultative planning and forecasts of the house of commons, but this planning is based on information about their activities provided by them, as the persons in sole control of their own activities. Industry, this complex of various self-managed enterprises and professional associations of all kinds of 'abilities', does not need advice from specially appointed political bodies and rejects their control or supervision. And industry makes sure of its independence by limiting the organization of the house of commons and the 'administrative' duties which it still possesses to the bare minimum.

Such a relation between society and government is, of course, typical of liberal *laissez-faire*. Moreover, it is precisely when Saint-Simon was writing his earlier works, from which this parliamentary model is drawn, that he was in the closest association with the 'industrialists' (of whom the workers themselves formed only one, though the most sizeable, part) and that his doctrine was almost indistinguishable from liberalism. But his doctrine soon acquired a second dimension as he developed the idea of the producers managing the society by themselves and, consequently, of the economy based on self-management. The doctrine then became 'industrialism'. Saint-Simon took special pains publicly and explicitly to distinguish between liberalism and 'industrialism'.[60] But his distinction did not, and should not, alter the principle that society, and the self-managed economy should be independent of, any political control. The more the accent is laid on self-management, the more inconceivable becomes the idea of controls from outside the sphere of the economy. Durkheim described the doctrine of Saint-Simon as workers' socialism. If we remove the pivotal role of the state as the main controller and organizer from the classic definition of socialism, Saint-Simon's 'industrialism' could indeed be workers' socialism.

The second reason why very limited functions are attributed to the house of commons and its 'administration' is that it is subordinated to the European Parliament. This is the third institution which Saint-Simon includes in his scheme of organization. One of his principles is that there should be two levels of administration: general and local. From this he draws the conclusion that, '*Europe could have the best possible organization, if each one of the nations which it encompasses were to be governed by a parliament, recognizing the supremacy of a general parliament set above all the national governments and invested with the power to judge their disputes*'[61] (italics in the text). But this European Parliament should not be merely a reproduction of the obsolete national parliaments. The European political system must be 'homogeneous', that is, it must be perfectly suited to an entirely new society, based on entirely new social, technical and economic

60. See *infra*, *The Catechism of the Industrialists*, p. 198.
61. See *infra*, *On the Reorganization of European Society*, p. 88.

structures, and operating on an entirely new territorial dimension.

The European Parliament, therefore, must not resemble the old national parliaments, although it should consist of a chamber of deputies and a chamber of lords. But, the chamber of deputies should 'make up the European *esprit de corps* and promote the general interest which must also be the corporate interest of the European Parliament.' It should be based on corporate representation. In so far as 'all the common interests of European society can be related to the sciences, arts, law, commerce, administration and industry', each million of the literate in Europe should return one businessman, one scientist, one administrator and one magistrate to the chamber of deputies. The election should be made by the corporations—and the members should be elected for ten years. In turn, the house of lords should be composed of men, or sons of men, who had done work considered to be of the greatest usefulness to the European society. And, as if to underline once more the constant archaisms and discrepancies on which his ideas were based, Saint-Simon proposed that the lords should be appointed by the king!

Notwithstanding these archaisms and discrepancies, and bearing in mind that these institutional models belonged mostly to his early works, one can nevertheless conclude that the organization proposed by Saint-Simon was doubly consistent. It was consistent with his entire theory of the 'politics of abilities'. It was also consistent with his idea of the future industrial-technological society. In fact, it was much more advanced and much more in tune with the modern industrial-technological Europe than are, even now, the institutions proposed for the European Community which came into being more than a century after Saint-Simon had devised his model.

(*c*)

Two points are made here. The first is that Saint-Simon above all abhorred the Jacobins and their direct heir, Napoleon. Usually, anti-Jacobinism is regarded as a conservative reaction typical of those who reproached the French Revolution with having destroyed the living tradition of the past. But Saint-Simon reproached the Jacobins for having destroyed the future or, more specifically, for having strangled the historic industrial revolution, and replaced it by a banal political revolution in which the old social and political system survived—but to the advantage of new and hungrier rulers. Thus, Saint-Simon's doctrine of industrialism is the exact antithesis of Jacobinism.

Saint-Simon's irreconcilable opposition to the Jacobins is based on the following fundamental arguments: the Jacobins had not put the producers in control of the means of production but, on the contrary, had allowed a new class, the bourgeois, to interpose themselves in the process of production and to divert it for their own benefit. They had not granted to the industrialists and the scientists their rightful positions of leadership in the society; instead they had put themselves at the head of the revolutionary government by forming the only organized political party. Thus, the Jacobins missed, or indeed misdirected the true revolution, and succeeded only in replacing one class by another in the old system. As a result, they had inevitably fallen back into the obsolete and no longer viable politics of power. They had reconstituted the nation state, thus ignoring the need for federalization into one single integrated community. And having achieved this, they were pushed further down the slippery paths of nationalism and sovereignty. They had advanced these reasons in order to build anew the institutions of centralized power: army, police and the hierarchy of economic and administrative controls, thus creating the perfect conditions for the revival of the old politics of power.

The second point made here is that the actual historical conflict between Saint-Simon and the Jacobins at the end of the eighteenth century is only the beginning of a perpetual incompatibility, which has manifested itself ever since, between industrialism and Jacobinism—taking Jacobinism to mean the way in which a political party, strongly organized for this purpose, can, by presenting itself to the people as the defender of the 'people's will', gain control of the central government and of its organs of coercion and use them to rule the producers. This conflict between 'the politicians and the economy', or between 'the industrial forces and the political party', or between 'state socialism and workers' socialism' has continued ever since the French Revolution in the capitalist world, and ever since the Russian Revolution—yet another victory for Jacobinism—in the communist world.

In Saint-Simon's historical interpretation, 'if one were to try to find one origin to the French Revolution, the date which should be taken as its true beginning should be the day when the emancipation of the communes and the study of the sciences of observation began in western Europe'.[62] This is one of innumerable statements by Saint-Simon on the historical origins and the course of the Revolution. It has been chosen

62. *Du Système Industriel*, I, p. 78.

here as one of the clearest and also because of the deliberate way in which it attributes French development to a series of causes common to western Europe as a whole, a point which has repercussions afterwards for his entire theory.

The progressive emancipation of the communes, which began in the twelfth century in England, France and the Low Countries, came to a head in the seventeenth century with the English Revolution, and in the eighteenth century with the French Revolution. These events represented, above all, the growing dominance of industrial society over feudal society or, more precisely, of industrial society over the feudal states. First, the emancipation of the communes created the class of the small proprietors and cultivators who, by their remarkable economic performance over the centuries, proved that they could assume responsibility for production in the agricultural sector. Then, the progress of manufacturing industry—the inventiveness, skill, production, profitability of the new craftsmen, artisans and heads of workshops and factories, as well as the new successes of merchants, bankers and financiers—demonstrated that those engaged in industrial production could become the natural leaders of society. They delivered the goods and produced the services: they should naturally be entrusted with the leadership of the most important sectors of modern production. But they should also share the leadership with scholars and artists, and especially with the scientists, who were assuming functional importance in a society increasingly based on the specialized advance and diffusion of positive science.

These forces in the new society should have given themselves a new organization. They should have started by dispensing with the leadership of the military and the nobility—until then, the self-appointed rulers of society. The industrial society was a society of production and therefore the producers should manage it. It was not one of aggression, or of defence against other aggressive nations, which required the supremacy of the military. It could have been an essentially peaceful society: peaceful externally because in its very essence the industrial society was international (European); peaceful internally, once the producers had become, on the one hand, the numerical majority of the population and on the other hand, had all come to participate in the functioning of the society[63] and its common

63. In Saint-Simon's expression they are '*des sociétaires*'. 'In the old system the people was regimented (*enregimenté*) by its chiefs; in the new it is combined with them. . . . In the first case the people was subject; in the second it is *sociétaire*. Such is in reality the admirable character of the industrial combinations that all who work in them are bound to collaborate.' *L'Organisateur*, II, p. 150.

goal: the public good. Those who refused to participate could be only unemployed or the drop-outs (*les désœuvrés*), who were either not qualified to find employment in an expanding society which required more skills and capabilities, or who refused to accept the self-imposed, rational or rationalized working of the organization of producers. Those whom Saint-Simon called the 'idlers' or the 'consumers'—i.e. the military, the nobility and the unproductive proprietors, all those who did not contribute to production, and were not useful to industrial society, but constituted superimposed parasitical layers of 'government'—should be deprived of representation in the decision-making processes and gradually absorbed or eliminated, and so should the *désœuvrés*.

Instead of which, what happened? The entire course of history was turned aside by the clever intervention of new people with old mentalities, the same mentalities of 'lawyers and metaphysicians' who might have been useful to the old régime of power politics, but who were not necessary in the new era. This meddling with the course of history started with the coming to power of the Jacobins.

The rather lengthy quotations which follow show the reasoning on which Saint-Simon's anti-Jacobin stand is founded. Thus:

The old government having been overthrown, it was Robespierre who seized *power*; and who was Robespierre? Yet another lawyer, and his principal lieutenants also *lawyers*. . . . They took the leading positions among the Jacobins; they created a club of the Cordeliers. . . . Always guided by the same *esprit de corps*, that of domination, they behaved accordingly in all our great political crises. They had to have power at any price, and in order to get as much of it as possible, these new Proteans knew how to assume all the shapes required by the circumstances.[64]

In contrast:

The *industrialists* have not played any active role during the *revolution*; they have not taken any part in the government or administration of public affairs; they have not tried to seize power. . . .

The political spirit which animated the *industrialists* since the beginning of their emancipation, that is since the enfranchisement of the communes, that spirit which they displayed throughout the course of their evolution . . . was: (1) to avoid political upheavals . . .; (2) to limit the action of power and to restrain it as far as possible.[65]

64. *L'Industrie*, II, pp. 162–3. (Italics in the text.) See complete text *infra*, pp. 126–7.

65. *L'Industrie*, II, pp. 166–7. (Italics in the text.) See complete text *infra*, pp. 127–8.

Then Saint-Simon explains how the Jacobins used the war to bring about the recreation of a centralistic government, dominated by the military. 'In such a state of things, government has necessarily been vested with unlimited power and the direction of affairs has been taken over by the military.'[66] This is how the Jacobins substituted their own social and political interests for 'the *interests of the revolution*'. Addressing himself to the industrialists, Saint-Simon explains: 'What is lacking, the party which has usurped your confidence will show you. . . . It has substituted in your minds the interest of all those who have enriched themselves at your expense since 1789 . . . for the industrial cause the triumph of which was the goal of the revolution.'[67]

It was this substitution which brought about the corruption of the *industrial* revolution by a new domination by *politicians*. The communes should have realized that the basic object of the revolution was the formation of a new political system . . .; they should have realized that the ablest scientists and industrialists were the only ones who could fulfil this task.[68]

Since Saint-Simon first denounced it, the incompatibility between Jacobinism and the industrial-technological society has continued. In both capitalist and communist industrial-technological societies today, the political parties which make use of the central government to impose their policies in the name of national interest are being challenged from within by the functional forces of modern societies: trade unions, technical and cultural elites, national and multi-national corporations, managers, planners, regional and ethnic as well as religious and cultural organizations. All these forces demand decentralization, self-management or self-adminstration, abolition or loosening of national controls and—above all—equal participation in decision-making. But whereas in the Western democracies, political parties try to adapt themselves to the new conditions of corporate pluralism, in the communist industrial societies, the Party rulers stiffen into typically Jacobin attitudes, determined to cling to their ways of 'controlling' the entire society from their central position of power.

66. *Sur la Querelle des abeilles et des frelons*, *Works*, Vol. II, p. 217. (See complete text *infra*, pp. 136–7).

67. *Du Système Industriel*, II, pp. 12–13. (See complete text *infra*, pp. 161–2.)

68. Ibid., I, pp. 82–3.

## 4. CONCLUSIONS

Saint-Simon's thought has very serious, and indeed obvious, drawbacks.

All the drawbacks, all the 'utopian' features in Saint-Simon's work have one very substantial cause: his inability to grasp the importance of capitalism. He failed to perceive, or perceived too late, how this historical phenomenon would distort the evolution of his cherished industrial revolution. As a result his work seems today particularly naïve and utopian. His vision has been shattered in the one hundred and fifty odd years which separate him from the present time. His estate of 'industrialists' or of 'producers', for instance, has been split into two antagonistic classes by the difference that ownership of the means of production brings about: the employers or exploiters and the employed (or indeed unemployed) or exploited.

This division has produced a heightened consciousness of class and of the class struggle. Proudhon's, Blanqui's and, last but not least, Marx's perception of the overwhelming importance of class consciousness has played and is still playing an enormous part in social evolution.

From another point of view, unholy alliances, which Saint-Simon would have rejected as inconceivable, have emerged as social realities. The alliance between the military and the industrialists, now commonly called the military–industrial complex', and taken by many authors to be a common feature of the industrial society in both constitional-pluralistic and socialist states, would have been anathema to Saint-Simon and an inconceivable contradiction. An earlier example of this contemporary phenomenon, i.e. the arms industry, provides an even more abominable affront to his cherished belief in the innate pacifism of industry.

Saint-Simon also underestimated the effects of the spiral of industrial concentration and of 'automation' on employment. *désœuvrés* (the idlers, incapables and drop-outs) were for him only a fringe, a marginal category. He did not visualize the recurring unemployment which concentration and automation, the two major processes of modern industry, inevitably produce. He believed that the wealth produced by industry would exceed the consumption of society and create an expanding need for labour.

Again, Saint-Simon failed to visualize the ugliness and the dehumanization which has overtaken industrial life since its expansion in earnest in the nineteenth century. The blind discipline of industrial organization, the ever-expanding conurbations, the increasing environmental pollution, the false worship of the 'consumer', the manipulation of societies by vast monopolistic companies controlling all markets, and the world-wide advertising techniques to which men of the last decades of this century may or may not become inured, make an incredible contrast with his almost pastoral vignettes of an 'industrial world', in which he saw industrialists consulting with workers, scientists and artists on how to increase yet more the prosperity and the welfare of mankind thus served by the genius of industry. All these objective factors, as well as the subjective factor of the growth of revolutionary class consciousness, helped by the revolutionary education provided by the new political or social organizations, made of the concept of 'class' the reality which we have known in the traditional industrial society.

But once we accept the enormous caveat of his omission of any reference to capitalism, and if we accept the argument that we have already entered the post-capitalist society, the relevance of Saint-Simon's work to contemporary politics appears in a different light.

Saint-Simon's analysis of industrial society foresaw four developments which are currently visible in the unstable order of industrial-technological societies in Europe.

The first development is the imposition on society of decisions made by corporate forces. Because of the diffusion of power, brought about by the coming of the industrial-technological society, groups, indeed corporations, whose purpose, in classical definitions, was to try to influence the decision-making processes, can now impose their own decisions on the society directly. This dispersion of the power of decision-making requires a change in the technique, or style of politics. The possession of specialized knowledge, from the very rarefied knowledge at the top to the more elementary but still irreplaceable skills at the bottom, adds to the likelihood of groups imposing their own decisions on the society, thus increasing the dispersion of power. This is a key problem in the politics of the industrialist-capitalist societies; one which frequently leads to situations of complete social deadlock. But even in communist industrial societies, the basic problem is the same—as the crisis in Czechoslovakia in 1968 showed so clearly. There is an increasing need for the communist party of government to 'bargain' under the counter with the productive forces who deliver the goods and provide the services in modern society.

The second development is seen in the hierarchy of the

industrial-technological society which is based on science and on the exercise of knowledge. This produces new differentials and splits in the structure of power of these societies. In both capitalist and communist societies the functional elites (or technical intelligentsia) come to the fore, and exercise more influence on the respective authority: the management in the enterprises, or the government in the society at large. These functional power groups grow increasingly broader, as specialization of technical skills spreads in modern production. The technique of decision-making, which Galbraith has felicitously called group-decision-making, is based on the indispensability of each expert group, or indeed individual.

Thirdly, there is the rapid extension of the new style of politics of abilities among modern European governments. They all experiment with different variations on the theme of 'partnership' with the corporate forces: social contracts, prices and incomes policies, medium-term planning, crisis-management, contractual devolution to national and multi-national corporations, regional autonomy, social and economic councils, tripartite government–employer–trades union bodies, etc., in all these variations the government, and the representative institution, themselves constitute only one factor in the complex process of decision- and policy-making.

Fourthly, the size and resources of the nation states, and in particular of the European nation States, both in western and eastern Europe, have now proved to be insufficient to enable them to maintain their positions in the competitive world market, and to control the internal centrifugal forces which the industrial-technological society unleashes. Saint-Simon's early advocacy, on these very grounds, of some form of European union seems to be vindicated. Integration, in the double sense of social and international integration, is the principal problem facing these states now. In western Europe it has led to the present half-way institutional arrangements which will come to life only when the European Parliament, foretold by Saint-Simon, comes into existence. In eastern Europe the prospect of integration has led to a definitive reaction in favour of the sovereignty of the individual East European states against the dangers of absorption into a federation forcibly led by the super-power.

However, rule by force, and indeed by military forces, in the bloc of states dominated by the U.S.S.R. is the sharpest reminder of Saint-Simon's ultimate alternative: the rule of sheer political and military power versus the rule of producers. It is easy to see that by keeping their societies under strict control, and forbidding strikes, associations and demonstrations, the communist régimes can keep order within their borders—while the Western world is in open disorder. One can also understand how, in some European capitalist countries particularly threatened by the clashes and conflicts from within the disorderly societies, the national communist parties with a steel-like organization might seem to emerge as the party of order.

Finally, we have also seen how, by military means, the U.S.S.R. has crushed other communist governments more inclined than the Soviet leadership to adjust Marxism–Leninism to the requirements of the modern industrial-technological society. The emergence of a military super-totalitarianism, of the Left or of the Right, fostered by the new cybernetic means of control and repression of all activities, is very feasible indeed. The suggestion that a gigantic military dictatorship could solve most of the problems of the industrial society has been increasingly heard in the Western world. But this only confirms Saint-Simon's basic premise: that, at the end of it all, the two forces which oppose each other in the industrial societies are the producers and the military, or the 'abilities' and the Jacobins, and that the ultimate choice in modern politics is between the politics of increased arch-centralistic and violent power as against politics without power and with increasingly free, consultative decision-making processes.

Lastly, there is one more general feature of Saint-Simon's vision of the industrial-technological society which is very relevant to contemporary life. This is his concern with the degradation of moral values in and by the industrial society and, following from this, his concern with education. Modern religious philosophers nowadays share this concern. They see the industrial-technological society as a 'post-Christian' society. Concern about the moral vacuum in a society which is geared only to the production and consumption of material things; the thought that such a purely functional society might be possible only when the men who form it have lost their moral strength or their basic faiths; these things have to be set against the satisfaction that mankind might otherwise derive from the hitherto inconceivable achievements of the progress of human science and human technology. The 1960s saw a great reconsideration of values. Simple populism and anarchism were propounded in a reaction against the gluttonous desire of the fifties for comfort, luxury and wealth. There occurred even a new kind of Christian revival, taking the form sometimes of the 'hippie' and 'superstar' style. This was the second Christian revival to occur since the Second World War. The first appeared immediately after the war, from the crucible of the Resistance and of the concentration camps, in the political doctrine of Christian Democracy and the philosophy of Christian existentialism. In both instances, what the new reformers tried to achieve was the restoration at the centre of human life of a set of Christian moral values, even if these were simplified and theologically imperfect.

This need or search was prefigured in Saint-Simon's spiritual journey through the industrial society of the future. The *New Christianity*,[69] is seen, with justification, as an unsophisticated criticism of the Christian churches of his time. But it is equally significant as an appeal for the restoration of Christian principles and values as the basis of social life. Saint-Simon says:

Great harm was done to the community by the neglect in which, since the fifteenth century, the study of universal principles and universal interests had been left. This neglect gave rise to the egoism which became dominant in all classes and individuals. This sentiment, dominating all classes and individuals, made it easier for Caesarism to recover much of the political force which it had lost before the fifteenth century. It is to this egoism that we must attribute the political malady of our own age, a malady which affects all the workers who serve the community.

It is clear that what Saint-Simon denounces here is the moral emptiness of *all* individuals and of *all* classes, which allowed Caesarism to gain the ascendancy in the affairs of mankind and from which originated 'the political malady of our own age'. He was concerned with the ultimate motivations of social action and with the values of those engaged in it.

The kind of rehabilitation of Christian values advocated by Saint-Simon has been partially realized in the trends towards 'Christian revivals' manifested by thinkers of our generation who see themselves as modern Saint-Simonians. For instance, one of Saint-Simon's genuine contemporary interpreters, the French economist and social philosopher François Perroux, in his book, *Le pain et la parole*, writes:

The man of earthly achievements is the man of progress . . . the élite knows the ambiguity of the progress of science, of technique and of industry. The élite fulfils its function when it suggests that man does not create himself only by transforming things, but that things cannot be transformed unless man reinvents himself incessantly. . . .

69. See *infra*, p. 204f.

The Christian and Catholic Church cannot forget that our species carries with it the most intense and the most efficacious forces of the cosmic evolution. The commandment to love is addressed to a man who is shown to us by the positive sciences as structurally predisposed to receive it, and armed with powerful means with which to make it a living reality. This commandment to love already permeated Saint-Simon's social doctrine which taught that the law of our species it to know and to love. . . . The technique and the industry increase the portent and the efficacy of such proofs of human solidarity and brotherhood as the renunciation of the surfeit of riches, the acceptance of some sacrifice, the discipline of common service (which replaces the pursuit of gain) in favour of the weak and feeble masses. Our holy rites of the Sacrifice, of the oblation and of the sharing of our Bread have now laid hold of the profane rites which men had to invent in the course of history.

# Notes on the Selection of Texts and on the Translation of Certain Expressions

The extracts from Saint-Simon's written work published here have been chosen as most representative of his political thought, rather than of his philosophical, scientific, historic or religious ideas. But since Saint-Simon's work is an amalgam of all these ideas, any attempt to divide the actual text rigidly is bound to seem arbitrary. In compiling the present selection the principle followed has been to include as many texts as possible—even where their political relevance was perhaps not absolute. The selection comprises the greater part of Saint-Simon's classical works, but it also includes other, less well-known passages which have been omitted from previous collections. Thus the reader can draw on a wider, if more generalized, range of examples.

The texts have all been translated anew from the 1869 French edition. This was decided on, in the first place, in order to ensure continuity of style throughout the entire unabridged passages, which are generally longer than previously published extracts. Second, a new translation was thought advisable in order to use, whenever possible, the technical vocabulary of political science, in the hope that this would throw into relief the hitherto neglected political significance of some of Saint-Simon's theories. The French text used for the translation is that of the *Œuvres de Claude-Henri de Saint-Simon*, published in six volumes in 1966, in Paris, by the Maison d'Editions Anthropos, whose permission to quote is here gratefully acknowledged. The Anthropos edition is a photographic reproduction of the Dentu edition of Saint-Simon, taken from the *Œuvres de Saint-Simon et Enfantin*, published between 1868 and 1876 in Paris, which is now out of print. However, each of the larger volumes of the Anthropos edition brings together two or more of the small Dentu format, each with its own pagination. Thus, references in the present edition reading for instance: I, 2, pp. 88–100 should be interpreted as Anthropos edition, volume I, Dentu edition, volume 2, pp. 88–100.

What this present selection has also attempted to do, is to include as far as possible only Saint-Simon's own original writings, as distinct from those of his disciples and secretaries.

Thus, chapters from *Le Politique* or from *L'Industrie* specifically referred to in the original as having been written by Augustin Thierry or by Auguste Comte have not been included here. In some cases this was to be regretted because a number of these passages were particularly relevant to the political aspect of Saint-Simon's discourse. In distinguishing between what Saint-Simon wrote and what Enfantin wrote, the present edition has followed with confidence Dentu's selection. Indeed, the editor's own and limited attempt to check, by working on the original editions available in the Bibliothèque Nationale and the Bibliothèque de l'Arsenal in Paris, whether there were disparities between these originals and Dentu's edition proved the latter to be as faithful as possible. But intensive research is still being carried on in this field and new attributions to the Master or to his disciples will still be made, presumably for a long while.

Seemingly paradoxically, this anthology of Saint-Simon's essentially political work has left aside some circumstantial and 'propagandist' portions of the work which concerned immediate political circumstances in French or European politics of the time. This again has proved to be a difficult and arbitrary operation. But to have left all the incidental contemporary references in the text would have amounted to drowning the essential 'theoretical' passages in a sea of irrelevant trivia.

Finally a word should be said here about the translation of some of Saint-Simon's key expressions, i.e. of those expressions which carry special conceptual weight in Saint-Simon's political philosophy, and which consequently recur frequently in the text. As will be seen from the examples listed below, the translator chose to use in such cases the more abstract English word, thus cutting across the anachronistic analogies. It was hoped in this way to retain Saint-Simon's characteristically conceptual and functional view of the industrial society.

The expression *charter* (*la charte*) is used in the strict sense of constitution granted by sovereigns to their subjects in contradistinction to those based on the 'will of the people'. Such was the Charter granted by Louis XVIII to France in 1814. In feudal times, charters of privileges were granted, not only by the crown, but by both ecclesiastical and lay lords to communities, boroughs and religious foundations as well as to individuals. (*Encyclopaedia Britannica*, 1912).

There were special difficulties in translating the expression *la commune*, in so far as in French the word can be used both for what is meant in English by *Parish* or by what is meant by

*Commons* in the context of 'House of Commons'. The French English *Larousse* warns us that: 'Commune has no exact equivalent in English and cannot really be translated'. The *Concise Oxford Dictionary of Common English* makes it clear that *commons* means only 'the common people, third estate in English or other similar constitutions represented by lower House of Parliament' while *commune* means 'a French territorial division' or 'a similar division elsewhere'. It was therefore decided to use in the translation *communes* for the medieval communes described by the *Encyclopaedia Britannica*, 1912 as 'a group of persons acting together for the purposes of self-government, especially in towns' and *commons* only in the exclusive context of the English House of Commons.

Saint-Simon's *cultivateur* might mean alternatively in English: farmer, labourer or, indeed, cultivator. It was translated here principally as *agriculturalist*.

In the Introduction, it was explained at greater length why and with what qualifications *industrialiste* was translated as *industrialist* and *science politique* as *political science*.

Probably the most difficult problem was raised by the translation in English of *politique des capacités* which, as contrasted with *politique du pouvoir*, is at the centre of Saint-Simon's political theory. *Capacité* by itself can be translated as capacity, competence or ability or, when taken as a collective noun, as men of competence or indeed elites. But the 'politics of elites' denotes the politics made by elites, or even in the interest of elites. This would be absolutely misleading for *politiques des capacités*. What Saint-Simon had in mind was the technique of the *politics of abilities*, when contrasted with the politics of power—thus coming nearest to such modern expressions as politics of 'bargaining', of 'corporate pluralism', of 'communication', or indeed of 'concertation'. It is in this sense that 'politics of abilities' is used in the translation.

Again, *propriétaire*, an essential expression in Saint-Simon's terminology, is used by him with different meanings; in English they are: landowner, owner, property-owner, bourgeois or freeholder. The basic meaning was translated here as *proprietor*, thus allowing for Saint-Simon's fundamental distinction between industrial and non-industrial proprietors (and properties)

*Savants* is used indiscriminately by Saint-Simon to mean in English: scholars, men of learning or scientists. In the context of the politics of the industrial-technological society, *scientists* is the most appropriate for and the nearest to Saint-Simon's meaning.

*Théologique* is another expression which Saint-Simon uses with different meanings; in English these are: theological, ecclesiastical or clerical. The frequent and basic expression *le systéme théologique et féodal* was consistently translated here as the *ecclesiastical and feudal system.*

The expression *Turkish Equality* is defined by Saint-Simon as follows: 'It is the very opposite of true equality, i.e. industrial equality, which amounts to any person's right to derive from society benefits exactly proportionate to that person's social contribution, or in other words proportionate to that person's ability and to the productivity of the means used by that person, including, of course, the capital used.' In *Du Système industriel* 111, 2, 17.

G.I.

# EXTRACTS FROM THE WORKS OF CLAUDE-HENRI DE SAINT-SIMON

TRANSLATED BY
VALENCE IONESCU

# I

# Letters from an Inhabitant of Geneva to His Contemporaries

*Lettres d'un habitant de Genève à ses contemporains* (a brochure of 103 pages without date or place of publication or author's name), Paris, 1803, I, 1, pp. 11–48.

This work is presented as an exchange of letters between the author of the 'project' and a friend.

## FIRST LETTER

I am no longer young, I have observed and reflected actively all my life and your happiness has been the end to which all my work has been directed; I have thought of a project which I think might be useful to you and I now propose to tell you about it.

Open a subscription in honour of Newton's memory: allow everyone, no matter who he may be, to subscribe as much as he wishes.

Let each subscriber nominate three mathematicians, three physicists, three chemists, three physiologists, three authors, three painters and three musicians.

The subscriptions and nominations should be renewed annually, although everyone should be completely free to re-nominate the same people indefinitely.

Divide the amount of the subscriptions between the three mathematicians, the three physicists, etc., who have obtained the most votes.

Invite the President of the Royal Society in London to receive the subscriptions for the first year. In subsequent years, entrust this honourable duty to whomsoever has given the highest subscription.

Make it a proviso that those who have been nominated should accept no posts, honours or money from any special group, but leave each man absolutely free to use his gifts as he wills.

Men of genius will in this way enjoy a reward which is worthy of themselves and of you; this reward is the only one which will supply them with the means to give you all the service of which they are capable; it will become the object of the ambition of the most active minds and will deflect them from anything which might disturb your peace of mind.

Finally, by doing this you will be providing leaders for those who are working for the progress of your enlightenment; you will be endowing these leaders with great prestige and you will be placing considerable financial resources at their disposal.

*Opinion of my friend*

You have asked me to share with you my thoughts about the plan you sent me; my pleasure in giving you my opinion is all the greater because the noble motives of its author strikes the careful reader; because his intention is sublime and because the project should meet with a favourable response from every thinking and sensitive human being. And, lastly, the author desires the happiness of mankind. He works for it. I love him for this.

His ideas are as new as they are philanthropic. He rightly sees men of genius as torches illuminating mankind, those who rule as well as those who are ruled; and it is by a well-reasoned principle of justice that he enlists mankind in a collective action to reward them. From another point of view, his project is equally good; it involves mankind in a *collective* action to reward men of genius, turning them away from concentration on the particular interests of a fraction of mankind which, because it pays them, paralyses a part of their energy.

The project creates finer positions than any which have previously existed; positions which will raise the man of genius to his proper place—above other men, even above those who are invested with the highest authority. The prospect of these positions will stimulate the man of genius who will, at last, enjoy rewards worthy of the love of glory, of the passion which enables him to bear uncomplainingly the strains attendant on study and profound meditation, which gives him the necessary perseverance to make his mark in the sciences and the arts.

Personal interest is a very powerful force in a man of genius, but love of mankind can also act as a spur to the performance of prodigious feats. How fine it is to work for the good of mankind! What a noble goal! Has man any better way of aspiring to the Divine? In doing this he finds within himself powerful compensation for the pains he must endure.

If I compare the high position in which mankind will place the man of genius to a seat in one of the academies, I see that HE WHO HAS BEEN ELECTED BY MANKIND will be in a far better position than the academician; he will enjoy the most unfettered independence and will be able to develop all his powers, unhampered by any personal considerations; no false prudence will slow down the progress of his genius or interrupt his work and his happiness. To keep the place which he has won, he will take fire; he will anxiously scrutinize the work of his predecessors; he will want to outdo them, to leave the beaten track and break new ground; his enthusiasm will grow by degrees and he will arrive at the true goal: to further the development of the human mind.

Such will be the path the man of genius will tread once he has become independent, while the academic mind will continue to take the opposite one; the academic spirit will always tend to cling to accepted opinions, seeing himself as the repository of the truth. He would be attacking his own so-called infallibility were he to change his mind. He will continue to see heresy everywhere and become intolerant rather than take a *backward* step to the profit of the enlightenment and happiness of mankind. How relentlessly the academics have persecuted men of genius, whenever the latter have disputed their opinions! Examine the course the academic spirit has followed: you will see how it has been both proud and servile; with what skill it has stifled arguments which could have enlightened mankind, whenever these have threatened its own existence. There are two reasons for this; one is that academicians are appointed for life, and the other is that they are dependent upon the government.

Cast your eye over the history of human progress and you will find that we owe nearly all masterpieces to lonely, often persecuted men. Once they have been appointed academicians, nearly all of them fall asleep in their chairs; and when they have written anything it has been in fear and trembling and has produced only a feeble flicker of truth. Independence alone can nurture love of mankind and desire for glory, the two powerful impulses which motivate the man of genius. Is it surprising that the academician, who is a slave, should produce nothing? Enslaved as he is, he believes that he has attained the height of glory; he is afraid of falling and this is precisely what prevents him from climbing higher.

A glance at the history of academics reveals that in England there are none and only two societies which are in any way linked with academic institutions, while absolute monarchies and also states given over to superstition and ignorance are teeming with them. And yet what country has produced more great men of every kind? Where have more truths been discovered? Where have they been published more courageously and adopted more promptly? Where have the authors of these useful discoveries been more liberally rewarded? In that island, love of personal freedom and independence of thought have caused the academies to be despised and excluded; as a citizen, the Englishman is conscious of his personal dignity; as a scientist, he would blush to prostitute himself to the powerful and to become a member of a body which owes its existence to them.

The despotic Richelieu was the founder of the first academy in France; he saw that the prospect of medals and academic chairs would shackle the writer; that the government would be able to use him to spread opinions favourable to its views, so that it could command public opinion. By so doing, it would thus turn the academies into the hidden well-springs of its despotism. And the outcome justified the views of the masterful minister. The first mother academy gave birth to a hundred others, which were still unable to raise France to the English level. Italy is stuffed with academies and yet has little standing among scientists; they merely distribute vast numbers of diplomas in arts and literature. And yet men are neither better nor more enlightened there. If all its academies were suppressed, perhaps genius in Italy would soar higher.

Nevertheless, I must admit that the academies have been of some use; that their establishment, imperfect as it is, has benefited the arts and sciences to some extent. I acknowledge also that there are a few academicians who have remained active. But the academic way of thinking lags too far behind present philosophical opinions for it to be preserved any longer. The progress of the human spirit, which has become more daring, seems to me to make possible the complete abolition of all the shackles which bind even the most learned academies. Mankind must not lose sight of the fact that it must reward those who enlighten it and that it should reward collectively those whose light is bright enough to illuminate the whole world.

The project impresses me in another very important respect. What obstacles have not been surmounted by men of genius up to now? Nearly all of them, at first, are turned aside from important ideas by their need to earn their living. How much experience, how many journeys necessary for the development of their ideas they have missed! How often they have been deprived of the collaborators they need if their work is to fulfil all its potential! How many felicitous ideas have been still-born because they were not revived with help, encouragement and reward!

And if, in spite of all these difficulties, some men of genius have been able to make their names and to win a reward, the reward has always been insufficient to pay handsomely for their work, to encourage the young whom they think are promising, and to subsidize those without private means. The man of genius alone is capable of discovering the first seeds, of developing them and of giving wisely the help they need.

Any post or salary which the man of genius acquires nearly always involves duties which distract him from his work to some extent; it forces him to remain in one place and, consequently, prevents him from going to see things or people which might provide with him opportunities for making new discoveries; the instability of the government from which he receives his salary makes him anxious about his future and frequently forces him to act merely with a view to keeping and being kept in his post; and, in spite of all his foresight, it often happens that a war or some upheaval in the financial sector leads to the suppression of all remunerations or, at least, to the suspension of their payment.

In fact, the man of genius who needs complete independence to work is always, to a greater or lesser extent, dependent on the government which pays him. He must adopt its outlook, subject himself to its forms and practices; he must think at second hand, instead of boldly following his own flights of imagination: he has to resort to timid compromise in the expression of his ideas and ends up by seeming much less what he really is, than what others wish him to appear; in a word, he has to pay dearly for the pittance accorded to him.

The position of the man of genius who accepts special benefits from a governor or anyone else is made even more irksome through the debasement into which he has fallen.

If the ideas, which are the guidelines of governments in all the various sections of administration, are examined, it becomes clear that they have all been discovered by men of genius. Men of genius enlighten those who govern as well as those who are governed.

I admit that often their discoveries have not been immediately suitable for use; but to acknowledge that their discoveries are only of use to the next generation, is not to say that those among whom they live should not reward them. And should mankind continue to allow those whom they will deify after their death to suffer, or at least to be inconvenienced?

Unless great changes are made in this direction, the human spirit cannot be expected to progress.

Among the educated nations, men of every age plant trees, while the inhabitants of ignorant nations (the Turks, for example) cut down trees and do not replace them. The tree planted by the generous old man gives him more pleasure than will ever be felt by the man who cuts it down for profit.

What is finer, more worthy of man, than to direct the passions towards the unique goal of increasing enlightenment! Those are happy moments when ambition, realizing that greatness and glory are only to be found in the acquisition of new knowledge, leaves the tainted springs at which it has tried to quench its thirst. Springs of misery and pride, which serve to quench the thirst of the ignorant, of heroes, of conquerors, of those who lay waste mankind—you will dry up through neglect and your philtres will no longer intoxicate those arrogant mortals! No more honours for the Alexanders of this world: long live the Archimedes!

My friend, what more fitting time at which to produce the project you have produced, than this in which genius, locked in a struggle with despotism, calls all philanthropists to its aid! In the generation which has grown up since the beginning of this struggle the number of those who act by mechanical routine has perceptibly decreased; the project will be understood by many; the reign of enlightenment is approaching; every intelligent man with an eye to the past and the future is convinced of this.

The project contains an elementary idea which could be used as a basis for a universal organization; it offers to mankind a conception which could help it to climb, without risk, one step higher on the ladder of abstraction.[1]

How fortunate that the tomb of Newton in whose honour this project is conceived, lies in England, that country which has always been the refuge of men of genius and scientists, persecuted elsewhere.

We cannot speak of Newton, without observing that he received from the government, by way of recompense, the post of Master of the Mint; from that moment onwards, this world citizen was merely an Englishman who employed all his energies in the job which had been entrusted to him; and that star, radiant with its own light, was presented to the world as an opaque body used to reflect the rays of the royal sun.

1. If the Abbé de Saint-Pierre had thought of this organization and if he had indicated it as a means of realizing his ideas on universal peace, these ideas would not have been treated as daydreams. Again, this idea provides the solution for a problem which has preoccupied moralists throughout the ages: which is to place a man in a position in which his personal interests and the general good always coincide.

Let us speak boldly: all men of genius who are given government positions will lose in practice as well as in prestige; for, in order to carry out their duties, they will neglect work which is more important for mankind or, if they cannot resist the force of their genius, they will often neglect the duties of their official positions.

One cannot avoid this double risk, harmful alike to mankind, to governments and to men of genius, unless the men of genius are left in the only place which the universal interest assigns to them; they must remain *themselves* and this truth must be powerfully impressed on mankind: that they are sent to be its torchbearers and not to be sold to the special interests which debase them and divert them from their true functions.

There are not so many men of genius that they can be diverted from their work by being taken out of their sphere. The author of the project, knowing how sparing nature is with them, only proposes twenty places for the whole world. If genius is an indispensable qualification for the occupation of one of these places, it is inevitable that there will often be vacancies.

I approve of the annual election, with the right to re-elect. By this means men of transcendant genius will be elected for life and those whose capacities approach genius will be given the greatest possible encouragement.

The method of election is such that *individual interests* cannot acquire enough strength to override the *general interest*.

Here, my friend, are my first impressions on reading your project.

Now I ask two questions. Will the project be adopted? If it is adopted, will it cure the present ills of mankind, ills which discretion forbids me to mention?

### REPLY

I thank you, my friend, for all the kind things that you have said to me in my capacity as the author of the project which I have made known to you. The vigorous way in which you have expressed approval in the opinion which you have taken the trouble to write, must have a powerful effect upon the readers. This observation will, I hope, assuage the anxiety which you have shown that my plan will not be adopted. I have addressed this project *directly* to mankind, because it is in its *collective* interest; but I am not foolish enough to hope that mankind will immediately put it into execution. I have always thought that its success would depend on how much support the most influential would decide to give. The best way to win their votes is to explain the matter as fully as possible. This is what I intend to do by addressing myself to different sections of mankind, which I have divided into three classes. The first, to which you and I have the honour to belong, marches under the banner of the progress of the human mind. It is composed of scientists, artists and all those who hold liberal ideas. On the banner of the second is written 'No innovation!' All proprietors who do not belong in the first category are part of the second.

The third class, which rallies round the slogan of 'Equality' is made up of the rest of the people.

I would say to the first class: everyone to whom I have spoken of the project I am presenting to mankind, has, after a short discussion, finally approved it. All have wished it well, but they have also all let me see that they feared it would not succeed.

This general conformity of opinion makes me think that I am likely to find everyone, or at least most people, of the same way of thinking. If this presentiment comes true, the force of *inertia* will be the only obstacle to the adoption of my views.

You, scientists and artists and those of you who devote some of your energy and your means to the furtherance of enlightenment, you are the section of mankind with the greatest intellectual force; you have the greatest talent for grasping new ideas. You are the most directly interested in the success of the subscription; it is up to you to overcome the force of inertia. Let the mathematicians, since they head the list, make a start!

Scientists, artists, look with the eye of genius at the present state of the human mind; you will see that the sceptre of public opinion has fallen into your hand; grasp it with vigour! You can create happiness for yourselves and for your contemporaries; you can preserve posterity from the evils from which we have suffered and from those which we still endure; all of you, subscribe!

To the members of the second class, I would then address the following words:

Gentlemen,

Compared with those who own no property, you are very few in number: how, then, does it come about that they consent to obey you? It is because the superiority of your intellect enables you to combine your forces (as they cannot), thus for the most part giving you an advantage over them in the struggle which, in the nature of things, must always exist between you and them.

Once this principle has been accepted, it is clearly in your interest to include those without property in your party; those who have proved the superiority of their intelligence with important discoveries; and it is equally clear that the interest being *general* for your class, *each* of the member who compose it should contribute.

Gentlemen, I have spent much of my time among scientists and artists; I have observed them closely and I can assure you that they will exert pressure on you until you decide to sacrifice your pride and the money needed to place *their* leaders in the most respected positions and to provide *them* with the necessary financial means to exploit their ideas fully. I would be guilty of exaggeration, gentlemen, if I allowed you to believe that I have found this intention fully formulated in the minds of scientists and artists: No! Gentlemen, no! I can only say that such an intention exists in a vague form; but I am convinced, by a long series of observations, of the existence of such an intention and of the influence which it can exert on the ideas of scientists and artists.

Until you have adopted the measure which I propose to you, you will be exposed, each in your own country, to the sort of evils which some of your class have suffered in France. In order to convince yourselves of the truth of what I have said, you have only to think about the events that have occurred in that country since 1789. The first popular movement there was secretly fomented by scientists and artists. Once the success of the insurrection had lent it the appearance of legitimacy, they declared themselves its leaders. The resistance they encountered to the direction they gave to that insurrection—a direction aimed at the destruction of all the institutions which had wounded their self-esteem—provoked them to inflame the passions of the ignorant and to burst all the bonds of subordination which, until then, had contained the rash passions of those without property. They succeeded in doing what they wanted. All the institutions which from the outset they had intended to overthrow were destroyed inevitably; in short, they won the battle and you lost it. This victory was to cost the victors dear; but you who were defeated have suffered even more. A few scientists and artists, victims of the insubordination of their army, were massacred by their own troops. From a moral point of view, they have all had to bear your apparently justified reproaches, for they were responsible for the atrocities committed against you and for the disorders of every kind which their troops were led to commit under the barbarous impulse of ignorance.

Once the evil had reached its height, the cure appeared; you no longer resisted. The scientists and artists, having learnt from experience, and recognizing that you were more enlightened than the propertyless,[1] desired to see sufficient power returned to you to restore the regular functioning of the social organization. The propertyless bore almost the whole brunt of the famine brought about by their own improvident measures. They were brought to heel.

Although force of circumstances had led the people of France ardently to desire the restoration of order, they could only be reorganized as a society by a man of genius: Bonaparte undertook this task, and succeeded in it.

Among the ideas I have put before you is the suggestion that you have lost the battle. If you remain in any doubt on this subject, compare the amount of prestige and comfort which scientists and artists now enjoy in France with their position before 1789.

Gentlemen, do not take issue with them, for you will be beaten in every battle in which you allow them to embroil you. You will suffer more than they during hostilities and the peace will not be to your advantage. Give yourselves the credit of doing something with good grace which, sooner or later, the scientists, artists and men of liberal ideas, joined with the propertyless, will make you do by force: subscribe to a man—it is the only way open to you to avert the evils which threaten you.

Since this question has been raised, let us be brave enough not to leave it without glancing at the political situation in the most enlightened part of the world.

*At this moment* in Europe, the actions of governments are not troubled by any open opposition from the governed; but given the climate of opinion in England, Germany and Italy, it is easy to predict that this calm will not last long, unless the necessary precautions are taken in time; for, gentlemen, you cannot conceal from yourselves that the crisis which faces the human mind is common to all the enlightened peoples, and that the symptoms which appeared in France, during the terrible explosion which occurred there, can be detected at the present moment by an intelligent observer in England, and even in Germany.

Gentlemen, by adopting the project which I am proposing, you will limit the crises which these peoples are fated to suffer,

1. I ask the reader to weigh this observation carefully. The proprietors command the propertyless, not because they own property, but they do have property and they command because, taken collectively, they are more enlightened than the propertyless.

and *which no power on earth can prevent*, to simple changes in their governments and finances, and you will spare them the general upheaval undergone by the French people—an upheaval in which all existing relations between the members of a nation become precarious; and anarchy, the greatest of all scourges, rages unchecked until it plunges the entire nation it afflicts into a depth of misery which finally gives birth, even among the most ignorant of its members, to the desire for the restoration of order.

I would appear to be underestimating your intelligence, gentlemen, if I were to add further proofs to those which I have just submitted, to prove to you that it is in your own interest to adopt the measure which I propose, in the light of the evils from which it can save you.

It is with pleasure that I now present the project to you in a light flattering to your self-esteem. Think of yourselves as the *regulators* of the progress of the human mind; you can play this part; for if, through the subscription, you give prestige and comfort to men of genius, one of the conditions in the subscription is that those who are elected are debarred from holding any position in the government, you will thus safeguard yourselves and the rest of humanity from the drawbacks of placing effective power in their hands.

Experience has shown that at the moment of their conception an admixture of harmful elements is generally found in new, powerful, just ideas, on which discoveries are based. Despite this, if their inventor had the power he would often demand that they should be put into practice. This is an example of one particular disadvantage. But I would draw your attention to another of a general nature. Always, if a discovery is to be put into practice which requires a change in existing customs and habits, the generation which has witnessed its birth can only enjoy it through its feeling for future generations who are destined to profit from it.

I conclude this little discourse which I have ventured to address to you by saying:

Gentlemen, if you remain in the second class, it is because you want to do so, for it lies in your power to climb into the first class. Now let us turn to the third class:

My friends,

There are many scientists in England. Educated Englishmen have more respect for scientists than they have for kings. Everyone can read, write and count in England. Well, my friends, in that country the workers in the cities, and even those in the countryside eat meat every day.

In Russia, if a scientist displeases the emperor his nose and ears are cut off and he is sent to Siberia. In Russia the peasants are as ignorant as their horses. Well, my friends, the Russian peasants are badly fed, badly clothed and are frequently beaten.

Until now, the only occupation of the rich has been to order you about; force them to enlighten themselves and to teach you; they make you work for them with your hands—make their hands work for you; do them the good turn of relieving them of the burden of boredom; they pay you with money; pay them with respect: it is a far more precious currency; happily, even the poorest owns some of it; spend what you have wisely and your lot will soon improve.

To enable you to judge the advice which I am giving you, and to appreciate the advantages which can follow from the execution of my project for mankind, I must go into some detail, but I will confine myself to what is essential.

A scientist, my friends, is a man who foresees; it is because science provides the means to predict that it is useful, and that scientists are superior to all other men.

All the phenomena we know of have been divided into different categories: astronomical, physical, chemical and physiological. Every scientist devotes himself more especially to one of these categories above the rest.

You know some of the predictions made by the astronomers: you know they foretell eclipses; but they also make a host of other predictions to which you pay no heed and with which I shall not trouble you. I shall confine myself to saying a few words about the use to which they are put, the value of which is well known to you.

It is by means of the predictions of astronomers that it has been possible to determine exactly the relative position of different points of the earth; their predictions also make it possible to navigate the farthest oceans. You are familiar with some of the predictions of the chemists. A chemist tells you that with this stone you can make lime and with this one you cannot; he tells you that with such a quantity of ashes from a particular tree you can bleach your linen just as well as with a far larger quantity from another kind of tree; he tells you that one substance mixed with another will yield a product with such and such an appearance, displaying certain properties.

The physiologist devotes himself to the phenomena of organic bodies; for instance, if you are ill, he tells you "You feel this symptom today; well, tomorrow you will be in such a condition."

Do not run away with the idea that I want you to believe that scientists can predict everything; of course they cannot. And I am even sure that they can predict accurately only a very small number of things. But you have convinced yourselves, just as I have, that scientists are men who can predict the most in their own field; and this is, of course, because they only acquire the reputation of being *scientists* by the *verifications* which are made of their *predictions*; at least this is so today, although it has not always been so. This means that we must look at the progress made by the human mind; despite my efforts to express myself clearly, I am not absolutely sure that you will understand me at first reading, but if you think about it a little, you will do so in the end.

The first phenomena which man observed systematically were astronomical. There were good reasons for this, since they were the simplest. In the beginning of astronomical research, men *confused* the facts which they *observed* with those which they *imagined*, and in this primitive hotch-potch they made the best combinations they could in order to satisfy all the demands of prediction. They gradually disentangled themselves from the facts created by their imagination and, after much work, they finally adopted a sure method of perfecting this science. The astronomers *accepted* only those facts which were verified by observation; they *chose* the system which linked them best, and since that time, they have never led science astray. If a new system is produced, they check before they accept it whether it links the facts better than the one which they had adopted. If a new fact is produced, they check by *observation*, that it exists.

The period of which I am speaking, the most memorable in the history of human progress, is that in which the astronomers drove out the astrologers. Another observation which I must make is that since then, the astronomers have become modest harmless people, who do not pretend to know things about which they are ignorant. You, for your part, have stopped asking them presumptuously to read your future in the stars.

Chemical phenomena are far more complicated than astronomical ones, so men only came to study them much later. In the study of chemistry, the same errors were made as in the study of astronomy, but eventually the chemists rid themselves of the alchemists.

Physiology, too, is still in the bad state through which the astrological and chemical sciences have already passed; the physiologists must expel the *philosophers, moralists* and *metaphysicians* from their midst, just as the astronomers expelled the astrologers and the chemists the alchemists.[1]

My friends, we are organic bodies; by viewing our social relations as physiological phenomena I conceived the plan which I am putting forward, and it is with arguments drawn from the system which I used to co-ordinate physiological facts that I shall demonstrate to you the value of this plan.

It is a fact, confirmed by a long series of observations, that every man feels, to some degree, the desire to dominate others.[2] What is clear, according to reasoned argument, is that every man who is not isolated is both *actively and passively dominant* in his relations with others, and I urge you to use that little portion of domination which you exercise upon the rich. . . . But before going further, I must discuss with you something which angers you deeply. You say: *we are ten, twenty, a hundred times more numerous than the proprietors and yet they exercise a power over us very much greater than that which we wield over them.* I can understand, my friends, that you are aggrieved. But notice that the proprietors, although fewer in number are more enlightened than you are and for the general good power should be distributed according to the degree of enlightenment. Consider what took place in France during the period when your comrades were in power. They brought about famine.

Let us now return to my plan. By adopting and putting it into practice, you will permanently entrust to mankind's twenty-one

1. I do not mean to say that the philosophers, moralists and metaphysicians have not been of service to physiology; but it is well known that the astrologers have been useful to astronomy: while the alchemists played a great part in chemical discoveries and yet everyone agrees that the astronomers did well in cutting themselves off from the astrologers, and the chemists in separating themselves from the alchemists.

One idea remains to be explored: the main business of the philosophers, the moralists and metaphysicians is to study the relation between those phenomena which are called physical and those which are called moral. When they are successful in this field, their research may be called physiological. But they try also to relate all the observed facts to a general system; it is very obvious to me that this is impossible, until physiology has been organized in the same way as astronomy.

I would add that only mathematics contain the materials which can be used to construct a universal system and that if it is impossible to apply calculation to phenomena which cannot be reduced to very simple terms, it does not seem to me that one should therefore abandon the hope of relating by satisfactory explanations, ideas which serve as a basis for the theories of the different branches of physics to the idea of universal gravitation.

2. Two paths can lead a man to a position of superiority; one combines both the individual and the general interest; my aim is to embellish this path and to sow a few thorns along the other.

most enlightened men, the two great instruments of power: prestige and wealth. The result will be that, for many reasons, the sciences will make rapid strides. It is well known that the study of the sciences becomes easier with every advance made, so that those who, like yourselves, can only devote a short time to their education can learn more, and as they learn more, they lessen the extent of the power exercised over them by the rich. It will not be long, my friends, before you see the resultant benefits. But I do not want to waste time in speaking to you of the remote consequences of a course of action which you have still not decided to take. Let us rather speak about what you can see before your eyes at this very moment.

You give your respect, that is to say you voluntarily give a measure of power to men who, in your view do things you consider to be of use to you. Your mistake, which you share with all mankind, is that you do not make a clear enough distinction between temporary and lasting benefits; between benefits of local interest and those of universal interest; between things which benefit a part of mankind at the expense of the rest, and those which increase the happiness of the whole of mankind. In short, you have not yet noticed that there is only one interest common to all mankind: that of the progress of the sciences.

If the mayor of your village obtains a concession for you over the neighbouring villages, you are pleased with him, you respect him; city-dwellers exhibit the same desire to exercise superiority over other towns in the vicinity. The provinces compete with each other, and there are struggles of personal interest between nations which are called wars.[1] Among the efforts made by all these factions of mankind, can we see any which aims *directly* at the common good? It is a very small effort indeed—which is not surprising, considering that mankind has not yet taken any steps to agree *collectively* on the subject of rewards for those who

1. Moralists are inconsistent when they condemn egoism and approve of patriotism; for patriotism is simply national egoism; and this egoism causes nations to commit the same injustices against one another as does personal egoism among individuals.

Opinion is still divided on the question of egoism. Although the subject has been hotly debated since the beginning of time, the solution of the problem lies in opening a way for both the individual and the universal interests. The preservation of organized bodies requires egoism. Every effort to *combine* the interests of individuals is a step in the right direction. All the arguments of the moralists which go beyond the reconciliation of interests and which try to destroy egoism are erroneous and the root of the error is easily recognizable. *Moralists often mistake words for things.* The first generation of mankind manifested the greatest individual egoism because individuals did not combine their interests.

succeed in doing something for the common good. I do not think that a better method can be found than the one which I propose, for uniting as far as possible all those forces acting in so many, often contrary, directions; for leading them as far as possible in the only direction which points to the betterment of mankind. Now, for the time being, enough about the scientists. Let us speak of the artists.

On Sundays, you find delight in eloquence, you take pleasure in reading a well-written book, in looking at beautiful pictures or statues or in listening to music which holds you entranced. Hard work is necessary before a man can speak or write in a way which will amuse you, or can paint a picture or carve a statue which pleases you or can compose music which affects you. Is it not fair, my friends, that you should reward the artists who fill the pauses in your work with pleasures which enlarge your minds by playing on the most delicate nuances of your feelings?

Subscribe my friends! No matter how little money you subscribe, there are so many of you that the total sum will be considerable; besides, the prestige bestowed on those whom you nominate will give them untold strength. You will see how the rich will hasten to distinguish themselves in the sciences and the arts, once they realize that this road *leads to the highest honours*. Even if you only succeed in diverting them from the quarrels born of their idleness, over how many of you should be under their command, quarrels in which you are always embroiled and of which you are always the dupes, you will have gained much.

If you accept my plan, you will encounter one difficulty—that of choice. I will tell you how I should set about making my own. I should ask all the mathematicians I know, who are, in their opinion, the three best mathematicians, and I should nominate the three who have gathered the most votes from those whom I had consulted. I should do the same for the physicists, etc.

Having divided mankind into three parts, and having presented each with what I thought were the reasons why they should adopt the plan, I shall now address my contemporaries collectively and lay before them my reflections on the French Revolution.

The abolition of the privilege of birth required an effort which burst the bonds of the old social system and did not present an obstacle to the reorganization of society. But the appeal which was made to all the members of society to carry out their duties of deliberation regularly had no success. Apart from the terrible atrocities which resulted from the application of this principle of equality, as the natural result of putting power into the hands of the ignorant, it also ended in the creation of an utterly impractical form of government, because the rulers, *who were all paid so that the propertyless could be included*, were so numerous that the labours of the governed were barely sufficient to support them. This led to a situation absolutely the contrary of what the propertyless had always wanted, which was to pay less taxes.

Here is an idea which seems to me to be fair. The basic needs of life are the most pressing. The propertyless can only partly satisfy them. A physiologist can see clearly that their most constant desire must be the reduction of taxes, or an increase in wages, which comes to the same thing.

I think that all classes of society would be happy in the following situation: spiritual power in the hands of the scientists; temporal power in those of the proprietors; power to nominate those called upon to carry out the functions of the great leaders of mankind in the hands of everyone; the reward for those who govern to be—esteem.

# II

# Letter to his Nephew

*Épître dédicatoire à mon neveu Victor de Saint-Simon*, from *Nouvelle Encyclopédie*, Paris, 1810, I, 1, p. 102.

I believe in God.
I believe that God created the universe.
I believe that God made the universe subject to the law of gravity.

I do not blame d'Alembert, Diderot nor any of their collaborators on the Encyclopedia for having publicly attacked belief in God, for at the time when they were at work this belief was so linked and intermingled with belief in revealed ideas that it was impossible to attack the one while respecting the other. But today, when revealed ideas are seen as being merely scientific insights produced by mankind in its infancy which are, as such, quite inadequate to govern the conduct of the human race now that it has reached its maturity; today, when the clergy have been stripped of all the benefits they dishonestly acquired, I think, I say, I profess, I shall profess all my life, that one must believe in God.

# III

# On the Reorganization of European Society

## TO THE PARLIAMENTS OF FRANCE AND ENGLAND*

*De la Réorganisation de la Société Européenne ou de la nécessité et des moyens de rassembler les peuples de l'Europe en un seul corps politique en conservant a chacun son indépendance nationale*, M. le Comte de Saint-Simon and A. Thierry, his pupil, October 1814.

My lords,

Until the end of the fifteenth century all the European nations formed a single political body, at peace within itself, and armed against the enemies of its constitution and independence.[1]

The Catholic religion, practised from one end of Europe to the other, was a passive bond in the European society; the Catholic clergy were the active bond. Spread everywhere and everywhere dependent only on itself, forming part of every people and with its own government and laws, it was the centre from which emanated the will which moved the great body and the force which activated it.

The ecclesiastical government was, like those of all the European peoples, a hierarchic aristocracy. The administrative centre of its leaders was a territory independent of all temporal power, too large for easy conquest, too small for those who possessed it to become conquerors themselves. By their power, which was held to be higher than that of kings, they curbed national ambitions; by their policy, they kept the balance of power in Europe, which was beneficial at that time but later became so harmful when the exercise of it passed into the hands of one people alone.

Thus, the court of Rome ruled over the other courts in the same way as those courts ruled their people, and Europe was a great aristocracy, divided into several smaller aristocracies, all dependent on it, all subject to its influence, its judgments, its edicts.

No institution founded upon a belief should outlive that

* I, 1, pp. 161–8.

1. When I say at peace, I mean in comparison with what has happened since and what is happening today.

belief. Luther, by shaking the old respect upon which the power of the clergy was based, upset Europe. Half the Europeans threw off the bonds of the papacy, that is, they broke the only political link which bound them to the great society.

The Treaty of Westphalia established a new order of things by a political operation which was called the 'balance of power'. Europe was divided into two confederations which had to be kept equal: this amounted to creating and constitutionally perpetuating war, because two associations of equal strength must inevitably become rivals and there is no rivalry without war.

Thenceforth, each power concentrated only on increasing its own military strength. Instead of the puny levies of soldiers, called up for the occasion and soon disbanded, formidable armies were to be seen everywhere, always ready, almost always engaged in action; for since the Treaty of Westphalia war has been the normal condition of Europe.

It was out of this confusion, which has been and still is called the basis of the political system, that England rose to greatness. More skilful than the continental peoples, she saw what the balance of power meant and by being doubly skilful she was able to turn it to her own advantage and to the disadvantage of the others.

Cut off from the Continent by the sea, England ceased to have anything in common with those who lived there when she gave to herself a national religion and a government which differed from all the European ones in itself. Her constitution was no longer founded upon precedent and custom but on what is universally valid for all times and places, on what should be the basis of every constitution, the freedom and well-being of the people.

Having established a sound, firm internal social structure, England turned her attention entirely outwards, in order to achieve great influence there. The aim of her foreign policy was universal domination.

She encouraged her own shipping, trade and industry, while hampering these activities on the part of other countries. Wherever despotic governments oppressed Europe, England supported them with her might and reserved liberty and its attendant benefits for herself alone. Her gold, her armies, her policy, were all set to work to maintain this so-called 'balance' which, by encouraging the forces of continental Europe to destroy each other, left her free to do what she liked with impunity.

It was from this double political system that the colossus of

English power has grown—a power which threatens to overwhelm the whole world. Hence it is that England, free and happy at home, harsh and despotic abroad, for a century now has played with Europe, overturning her at will.

Such a state of affairs is too monstrous to endure for long. It is in Europe's interest to free herself from a tyranny which is torturing her. It is in England's interest not to wait until Europe has freed herself by force of arms.

Let there be no mistake: these are not the kind of evils which can be cured by secret negotiations or by the petty operations of closet politics. There can be no peace or happiness in Europe until there is once more a political bond attaching England to the Continent from which she has been separated.

Formerly, Europe was a confederative society, united by common institutions, under a general form of government, which was to the people of Europe what the national governments are to individuals. A similar state of affairs is the only one which can put things right.

Of course, I do not suggest that that old organization, which still encumbers Europe with its useless ruins, should be raised from the dust: the nineteenth century is too far removed from the thirteenth. A constitution, strong in itself, grounded in natural principles and free from ephemeral beliefs and opinions is what Europe needs and this is what I am now proposing.

When the revolutions in empires are caused by the advance of enlightenment, they will always lead to a better state of affairs; in the same way the political crisis which has broken up the great European body is paving the way for a more perfect organization for Europe.

This reorganization cannot come about suddenly, or all at once; for it takes more than a day to destroy old institutions completely and to fashion better ones from their ruins. The new can only arise and the old can only crumble slowly and imperceptibly.

The English, whose island position encourages them to be more of a sea-faring people than the other Europeans and are therefore less bound by innate prejudices and customs, took their first forward step when they rejected feudal government in favour of a hitherto unknown institution.

The half-destroyed remnants of the old European organization continued to exist on the continent; the governments retained their original form, although here and there they were slightly modified; the power of the Church, disregarded in the north, survived in the south as nothing more nor less than an instrument to oppress the peoples and as a tool of despotism for the princes.

And yet the human mind did not long remain inactive: enlightenment was spreading and completing the destruction of the old institutions everywhere; abuses were corrected, errors destroyed, but nothing new was built up in their place.

It was necessary for the reforming spirit to be backed by a political force and this force, present only in England, could not fight against the forces of the whole continent, which acted as a bulwark for all that remained of the despotic régimes and papal authority.

Today, when France can join with England to be the mainstay of liberal principles, all that remains is for Europe to reorganize itself to unite their forces and make them act.

This union is possible because France, as well as England, is now free. It is necessary, because it alone can ensure the peace of the two countries and save them from the evils which threaten them. This union can change the face of Europe, because England and France together are stronger than the rest of Europe.

All that the author can do is to show what is useful; only those in power can bring it about.

My lords, you alone can hasten this revolution in Europe which began so long ago; it will be accomplished by the pressure of events, but it will be disastrous if it proceeds at a slow pace.

You should be drawn to do this, not only by the prospect of the personal glory it will shed on you, but—for a more compelling reason—for the peace and well-being of the peoples whom you govern.

If France and England continue to be rivals, their rivalry will be responsible for the greatest disasters befalling themselves and Europe; if they unite their interests, as they are already united in their political principles and the similarity of their governments, they will be peaceful and happy and Europe can hope for peace.

The English nation no longer has to strive for its freedom or its greatness; the freedom and progress of all should be its aim: that is what the English should seek to create; but if they persist in their despotism, if they do not renounce their policy of hostility towards all prosperity other than their own . . ., well, we know how Europe punished France for a less tyrannical ambition.

## ON THE BEST POSSIBLE CONSTITUTION*

My object is to discover whether there is a form of government which is intrinsically good, founded upon reliable, absolute and universal principles, valid for all times and places.

Were I to try to solve this problem in the way in which political questions have hitherto been dealt with, I should simply be opening up a new field for endless debate. So, leaving aside all that may have been said on this subject, in this enquiry I will use the only two principles which can be relied upon to produce absolute proof: reason and experience.

All the sciences, no matter which they may be, are no more than a series of problems to be solved, of questions to be analysed and they only differ in the nature of the questions they pose. Thus the method applied to some of them should be applicable to all, just because it can be applied to some; for, this method is no more than a tool, completely independent of the objects to which it is applied, and whose application does nothing to change their nature.

Furthermore, it is from the application of this method that all science derives its certainty. It is through it that science becomes positive and ceases to be conjectural; and this only comes about after many centuries of hazy knowledge, errors and inaccuracies.

Hitherto, the method of the observational sciences has not been applied to political questions. Every man has brought to them his own point of view, method of reasoning and judgement, and as a result there has been neither accuracy in the solutions found for political problems nor universality in the results applied in this sphere.

The time has come to bring this infancy of science to an end and it is certainly desirable to do so, for the lack of knowledge of politics are the cause of unrest in the social order.

What is the best possible constitution?

Taking the constitution to mean any system of social order aiming at the common good, the best will be the one in which institutions will be organized and power distributed so that every question of public interest will be dealt with in the most thorough and complete way.

## CONCLUSION†

The method of the experimental sciences should be applied to politics. Reasoning and experience are the elements of this

* I, 1, pp. 182–3.
† I, 1, p. 195.

method. When, by reasoning, I tried to discover what was the best constitution I was led to the parliamentary system; and when I questioned experience, experience confirmed what reason had proved. During the hundred years or so since England, her revolution achieved, established this form of parliamentary government in all its fullness, have we not seen her prosperity and power constantly increasing? What people is freer and richer at home, greater abroad, more skilled in the arts of industry, shipping and commerce? And to what can this power, unequalled by any other country, be attributed if not to the fact that this English government is more liberal, more vigorous, more beneficial for the happiness and glory of a nation than all the European governments?

## ON THE NEW ORGANIZATION OF EUROPEAN SOCIETY*

I have analysed the old organization of Europe. I have shown its advantages and disadvantages and indicated how the former could be preserved and the latter abolished. I went on to show that there is a form of government which is inherently good and that is none other than the parliamentary system. The acceptance of these facts leads naturally to the following conclusion.

That wherever the old hierarchic or feudal orders are replaced by the parliamentary system of government, this simple substitution brings about a new system which is more perfect than the one which went before; it is no longer transitory, as the previous one was, because its worth does not depend upon a particular stage in the development of the human intellect, which is bound to change with time, but on the nature of things which never varies.

Thus, to sum up all that I have said, *Europe would have the best possible organization, if each one of the nations which it encompasses were to be governed by a parliament, recognizing the supremacy of a general parliament set above all the national governments and invested with the power to judge their disputes.*

I shall not speak here of the setting up of national parliaments. We know by experience how they should be organized. I shall indicate only how the common European parliament could be formed.

* I, 1, pp. 196–7. This is taken from the Second Book which has the heading: 'That all the European nations should be governed by a national parliament and combine to form a general parliament which would decide on the common interests of Europe.'

## ON THE CHAMBER OF DEPUTIES OF THE EUROPEAN PARLIAMENT*

Every man, born in a country and a citizen of that country, always acquires, through his education, his relationships and the examples set before him, certain more or less deeply engrained habits which encourage him to set his sights beyond the limits of his own individual well-being and merge his own interests with those of the society of which he is a member. Through habit, strengthened and transformed into sentiment, he develops a tendency to generalize his interests, that is to say, to see them always as a part of the common interest; this propensity, which can sometimes grow weaker but which never disappears, is what is called patriotism.

In every good national government, the patriotism which is part of each individual changes into an *esprit de corps* or corporate will the moment the individual becomes a member of it, since what is essential in good government is that the interests of the government should coincide with those of the nation.

It is this corporate will which is the soul of the government, which unifies all its actions and harmonizes all its movements, so that they all work towards the same goal and all respond to the same driving force.

This is as true of the European government as it is of the national governments; there can be no action without common purpose. Now this common purpose which, in a national government springs from national patriotism, in a European government can only arise from a more universal outlook and a broader sentiment, which can be called European patriotism. Montesquieu said that men are formed by institutions; thus, this tendency of patriotism to extend beyond the frontiers of country, this habit of considering European interests before national ones, will be an inevitable result of the establishment of a European parliament for those called upon to form it.

This is true; but it is also true that men mould institutions and that the institutions cannot be established unless men are completely ready for them, or at least in a state of preparedness.

It is therefore essential to admit to the chamber of deputies of the European parliament—that is, to one of the two active powers of the European constitution—only those men whose wider contacts, freedom from parochialism, participation in activities whose uses are not purely national but extend beyond their own country, make them better able to achieve the

* I, 1, pp. 197–201.

universal outlook, which should make up the European *esprit de corps*, and to promote the general interest which must also be the corporate interest of the European parliament.

Business men, scientists, judges and administrators only should be called upon to form the chamber of deputies of the great parliament.

For, indeed, everything which tends to the common good of European society can be related to the sciences, arts, legislation, commerce, administration and industry.

Out of every million men who can read and write in Europe, one business man, one scientist, one administrator and one judge should be sent to the chamber of deputies of the great parliament. Thus, assuming that there are in Europe sixty million men who can read and write, the chamber of deputies would be composed of two hundred and forty members.

The election of each deputy will be made by the corporation to which he belongs. Deputies will be appointed for ten years.

Every member of the chamber of deputies should have an income of at least 25,000 francs from landed property.

It is true that property makes for stability of government, but only when property is allied with enlightenment can the government be solidly based on it. The government must therefore include and allow a share of property to those men of outstanding merit who do not have property, so that talent and the possession of property will no longer be separated; because talent, which is the greatest and most active force, would soon seize property if it were not allied with it.

Thus, at each new election, twenty members, chosen from the most distinguished scientists, business men, judges and administrators who do not own property, should be admitted to the chamber of deputies of the European parliament and given an income of 25,000 francs from landed property.

## ON THE ESTABLISHMENT OF THE EUROPEAN PARLIAMENT AND THE MEANS BY WHICH ITS ESTABLISHMENT CAN BE HASTENED*

Men can fail to recognize what is useful to them for a long time, but the time always comes when their eyes are opened and they realize the truth.

The French gave themselves an English constitution and all

* I, 1, pp. 206–8. This extract is taken from the Third Book, headed: 'That France and England having a parliamentary form of government can and should form a common parliament to manage the affairs of the two nations—Action of the Anglo-French parliament upon the other European peoples.'

the European peoples in turn will do the same as soon as their eyes are opened to its benefits.

For, that point at which all the European peoples are governed by national parliaments will undoubtedly be the time when the general parliament can be set up without difficulties.

The reasons for this statement are so obvious that it is pointless to reproduce them here.

But this time is still remote from us and between then and now Europe must suffer terrible wars and very many revolutions. What should be done to protect Europe from these new evils, sad fruits of her continued disorganization? We must use all our skill and find, in a time nearer to our own, the means to destroy them at their roots.

I repeat what I have already said. The establishment of the European parliament will take place quite easily, the moment all the European peoples live under parliamentary systems.

It follows from this that the European parliament can begin to be established as soon as that part of the European population which enjoys representative government finds itself stronger than the part which has remained subject to despotic governments.

Now this is precisely the present state of Europe: the English and the French are incontestably superior in strength to the rest of Europe, and the English and the French have a parliamentary form of government.[1]

It is therefore possible to begin to reorganize Europe from this very day.

Let the English and the French join together to establish a common parliament; let the chief aim of this new organization be to expand by attracting the other peoples to it; consequently, let the Anglo-French government encourage the supporters of a representative constitution in all the other nations; let them support them with all their might, so that parliaments can be set up by all the peoples subject to absolute monarchies; let every nation, the moment it has adopted the representative form of government, join the organization and send its deputies to the common parliament, and the reorganization of Europe will be accomplished imperceptibly without wars, without catastrophes, without political revolutions.

1. I take the political strength of the English and the French to include their superiority in diplomacy, and the means of corruption available to them through the sums of money at their disposal, which enabled them to ensure the success of their undertakings.

### ON THE ANGLO-FRENCH PARLIAMENT*

The composition of the Anglo-French parliament should be the same as that I proposed for the great European parliament.

The French will only have one third of the representation, that is to say, England should send two deputies and France one for every million men who can read and write.

This arrangement is important for two reasons. First, because the French are still unskilled in parliamentary politics and need to be schooled by the English, formed by a longer experience; secondly, because in agreeing to this establishment, England must make some sacrifices, whereas France can only gain advantages.

### THAT IT IS IN THE INTEREST OF FRANCE AND ENGLAND TO UNITE BY MEANS OF A POLITICAL LINK†

The union of France and England can reshape Europe. This union, hitherto impossible, is practicable now that France and England have the same political principles and the same form of government. But for the benefits of the arrangement to be felt, is it enough that it should be possible? Indeed no; what is necessary is that it should be willed.

Both England and France are threatened by great political upheavals and neither of them alone can find the way to avert them. Both will certainly totter, if they do not lend each other mutual support; and by a strange but happy chance, the only resort they possess against an inevitable revolution is this union which must increase the prosperity of both and bring the misfortunes of Europe to an end.

### SUMMARY OF THE CONSIDERATIONS RELATING TO FRANCE AND ENGLAND‡

I have adjusted my point of view to that of the common interest of France and England. Let those who have followed me attentively, who have adjusted their sights with me and who have discerned from this point of view the cure for the ills of the two nations, make a further adjustment to consider those combinations of national interest which have only been thought about before and which we are going to begin to think about again. What do we see? Rivalries, wars, evils at home and abroad.

England, frightened by the approach of a revolution re-

* I, 1, p. 209.
† I, 1, pp. 209–10.
‡ I, 1, pp. 236–8.

doubles her efforts; she coldly contemplates new wars in Europe and new misfortunes for France. She supports the cause of the negroes and devastates the soil of her brothers. The whole of Europe was outraged by the news of the burning of Washington. Yet not all her wiles, nor her oppressive policy nor the crimes at which England herself trembles but which she believes she is forced to commit, will save her. The most they can do is to delay the crisis which threatens her.

Let us imagine England busy crushing everything that rises up; incurring debts in order to impoverish others; weakening herself in order to weaken them, as though her only salvation lay in general poverty and ruin. Let us see her, shocked by her own outrages, yet still preparing new ones, and finding herself the target for the hatred of every human being, in order to prolong for a few days this tragic state of uneasy ferment and ever-growing fears, vainly hidden behind the appearance of external strength and prosperity. Let us now imagine her united with France, and by this union saved from inevitable bankruptcy; powerful and happy, without crimes and without fears, the prosperity of others detracting not at all from her own; and tell me which of these two states is preferable.

Since the crisis which overturned her old political system, France has not succeeded in creating a new one for herself.

In a generous gesture, let France regard England's debt as the result of the efforts which had to be made to ensure a home for freedom in Europe, from which it could spread to all the nations; and let her agree to share the burden of a sacrifice whose fruits she also shares; and on a no less noble impulse, let England share with France the benefits accrued from a hundred years of liberty.

The immensity of this debt should not be allowed to frighten either of the two peoples. It will lessen all the time; for each time a free nation joins the Anglo-French society, it will assume a share of the debt proportionate to its wealth.

It will thus be in the interest of the Anglo-French confederation to promote by every means in its power the reorganization of Europe.

The less one thwarts the interests of others in working for one's own, the less resistance one encounters, and the more easily one reaches one's goal. Thus, the oft-repeated maxim. *One can only be truly happy in seeking for happiness in the happiness of others*, is as true, as positive as: *a body launched in a certain direction is stopped or delayed in its course if it meets other bodies on the way, launched in the opposite direction.*

## ON GERMANY*

There is a European people whose form of government would seem to relegate it to the lower ranks of the European nations but who is infinitely removed from them by virtue of character, knowledge and philosophy.

The purest morality, a flawless sincerity and unimpeachable probity are all to be found in the German nation. Even in circumstances of the most terrible wars, the most atrocious hostilities and the most unbearable oppression this character has never been belied. No French soldier has ever perished through treason in this country which France has laid waste.

Almost entirely deprived of maritime trade, Germany has been preserved from the mercantile spirit which puts calculation before noble sentiments and leads to egoism and forgetfulness of what is great and noble. In Germany one does not say, as in England, *How much is a man worth?*, when asking, how much does he own? Worth is not measured in wealth.

Moreover, it is remarkable how this natural goodness, this simplicity of manners which is characteristic of the German people extends to the government: arbitrary power is gentle and paternal in that country.

A nation can be regarded in three ways; it can be found in three different situations. The first is that of bowing down under a despotic government; taking pleasure in servitude and thinking that there is nothing more desirable than the good opinion of those who govern and nothing nobler than the honours which this good opinion bestows.

The second is knowing how to rise above one's social estate through philosophical enlightenment and noble sentiments; rooting out any ideas of purchasing favours through lowering oneself; perceiving that man has a worthier destiny and striving towards it by fighting against the course of events, without, however, trying to change it.

The third, and by far the best, is making a government of which everyone can be a member, if he is worthy; and devoting all the nation's concern, work and enlightenment to maintaining and improving the established social order. This last state of affairs prevails in England and France, and the second in Germany.

It is no doubt a fine thing to have raised oneself to the height of the noblest sentiments from the midst of the lowest servitude; through independent thought, to have cast off the constraint of

* I, 1, pp. 239–41.

absolute domination. But it is a finer thing, it seems to me, to have known how to create a free government for oneself, on which one can rely, without baseness or shame.

Germany has risen above her social estate and has left it behind her. England and France have raised themselves and their governments to their own level.

### CONTINUATION*

A great ferment is now making itself felt in Germany. The seeds of freedom are germinating in every breast, and everyone is saying that there will soon be a revolution.

The memory of the revolution in England and the more recent memory of the French Revolution frighten the German nation. Germany does not dare to believe that there is so much evil in store for her and she hopes that her character will save her. She is deceiving herself.

National character, regardless of what it may be, can do nothing against the force of circumstances and it is this force which is at work here. There is no change in the social order without a change in proprietorship. Zeal for the public good can at first create consent for the sacrifices demanded by this change and this is the first stage of any revolution. But people soon repent and resist and this is the second stage. Now the resistance of the proprietors cannot be overcome unless the propertyless arm themselves, and from this comes civil war, exile, massacres.

What can preserve a nation from these calamities? Nothing, save an external protection which sides with the partisans of the new social order and restrains the proprietors who oppose the revolution.

The evils of the English revolution were inevitable because at that time there was no force in Europe which could support the establishment of a free government.

France could have been saved by England, but England refused its help. Far from putting out the fire, England tried to stoke it and France was drenched in blood.

What England and France have been, Germany is today. The same evils threaten her; the same help can save her.

Furthermore, one circumstance which is peculiar to Germany must increase the violence of its revolution. Germany has more to do than either England or France. Not only must her constitution be changed, but she must compress herself into a single body and reunite under the same government a host of scattered

* I, 1, pp. 241–4.

governments. Germany divided is at the mercy of all; it is only by unifying that she can become powerful.

The first task of the Anglo-French parliament must be to hasten the reorganization of Germany by making its revolution shorter and less terrible.

The German nation, because of the size of its population, which is nearly half that of Europe, its central position and even more its noble and generous character, is destined to play the leading rôle in Europe as soon as it is reunited under a free government.

Once the Anglo-French association has been enriched by the reunion of Germany and a parliament common to the three nations has been established, the reorganization of the rest of Europe will become quicker and easier, because those Germans who will be called to take part in the common government will maintain in their opinions that purity of ethics, those lofty sentiments which distinguish them; they will raise to their level, by the force of their example, the English and the French whose commercial activities make them more selfish and less detached from their own interests. Then the principles of parliament will become more liberal, its operations more disinterested, its policy more favourable to the other nations.

### CONCLUSION*

In this work I have tried to prove that the establishment of a political system appropriate to the present level of enlightenment, and the creation of a common authority invested with sufficient strength to curb the ambitions of peoples and kings are the only things which produce a peaceful and stable order in Europe. In this respect, my proposed plan of organization is only of secondary importance, because if it were to be rejected, or were found to be essentially bad, I would still have achieved what I have undertaken to do, if some other plan were accepted.

From another point of view, my proposed plan is the most important part of this work. For a long time it has been generally agreed that the political system has been destroyed at its roots and that a different one must be set up. And yet neither this widely-held opinion nor the fact that men, exhausted by revolutions and wars, are ready to grasp at any means to restore order and peace, have shaken people out of their old ways. The old principles still hold sway as though there were no better ones. The elements of the old system have been combined in a thousand different ways, but nothing new has been thought

* I, 1, pp. 244–8.

of. The plan of organization which I have described is the first to have a new and comprehensive character.

It would, no doubt, have been desirable for the plan for the reorganization of European society to have been conceived by some powerful sovereign, or at least by a statesman skilled in affairs of state and renowned for his political talents. Such a plan, supported by great power and a great name would have attracted support more quickly; but the frailty of the human intellect prevented matters from taking this course. Those who in the day-to-day conduct of their affairs were forced by circumstances to base all their thinking on the principles of the old system which they supported, for want of a better one, could not take two different directions at once; and while they concentrated on the old system and the old methods, how could they conceive and nurture the thought of a new system and new methods?

As a result of strenuous efforts and great labours, I have adopted the viewpoint of the common interest of the European peoples. This viewpoint is the only one from which one can perceive both the evils which threaten us and the way to avert them. Let those who are in charge of our affairs climb to the same vantage-point as I and they will see all that I have seen.

The divisions in public opinion arise from the fact that everyone's point of view is too narrow and none dares to depart from the standpoint from which he habitually judges things.

For noble spirits, there is only one way to reason, and there is only one way to see things, if they look at them from the same point of view. If men, who have the same lofty sentiments, the same upright judgement, the same love of the public good, the same devotion to the king, hold different opinions, it is because each has his own point of view which he will not relinquish. Let us raise our sights: let us stop short at the point where I have tried to place human minds, and all those opinions will merge into a single opinion.

Then, through a happy change, whose results will benefit the state, we shall see the loftiest spirits, all the most enlightened minds, the Montesquious, the Raynouards, the d'Ambrais and the Lanjuinais, and many others who are divided by their opinions but united in their sentiments, joining together and marching towards the same goal, helping each other along the common road.

There will no doubt come a time when all the peoples of Europe will feel that questions of common interest must be decided before questions of national interest. Then evils will start to decrease, troubles to abate, wars to die away. Towards this moment we strive unceasingly; towards this moment the progress of the human mind bears us along. But which is worthier of man's discretion: to be dragged towards it or to run?

Poetic imagination has called the infancy of mankind the Golden Age, setting this amid the ignorance and brutishness of primitive times. This time would have been more aptly named the Iron Age. The Golden Age of mankind does not lie behind us, but before; it lies in the perfection of the social order. Our forefathers did not see it; one day our children will reach it. It is for us to clear the way.

# IV

# Industry (1)*

### DECLARATION OF PRINCIPLES*

In our view, society is the whole unified body of men who are engaged in useful work. We cannot imagine any other kind of society than this.

Society has two enemies, which it fears and detests equally: anarchy and despotism.

The constitution is the only barrier which the thought of the political writer must respect; against and outside it, no work is useful. Within the limits which it lays down, the widest freedom can do no harm. This freedom belongs to the writer, as the constitution itself belongs to the nation and the government.

### THE OBJECT OF THE UNDERTAKING

Men who are engaged in industry, and who collectively form the legitimate society, have only one need: freedom. For them, freedom means to be free to produce and to be unmolested in the enjoyment of what they have produced.

Man is naturally lazy. A man who works is only forced to overcome his laziness by the need to supply his wants or the desire to provide for his pleasures. Thus, he works only to satisfy his needs and his desires. But in society, the pleasures which invite him are manifold and far greater than his productive capacities, so that he is forced to exchange some of what he can produce for certain products which he cannot obtain directly from his labour. This necessity (which becomes a source of wealth for him) is the only one he recognizes, the only one to which he willingly submits. Thus the industrious man as such is only really subject to one law, that of self-interest.

* I, 2, pp. 128–38, Paris, 1817. *L'industrie littéraire et scientifique liguée avec l'industrie commerciale et manufacturière*, was published in 1817 in Paris, in two volumes. The first volume, Second Part, entitled *Politique* was published under the name of A. Thierry, 'adopted son of Henri Saint-Simon'. The second volume, from which the following extracts are taken, appeared also in 1817. In the Dentu edition, which is used in this translation, the editors themselves introduced the second volume with the following note: 'We extract from this volume of 346 pages, only what was actually written by Saint-Simon himself.'

But a host of parasites[1] surrounds society, drawing nourishment at its breast, and with the same needs and the same desires as the others, but who have been unable to overcome their natural laziness, as the others have done and who, producing nothing, consume or want to consume as though they did produce. These people must inevitably live on the work of others, whether it is given to them or because they take it. In short, they are idlers, that is, thieves.[2]

Thus, the workers are in danger of seeing themselves deprived of the good things for which they work. Out of this danger arises a need of a special kind which calls for a form of work distinct from any other and which is designed to combat the violence offered to industry by idleness.

In the eyes of industry, government exists simply to carry out this task. Idleness is the concern of government. The moment government activity moves outside this sphere, it becomes arbitrary, usurping and thus tyrannical and hostile to industry. It promotes the very evil it is supposed to prevent. Since a man works for himself, he wants to work in his own way. Whenever an action from above, external to industry, interferes with it and claims to rule it, industry is hampered and discouraged. Industrial activity ceases in proportion to the constraint it suffers.[3] If those engaged in industry can be ruled, it is not in their capacity as industrial workers.

If the activity of the government is considered useful to society, then society must agree to pay for this service.

While the sailor sails across the oceans, he is not ploughing the fields; while he who governs watches over the safety of the producers, he is not producing. But the sailor and the governor each pay their share in useful work. Both earn their share of what is produced. The share of the sailor is easily assessed by the law of supply and demand. What should that of the government be?

The solution to this problem is of the greatest interest to

1. In France there are far fewer unemployed than there were before the Revolution; there are far fewer in England than there are in France and far fewer in America than in England. The number of those unemployed has always decreased in direct proportion to the advance of civilization, so that one can foresee a time when there will be no more men who voluntarily do not work.

2. Idlers who are not thieves become beggars. The latter are scarcely less despicable and scarcely less dangerous than the former.

3. If industry, since the emancipation of the communes, has made continuous progress, it is because it has been less and less affected by the activity of the government.

industry because if it does not make the necessary sacrifices, the service will slow down and the security required by industry will not be complete.

If, on the other hand, for lack of sufficient evidence to assess the value of the service, industry pays far more for it than it should, two disadvantages result. In the first place, industry withdraws part of the capital needed by its productive occupations if they are to prosper; and, in the second, it allows the government an excess of strength and of scope for action which cannot fail to affect industry itself and be harmful to it.

Industry needs as little government as possible and there is only one way to ensure this, which is to be governed as cheaply as possible.

Let a search be made in industrial society for the man with the lowest intelligence, whose ideas do not extend beyond his own private affairs, and tell him that most of the tax he pays goes to reward the man who safeguards his peace and sees that he is not molested in the enjoyment of his possessions; then ask him the following question:

If it were possible for you to have, at a lower price, the same advantages for which today you pay so much, would you not agree to this?

And if it were clear to you that by paying less for it, peace would thereby be made even more complete and secure, would you not be even more in favour of the cheaper bargain?

There is no doubt what his reply would be. Of course, he would say, this is what we want you to bring about, this is what the whole of society naturally wants, just as you do. This is what we all want and is the end for which we are working.

It was while I was in America, fighting for the cause of industrial freedom that I first conceived the desire to see this plant from the New World blossom in my own country. This desire has dominated my thoughts ever since. Ceaselessly, in my study of the course of events, I became increasingly convinced that the advance of civilization has no other end; this end is genuine liberty, genuine public happiness, and I most ardently desired it. Every event which seemed to lead to it was for me a new joy and a new hope. The French Revolution broke out. At first it seemed to be completely industrial, but it soon lost this character and the many generous efforts which should have produced liberty, resulted only in the tyranny of the Jacobins and military despotism. A happier time has begun for us. At last, a government has been established which has declared that it wants to base its power on public opinion and *France has been restored to common sense, that is to say, to the free discussion of its common interests.*

One condition above all seems to be necessary for this discussion to be as complete as possible, for it to achieve results both accurate and important; I believe that that condition has been fulfilled.

We have seen that there are two orders of workers in society; those who produce and those who guard the producers. There is a third, composed of those whose profession it is to think about the general interests of society. They are the political writers. Now it is the government which is empowered to administer the general interests of society, so this order of workers finds itself naturally in touch with the government.

This state of affairs would present no drawback if the government turned to the writers only as advisers, whose knowledge could illuminate and facilitate its work. But this is not what happens; the interest of governments does not coincide completely with the general interest. The interest of the government is even, in some ways, by its very nature, opposed to the general interest.[1] Thus, governments are far less eager to seek counsel about what is advisable and what it would be best to do, than to secure approval of what they have done and what they want to do. And so they are seen to bring all their influence to bear, not to encourage the expression of opinion, but to mould it; they search for men who approve and explain, not for those who air their own views; for advocates, not for counsellors.

Writers, it will be said, obey nothing but their consciences and serve only the truth. They only approve and support the action of the government when they believe it is for the good of the governed. We believe, we know even, that the writers who work under the supervision and influence of the government, only work, or at least claim that they only work, for society as a whole and they are offended if the contrary is suggested. Nevertheless, we still think that the governed must know better than anyone else what they want and what benefits them. We believe that the government is an intermediary which serves no useful purpose between those who reflect on the public interest and those who feel it; between the writers on politics and industry.

1. Industry wants as little government as possible and those who govern, inevitably, want to govern as much as possible. Industry wants to pay as little as possible and those who govern want to get from industry as much money as possible.

What seemed to me to be necessary was that some way should be found to eliminate this useless and often dangerous intermediary and that direct relations should be established between industry and the men of letters. Moreover, liberal-minded men, who believe that governments exist for the governed and not for the governments, should not have to look forward to neglect and poverty as the only reward for their timely courage. In a word, it was necessary to establish alongside the favour and protection offered by power, national favour and protection.

But this is precisely what industry wanted when it formulated the project which we now proclaim;[1] This is the character that industry now assumes. This is the *personal stake* which industry brings to the association it proposes, into *the league formed by the manufacturing and commercial industries with the literary and scientific industry*.

Industry makes common cause with the political writers. On the one side, work, on the other sacrifices: these are the elements of their union; this is the condition, the link which binds them. Industry has understood this, and has promised to show literature in what esteem she holds her services.

## SIXTH LETTER*

It was a passion which began the French Revolution.–It can only be brought to an end by another passion.–The true object of the Revolution.–We are entering upon a revolution common to all mankind.

When I examine the passion which caused the French Revolution and which class of society was most violently moved by it, I see that the passion was for equality and that it moved most deeply men of the lowest class, whose ignorance and self-interest compelled them to fall violently under its sway. The effect of the passion for equality was to destroy the social organization which existed before the Revolution erupted. I

1. Industry here must be taken to mean only a few of the more important concerns which, moved by a feeling for the common good, make personal sacrifices which they think are for the well-being of everyone; the common good has always been served in this way and it is still today the only way in which it can be served.

Industry is only a single and vast body in which all the members are responsible for each other. The well-being and misfortune of one part affects all the others. There is only one interest, one need, one existence everywhere. But if the sentiment belongs to the whole body, it is the head alone which thinks for the entire body. It is there that revolutions are made, that needs make themselves felt, that desires declare themselves.

* I, 2, pp. 163–8.

now ask whether, once everything has been destroyed, another passion is not necessary to begin the work of rebuilding? In other words, I am asking if it is through passion or through moderation that a revolution can be brought to an end?

Habits acquired under the old institutions place great obstacles in the way of establishing a really new system. The establishment of such a system demands great philosophical labours and great financial sacrifices. A strong, single-minded passion is required to move men to great efforts.

Moderation is not an active force. It is essentially timid; it is far from conducive to the destruction of ingrained habits; instead it tends to tie us to them.

Moderation advises us to seek a compromise between habits inculcated by arbitrary and ecclesiastical institutions and liberal and industrial ideas and institutions. Now it is in the nature of the latter to be exclusive, and nothing can be done until they have gained the upper hand; until they are completely free from all alien elements, from the rust which corrodes their joints.

We exaggerate when we say that the French Revolution completely destroyed ecclesiastical and feudal power. It has not done away with them; it has only diminished confidence in their basic principles to a great extent, so that today those powers no longer have enough strength and credibility to bind society together. What ideas, then, can supply this vital and organic binding force? It is to industrial ideas, and to them alone, that we should look for our salvation and the end of the revolution.

Yes, Sir, in my view the unique goal to which all our thoughts and efforts should point *is the most advantageous organization for industry*; for industry in the widest sense, embracing every kind of useful work, theoretical and practical, intellectual as well as manual. The organization which is most advantageous to industry is a government whose political power has only that scope of action which is needed to ensure that useful work is not interrupted; a government in which everything is ordered so that the workers who make up the true society can exchange the produce of their different labours directly and with complete freedom among themselves; such a government, in fact, that allows society, which alone knows what suits it, what it wants and what it prefers, to be the sole judge of the value and utility of work; a government, moreover, under which the producer will receive the salary for his work, the reward for his service or whatever name he chooses to give it, only from the consumer.

Indeed, we want only to facilitate and illuminate the inevitable progress of events: in future, we wish men to do consciously, with more immediate effort and more fruitfully, what they have hitherto done without knowing it, slowly, indecisively and with little result.

After the enfranchisement of the communes, when the industrial class had regained its freedom, it succeeded in acquiring one political power. This power was that of being taxed only with its consent. The industrial class gradually increased its power and became more important. Its social condition improved in every respect: while those classes which can be called clerical and feudal continued to decline in prestige and in real power; from which I conclude that the industrial class must continue to grow and will at last spread throughout society.

This is the direction in which events are moving; this is where we are going, and those old institutions which are already too weak to sustain the power they had built up will fall for ever and disappear.

Some revolutions are only limited and national at first. There are partial revolutions, affecting only one of the social institutions. These successive revolutions combine to bring about a general revolution later.

From the philosophical point of view, ever since the Arabs first introduced the physical sciences into Europe and, from the political point of view, ever since the enfranchisement of the communes, mankind has clearly been advancing towards a general revolution; that is to say, it has taken the course which leads to a situation in which its existence will be greatly improved.

In the chain of events which have taken place since the two memorable epochs just cited, the most important links are: Luther's revolution, the revolution in England under Charles I, the expulsion of the Stuarts, the American and French Revolutions; and, now, in my view, the time is ripe for the general revolution, the revolution common to all civilized peoples of all lands.

Governments will no longer lead men; their functions will be restricted to preventing the disruption of useful work. They will command only limited power and limited financial resources; for limited power and money are enough to accomplish this aim. The financial resources essential for work of greater or lesser utility will be supplied by voluntary subscriptions and the subscribers themselves will supervise the way in which their money is used and administered.

EIGHTH LETTER*

## *THE SEARCH FOR A GENERAL PRINCIPLE IN POLITICS*

Sir, the question is therefore one of finding a new system of political organization.

How far has this work gone?

If it were enough to have assembled a great mass of material, it could be said that it was nearly finished. A great many ideas have been amassed; these ideas are even linked to some extent; but has the most important condition been fulfilled? Have we got a basic principle? An agreed principle to which we are led by new truths and from which these same truths may be deduced. This is what is lacking: this is what we must have.

Of all those who have worked on this research, it seems to me that the scholars who have written on political economy have done the most useful work, and M. Say's treatise on political economy seems to me to be the book in which the greatest number of positive, co-ordinated ideas are to be found.

This author, so rightly renowned, in my opinion comes nearest to the goal, without quite having reached it.

Here are the first two pages of his preliminary discourse. It contains his whole theory. It is the most general idea and, if I can express it in this way, the philosophy of his work.

A science only makes real progress when the field of research has been well defined as well as the object of the research. Otherwise one fastens here and there upon a small number of truths, without being aware of the connections between them, and upon many makes mistakes, without being able to discover where the error lies.

For a long time, *politics*, properly speaking, the science of the organization of societies, has been confused with *political economy*, which teaches how wealth is created, distributed and consumed. However, riches are essentially independent of the political organization. A state may prosper under any form of government, provided it is well administered. Nations have grown rich under absolute monarchs, and have been ruined under peoples' councils. If political freedom is more advantageous for the development of wealth, it is indirectly because it is more favourable to learning.

By mixing in the same study the principles of good government with those upon which the increase of wealth, either public or private, is based, it is not surprising that many ideas have been muddled together rather than clarified. Stewart can be reproached for having entitled his first chapter: *On the government of the human*

* I, 2, pp. 182–91.

*species*; the same reproach can be levelled at the group of economists in nearly all their writings, and against Rousseau in the *Encyclopedia*.

It seems to me that since [the work of] Adam Smith, these two doctrines have been firmly differentiated; the name of *political economy* has been kept for the science which deals with wealth, and that of *politics* has been reserved to describe the relations which exist between governments and peoples and between government and government.

It is clear that M. Say makes two distinct and separate subjects of politics and political economy. But at the same time, those who have read his work or listened to his public lectures are aware of the importance he gives to his discipline, and how often he reverts to the statement that it alone gives ethics and politics their qualities of certainty and reality.

This contradiction proves that the author has felt, vaguely and as if despite himself, that political economy is the genuine and sole basis of politics; but he has not seen it clearly enough, for he hints at it in the details of his work, while denying it in his general considerations.

Be this as it may, his work has been of the greatest use. It contains everything that political economy has discovered and proved up to now; for the time being it is the *nec plus ultra* of this discipline in Europe.[1]

The following seem to me to be the most universal truths and, consequently, the most worthy of being clearly stated for all to see:

1. That the production of useful things is the only reasonable and positive goal which political societies can set themselves and, consequently, that the principle of *respect for production and the producers* is infinitely more fruitful than that of *respect for property and property-owners*.

2. That governmental interference in industrial affairs is always harmful, even when it is an attempt to encourage them; from which it follows that governments should merely

1. Before Adam Smith, political economy, still in its infancy, cunningly presented itself as the auxiliary of governments, and was thus confused with politics. As it increased in strength, by the power of truth and the authority of common sense, it took on a more open and decided character and declared its independence of politics.

A little more courage still, a little more philosophy and soon political economy will take its true place. In the beginning, it leaned upon politics, and soon politics will lean upon it; or rather, it alone will comprise the whole of politics. This time is not far off.

concentrate on preserving industry from any kinds of disturbance and difficulties.

3. That those who produce useful things being the only useful members of society, they alone should agree upon how society is to be managed; being virtually the only ones who pay taxes, they should be the only ones who have the right to vote them;

4. That production is always harmed when men clash with each other; that wars, therefore, no matter what their object, are harmful to the whole of mankind and that they hurt even the victors.

5. That the desire of one people to exercise a monopoly over other peoples is wrong, because since a monopoly can only be won and kept by force, it must reduce the total amount of production even of that people which enjoys the monopoly.

6. That morality grows in relation to industrial improvement; that this is true whether we look at the relations of peoples to peoples or at relations between individuals: that, in consequence, the teachings we should spread, the ideas we should inculcate in all minds are those which tend to increase every man's productive activity and respect for the production of others.

7. That since the whole of mankind has a common aim and interest in his social relations every man should see himself uniquely as taking part in a community of workers.

This, I believe, is a summary of all the observed facts of political science. But what general idea emerges from them? To what common conclusion do they lead us? Because it is at that point that we can find, that we will inevitably find, the principle of all politics.

There is an order of interests experienced by all men; these are the interests concerned with the maintenance of life and well-being. This is the only order of interests upon which all men agree and need to agree. It is the only one they should discuss, on which they need to act in common; the only issue around which politics should centre and which should be taken as the sole criterion for judging all institutions and social matters.

To sum up in two words, therefore, politics is *the science of production*—that is to say, that science whose object is the creation of an order of things most favourable to every kind of production.

A principle is a starting point. If this point which we have just recognized, and to which the facts have led us, if this point, I repeat, is genuine and well-marked, politics from now on will no longer be a matter of vague conjectures, a plaything of circumstances. Its fate will no longer be determined by any power, form or prejudice. The ground it covers will be known; the way it is conducted will be respected; and the science of societies will therefore have a principle. It will at last have become a positive science.[1]

Let political philosophers take all the individual proved truths and apply them, one after the other, to the principle we have just drawn from them; then we will ask them first to judge the principle by their own truths, then we will ask them to judge these truths by the principle we have laid before them. We shall ask them whether these truths do not gain a new strength from the principle, a new existence; we shall ask them, finally, if this principle is not the most universal, the truest which has ever been put forward and, consequently, the richest in proved and useful results. Besides, one does not create a principle. One sees it and one demonstrates it. The one which I have just established is not the outcome of my work; it is derived from the writers and scholars whom I have mentioned. In their various treatises, they have established it indirectly, without looking for it and without knowing it. I have not established it, but I looked for it, I saw it and I proclaim it.

Doubtless, you will tell me, Sir, that I have only done half the work so far and that having climbed to the principle from the observation of the facts, I ought to descend again to experiments with this principle and thus submit my operation to proof. I agree with you; but as this last part of my task is simply, in my view, the discussion of all political questions; as these are the questions with which I concern myself, I shall say nothing from now on which is not a development and an application of this principle which, for the time being, I am content to have put forward.

1. We cannot be too distrustful of words, when we are working with ideas and we think that the reader's attention should be drawn here to the word *principle*, lest he confuse it (as is usual) with that of *precept*. We do not say that politics, having reached this point, has a precept, only that it has a principle. The principle may possibly become a precept, but that is not the business of the philosopher. Once the principle has been discerned, the rest follows inevitably. If the principle is true it naturally turns into precept and the substance will have found its form. If it is false, it will not influence anyone and the form will not give it a virtue which it does not have of itself.

# V
# Industry (2)

## THE POLITICAL STATE OF ENGLISH INDUSTRY

1817; vol. II, 1, pp. 49–61.

Industry has long played a political rôle in England, but it only won a free, positive, and guaranteed part in the administration of the public good at the time and as a result of the revolution of 1688. Now, at that time, feudalism and the Church were still very influential. Industry, having established its political power in these circumstances, necessarily therefore felt the repercussions of this anti-industrial reaction. Moreover, it was in an inferior position in all questions relating to the great political combinations. Two of the three parties in the English parliament are essentially feudal; only the House of Commons acts in an industrial spirit; and the two feudal sectors are two distinct powers, not only formally according to constitution but also in fact and in the public's opinion. The peers in England have a special strength; all have vast estates, privileges, and vassals. Thus, each of them has an effect on the industrialized House of Commons which is very different from the effect of royal action, but which is equally opposed to the interests of the advance of industry. Industry is, therefore, in a minority in the English parliament. It must always fight against two powers and, as a result, it is always dominated by them, when it comes to important measures which affect the mass of the nation. It cannot alter anything on the general political plane which is blocked by the royal power and the body of peers. In a word, it plays no part in the combinations which affect external relations; in all of them the feudal spirit is dominant. Also, we have seen that until now the foreign policy of England has never been directed towards the furtherance of industrial interests. The dominant spirit of this policy has been the mania for conquest, the passion to dominate, which is the essential characteristic of feudalism. The feudal spirit is completely warlike; that of industry is necessarily peaceful. England, compared with the continental powers, has always been prepared for war, proof positive that it is not industry which conducts its foreign policy and that feudalism is predominant in that sphere. Also, we have seen that on the most important occasions, in the struggle against the American colonies and in the war with France, these disastrous steps were taken against industry's will; that it was despite industry, despite its wishes as expressed by the House of Commons, that most of these wars were fought. We see, therefore, by the very fact that English industry does not conduct the foreign policy of the English government, that it does not influence the policies which affect the mass of the nation and that, in the great social combinations, it is feudalism which is dominant. This fact being established *a posteriori*, we have given the reason for it *a priori*, in the circumstances under the influence of which English industry acquired its political character. This influence means that feudalism has a majority in the English parliment.

But if this is so, what is the political strength of industry in England? What part has it played?

The English constitution has conceded to industry the right to vote taxes, liberty of person and of conscience, the maintenance of property. These rights are guaranteed by the constitution and industry is most surely safeguarded against feudalism in respect of them. In all domestic affairs, an Englishman is genuinely free; he never has to fear any violation of his property. He can speak his mind in public absolutely freely. He has unlimited freedom to use his abilities. He never has to fear illegal arrest or unjust expropriation. Industry, having won these precious rights in England, defends them against all usurpations because all the producers know how to agree among themselves, because an injustice to one of them affects the whole body of the nation, the whole industrial class.

Thus, English industry has taken the greatest advantage possible of the position in which it has been placed by the force of circumstances. Obliged to confine itself within a narrow circle, it has won all the advantages open to it. Industry has acquired some excellent national habits which guarantee to it for ever the possession of what it has known how to win and it is by virtue of these domestic habits that industry has prospered in England far more than in any other country, no matter how contrary to the interests of industry the foreign policy of the English government may have been.

To sum up, we see that English industry has not been able to break the influence of feudalism upon the masses but that it has protected itself satisfactorily against any arbitrary exercise of power which might threaten individuals.

THE POLITICAL STATE OF FRENCH INDUSTRY

The position of industry in France is completely different. French industry took shape at a time when feudalism had been destroyed and therefore it is industry which has the upper hand in the whole administration of public affairs. The house of peers is in no way feudal. It is only aristocratic in name and constitution, but not at all in fact and opinion. The peers of France have neither great territorial possessions nor the privileges of feudalism, nor do they have vassals. Nothing remains of feudalism except the monarchy and, because of this, there are in reality two industrial chambers, that is, two chambers which think and act on the side of the interests of industry. The members of the so-called aristocratic chamber have no interests other than their own; they are no longer a separate power; they are, properly speaking, an extension of the body which represents industry. From one point of view, they can be seen as an extension of the royal power, for they depend upon it for the most part for their livelihood; but this is only a temporary matter, of little importance. Even it it were true that a peer who receives favours from the court will always vote on the same side as royalty, it is clear that were these favours to be withdrawn, he would vote on the side of industry; while in England, a peer who has fallen from grace does not necessarily vote in the interests of industry because, as a peer, he has anti-industrial interests which are completely separate from any which he might have in his rôle as courtier.

Thus, industry in France, because of the influence of the age in which it took its place in the government, plays a more important political rôle than that of English industry. Industry in France has only to fight against one power; because even if we consider the house of peers as an extension of the royal power, whereas it is really an extension of industrial power, it would always be true to say that there are only two distinct political powers in France, the power of the monarchy and that of industry. This is why French industry plays an active part in the important social combinations; why it has a direct influence upon the general political plan, according to which foreign policy is conducted, and why a disastrous war cannot be waged against its wishes.

It thus enjoys a more favourable political position than does industry in England. But this superiority is offset by the fact that it lacks the advantages which English industry possesses to a high degree.

Industry has not existed for long enough in France to have formed good national habits. It has not developed that public spiritedness, that feeling for the common interest which reigns in England, and which, unless when it is produced temporarily by an upsurge of enthusiasm, can only be created by time. Every Frenchman cherishes his freedom and the maintenance of his possessions, but we have not yet acquired as strong and clear a feeling for our rights as has the lowliest Englishman. We do not yet know how to combine the interests of the individual with the common interest. In France, a despotic action is only resented by those who are its victims; it does not occur to the mass of people that it is their duty to fight it. And even the victim of a despotic action acquiesces in it unprotestingly, although he may complain later when he has already suffered the greatest trials.[1]

To sum up all that we have just said about French industry, we see that, because of the effect of the age in which it became part of the government, it has a more favourable political position than that of English industry, but that it has not realized

1. In France everyone says that the laws alone should be obeyed, but no one thinks of putting up the slightest resistance to the most insignificant representative of authority who has committed an illegal act. We have not yet acquired that spirit of independence which is characteristic of the English. To us, independence is simply a principle; to the English it is action and they carry it wherever they go; in every country they are ready to resist anything which does not emanate from the law. Among many examples which can be cited of this, we are content to recount the following anecdote which took place in France very recently:

'Shortly after 20 March, an Englishman bought the Hôtel de Noailles. When Bonaparte came to power, because the Englishman had only paid a deposit, the administration began to put into effect the imperial decree concerning the possessions of émigrés and to eject the buyer.

'On receiving the order to vacate the premises, which was brought to him by a bailiff, the Englishman replied only that this was his home, that the civil act which gave him the right of ownership could only be annulled by another civil act; this was the law.

'The next day another bailiff presented himself and received the same reply as the first, ending with these words:

' "Say to those who sent you that I will not leave here except by virtue of a court hearing; that I demand a court hearing. They say that you are free in France; I shall soon know if you are. I shall do what in the same circumstances I would do in England: the home of a citizen is inviolable; my house will be barricaded, my people armed and we shall fire upon anyone who approaches, as you have done, Sir, to commit violence against me in the name of an authority which is not based upon law."

'And, in fact, the house was barricaded, the doors barred, the servants armed. The incident became known; it was brought before the *Conseil d'État*. The Englishman was left in peace in his house.

'What Frenchman would have dared to show such resolution?'

in that position all the advantages open to it. In contrast with English industry, it wields enough influence to prevent arbitrary power being used against the masses, but it has not yet developed those national habits which are necessary to stop it from acting despotically towards individuals.

## CONCLUSION

From all that we have said up to now it follows that English and French industry represent two different political states; that they each enjoy a particular kind of influence in the direction of their respective affairs. English industry is safeguarded against action towards individuals, but is not secure from acting thus towards the mass of people. French industry, on the other hand, is secure against despotism towards the masses, and does not know how to safeguard itself against oppression of the individual. Does it not follow that it would be in the interests of both English and French industry to unite and combine their forces? As producers, the industrial workers of France and England have no grounds at all to hate each other; they are, on the contrary, drawn together by the general interests of industry; furthermore, by virtue of their particular political position, they have the most powerful motive for uniting. French industry and English industry are in relation to their respective governments, in the precise position in which each is able to supply what the other lacks in political strength. Re-united, they would thus have all their strength; isolated, they will both continue to suffer, each from their own lack of strength.

The coalition of all the national industries is necessary to prepare for the establishment of an industrial system. But this coalition cannot be formed suddenly all over the civilized world. It should begin with the union of French and English industry, as they, above all, have the most obvious interest in combining their efforts. Their union is possible; once again, this is because all industrial workers are friends. It is advantageous to both because the strengths which are lacking in one are to be found in the other; on the other hand, industry, as we have often said, possesses all the genuine power. English industry and French industry can and ought to form the firm intention to unite, and it is in their power to do so. What obstacle can stand in the way of this union? None, except ignorance of the way in which they should combine their efforts.

## APPENDIX

As we have shown, the industrial body is composed of two great families; that of the scientists or the theoretical industrialists and that of the direct producers or the empirical scientists. In all that we have said, we have dealt only with the practical industrialists. We can draw analogous conclusions with respect to the theoretical industrialists.

The English scientific class and the French scientific class find themselves also in a situation in which each can supplement the other's deficiencies.

French theoretical industry is constituted and the organization of the body of French scientists, the academy of science, is complete, with the exception of philosophy which it does not have, which it could not have until now, but which it will undoubtedly have soon. What does this body need before it can profitably join the general industrial league and work to establish the industrial régime? Only one thing is missing! This is to be free, to cast off all government influence.

This is what the English learned body has done. The Royal Society is free; its relations with the class of direct producers are more intimate. But, on the other hand, its organization is far from being as complete, as well integrated as those of our institution.

Thus, English theoretical industry and French theoretical industry, like the empirical industries of both countries, enjoy respectively advantages which one or the other lacks. They have thus, as have the practical industries, a powerful motive to combine.

## OF THE PRESENT STATE OF CIVILIZATION*

We attach too much importance to the *form* of *governments*; it would seem that this is the essence of all *politics* and that once the division of *powers* has been firmly established, everything has been arranged in the best possible way.

In *Europe* there are two peoples who live under an absolute monarch: the *Danes* and the *Turks*. If there is a shade of difference between them, it is that in *Denmark* despotism is stronger than in *Turkey*, because it is legal and *constitutional*; and yet, under the same form of *government*, what a difference there is in the condition of the governed! There is no people more unfortunate, more harassed, more oppressed, in short, more unjustly and expensively governed than the *Turks*; while there

* II, 1, pp. 81–4.

is no place where liberty is more widespread than in *Denmark*; there is no place, England included, less affected by arbitrary power, or whose administration costs less. Where does the difference lie? It is certainly not in the *form* of the *governments*, since that form is the same in both countries. Tyranny, then, must spring from another cause; this is the cause: due allowance being made, the *King of Denmark* is the poorest of all the European princes; the Turkish Sultan is the richest of all, since he is the only *landowner* in *Turkey*, just as he is the only master.

This example proves that the law which establishes the powers and form of government is not as important and does not have as much influence on the well-being of nations as the law which establishes and regulates ownership.[1] Do not imagine, however, that we would conclude from this that the law establishing the *division* of *powers* is not vital. We are far from professing such heresy. Of course, the form of *parliamentary government* is preferable to all the others; but it is only a *form* and the establishment of *ownership* is *basic*. Thus, it is this *establishment* of *ownership* which is the true basis of the social edifice.

Thus, the most important question to be resolved is, in my view, that of knowing how ownership should be established for the greatest good of society as a whole, with regard to both liberty and wealth.

Now the supplementary question which we are about to deal with here is attached to this general question.

So long as the *consumers* are in a majority in the debates about what their part should be, that part will be very strong, as strong as they want to make it; that is to say that, in spite of your *parliamentary forms*, you will be governed in an *arbitrary way*. On the other hand, the moment the *industrialists*—that is to say the people interested in public liberty and the economy—have won the exclusive right to vote taxes, they will only give what they really want to give and they will really be free to exercise their rights to the fullest extent. And, again, what must be done in order to reach this point? The nature of the right to *property*

1. We are not saying that the *right of property* was not dealt with during the *Revolution*. Of course, this right was discussed when the property of the Church was *nationalized*, for this decision was the result of a debate on the right of the *Church* to property. But the *right* to *property* was discussed only in general terms, by studying how *property* should be constituted for the greatest good of the *nation*. We ask the reader not to lose sight of the fact that we have always declared *disorder* to be the greatest of all evils, and have said that the maintenance of *order* demands, whatever side one takes, whatever advantage it may ensure, that a law should never be retroactive because the disadvantages in such a case will always outweigh the benefits.

must be understood, and this right established in the way most favourable to the growth of the wealth and the liberties of *industry*. Now this is the condition which we intend to bring about through the legislative measures set forth in this *work*, the examination of which we now leave to public opinion, that is, to *industrial* opinion.

The *declaration of the rights of man*, which was seen as the solution to the problem of *social liberty*, is really only a statement of the problem. Has this problem been solved? Will it ever be? What is certain is that it is not in organizing, in constituting or in combining the *three powers* that this can be achieved.

## POLITICAL PROGRESS OF INDUSTRY*

To clarify the political ideas of the *industrialists*, to discover what *industry* must do today to improve its standing in society, it is necessary to enquire what point *industry* has reached at this moment in its political career. Now this can only be done by looking back at the *past*, by a brief recapitulation of the successive steps which *industry* has taken until now.

If we go back in the *history* of *industry* to the *Greeks* and *Romans*, we find among these *nations* that the *industrial class* was completely *enslaved* by the *military class*.

The enslavement of *industry* continued under the *warriors* from the *north* who destroyed the *Roman empire*, and who established themselves in western Europe in the place of the old masters or conquerors.

This revolution which at first sight appears to have meant only a simple change of masters for *industry* was, nevertheless, of the very greatest importance to it, because of the fortunate result of the change of masters.

The nature of the enslavement of the *industrial class* changed and became the *enslavement* of the soil. This was a great improvement. Moreover, the conquerors spread to the *countryside* and the *workers*, who were established in the *towns*, were no longer subjected to the immediate and continual supervision of their masters. This was also a great advantage to them.

Thus, for these two reasons, the *conquest* of the *Roman empire* by the *peoples* of *northern Europe* produced the first important improvement in the lot of *industry*.

The second improvement in the lot of the *industrial class* lay in its *enfranchisement*.†

The benefits accruing to *industry* from the destruction of the

* II, 1, pp. 141–68.

† See note on translation, p. 59–60.

*Roman empire*, as we have just seen, allowed it to develop in a certain way until it gradually reached the point of being able to regain its freedom. This redemption was the most important of all the steps which *industry* has taken and will take in the future. It was the most important turning-point for industry; it was the beginning of its *political existence*, the development of which we are now going to follow.

This important *step* is usually known as the *enfranchisement of the communes*.* The expression is an apt one, as the *communes* and *industry* are one and the same thing: the *communes* were originally composed entirely of *artisans* and *merchants*, who established themselves in the towns. This is an important *fact* to note and one which must not be overlooked, if we are to have a true idea of what we should today understand by the *communes*.

After the *industrialists* had regained their *freedom*, their lot was improved in that each was freed from the immediate and despotic rule of the *lord* upon whom he had been dependent before the redemption of his freedom and this undoubtedly made things easier for them. But in the main these redeemed men were still dependent upon the *clergy*, the *nobility* and the *military*; they were still forced to give them a great part of the produce of their labour and to bear the frequent oppressive acts to which their position exposed them. This is how *industry* was freed from the second kind of arbitrary rule.

The privileged, who alone composed the whole of *parliament*, and who had no intention of sharing their power, had the idea of calling the *deputies* of the *communes*—that is to say, of *industry*—to make them give an account of what they possessed in order to take more by organized tax collecting than they had been able to obtain by oppression. This is the true origin of the *parliamentary communes*, which bear no relation to the *assemblies* of *soldiers* on the *Champ de Mai** which have existed in France since the time of the *conquest* by the northern peoples of Europe.[1]

The establishment of this custom must be recognized as being highly advantageous to the *industrial class* as it was the beginning of all its subsequent political successes. However, at first, the *communes*—that is, again, *industry*—regarded the obligation to send *deputies* to *parliament* as a burdensome one, because the *deputies* enjoyed no rights, and their mandate was limited to

* *Champ de Mai*, political assembly under the Carolingian kings [Translator's note].

1. We shall certainly be reproached for confusing in our recapitulation what took place in France with what took place in England. Our answer is that this is not a *national question* we are dealing with but a *European question*.

declaring by how much the wealth of their constituents had increased. But matters did not remain in this state, nor could they do so. *Industry*, in spite of the outrages and harassments of every kind with which the *military* and *feudal* class oppressed it, succeeded in the end in enriching itself through work, patience and thrift. It gained in importance and respect as its numbers grew, because marriages between the *industrialists* and the *military* drew together the interests of many individuals from the *military class* and many *members* of the *communes*. Because of this and many other reasons, and above all because *industry* was able to make the *military class* see that they could make money from industry at the same time as they allowed industry to pay fewer taxes; in a word, through the *financial ability* shown by industry which it represented to the military as something which could be useful to it, industry won a *deliberative voice* in *parliament* for the *communes* from the military class.

This great stride made by *industry* should be studied carefully because it is, in a way, the beginning of a *new era* for mankind. From this point, the *law* of the greatest *force* ceased to be the only law; or rather, *strength* and *cunning* ceased to be the only elements which composed the *law*: the *general interest* had also begun to be considered.

The next step which *industry* took, the last one it took until today, from the purely *political* point of view, was after the *English revolution*. It occurred when the custom was introduced that the House of Commons, [in England] completely alone and exclusively of any other power, voted the *budget*. The great *European revolution* would have been complete and the peaceful *industrial régime* would have been established at that moment if, on the one hand, the commons of England had been represented solely by *members of industry* and if, on the other, English *industry* had felt that, in the nature of things, it was more closely bound by common interests to the *industrialists* of other countries than to *Englishmen* of the *military* and *feudal* classes.

But at that time, *feudalism* was still a very powerful force and *industry*, knowing little about its own interests and the course it should take, allowed itself to be dominated by the *feudal spirit*, which is essentially *a spirit of conquest*.

The natural order of things, the progress of *civilization* have reserved for *French industry* the glory of establishing the *great European revolution*, because French industry, having taken the step we have discussed much later than *English industry*, made its move more completely and more decisively, and it was successful at a time in which the strength of *feudalism* was failing and when *industry* could easily recognize its interests and follow a well thought-out course.

Here we shall end our *recapitulation* of *industry's political past*. Let us now look at the civil successes it has won since the House of Commons found itself secure in the exclusive right to vote taxes.

Since this time, industry has increased immeasurably in importance. It has expanded everywhere; it has become master of all. By improving its products, it has accustomed men to luxuries which have then become necessities. But above all, it is the *government* which has become the subservient to *industry*, and has become especially dependent on it. Does the *government* want war? Its first priority is not to acquire soldiers; it turns to industry first and appeals to industry for money and then for all the other things it needs, which it buys from industry with the money it has obtained from industry. It is industry which supplies the *cannons*, *guns*, *gunpowder*, *uniforms*, etc., etc., etc. *Industry* has taken over everything, even *war*.

One happy and necessary effect of the improvement in the *art of war*, is that *war* itself has become more and more dependent on *industry*, so that today the real *military strength* is in the hands of the *industrialists*. The military strength of a country no longer resides in its *armies*, but in its *industry*. The *armies* of today (and by an *army* one must understand all the *soldiers* from the simple *private* up to the most illustrious *general*), the *armies*, we repeat, perform no more than a supporting rôle; for their value lies only in their use of the products of *industry*; the best-equipped army always gains the advantage, unless the *generals* are utterly incompetent. And the *French Revolution* has certainly proved that it is neither very rare to find nor very difficult to learn the *art of good generalship*: it can even be said that military effectiveness, at least for those bodies which today make up the main strength of the *armies* and on which, in great measure, the winning of battles depends, is a product of *industrial theory*.*

Industry has taken over finance in the same way: today, in France and England, it is industry which advances the money for the needs of the *public services*, and it is into its hands that the bulk of the *taxes* flows. The results of this *summary* of the advance and *progress* of *industry* are as follows:

1. That from the *political point of view*, the *industrial class*, originally enslaved, has gradually raised and enlarged it social condition so that today it is at last in a position to assume general

* In the original: *est un produit de l'industrie théorique*—translator's note.

power, since the *House of Commons*, having the *exclusive right* to vote *taxes*, possesses through this great *social power* upon which all the others depend; and that, consequently, if great *political power* is not yet in the hands of *industry*, this is solely because the *House of Commons*, the *members of the commons* (that is to say, of *industry*) do not yet form, as they should do, a majority in the lower house.

2. From the *civil point of view*, the real power today resides in *industry* and the *feudal class* finds itself dependent on *industry* for all its needs.

### ON WHAT HAS UNTIL NOW RETARDED THE PROGRESS OF INDUSTRY

If the *progress* of *industry* has hitherto been very slow; if even today *industry*, in spite of numerous and important achievements, finds in reality it is an inferior position; and if society is still governed, to a great extent, by the *feudal class* or at least by the *feudal spirit* (which comes to almost the same thing); the reason is that until now the *communes* have had no *principles* of their *own*; that they have only progressed and won victories by means of a kind of *practical* and *routine instinct*.

By principles of *industry*, we mean knowledge of the way in which industry should use *power*. Until today *industry* has lacked this knowledge, which is simply a *political plan* drawn up along lines suitable to industry and incorporated in its interests. Now it is clear that this knowledge is indispensable to *industry*, if *overall power* is to pass to it and that so long as these *principles* are missing, *industry* can only play a subordinate role.

The *military* or *feudal class* has its own *principles* and this is how it has held on to *overall power*. But without *principles* of its own, *industry* up to now has done, and still does, nothing except criticize the *feudal system of government*. It has been unable to take the initiative for itself and exert any influence.

All its *principles* can be reduced to the vague desire to be *governed well*, that is to say, to be governed in a way which accords with its interests; but it is clear that this desire, without the knowledge of how to govern in the interests of industry, can lead only to *acts of criticism*.

The *principles* which the communes have lacked for so long, have at last been produced by the immortal *Adam Smith*; for these *principles* are simply the universal truths enunciated by the science of *political economy*.

For more than forty years, men of the greatest merit have worked exclusively on these principles: they have not only influenced producers, but have also prepared *public opinion*, to welcome this important innovation; they have prepared public opinion to deliberate on affairs of *state* in exactly the same way as they would deliberate on matters concerning the interests of a particular individual; to consider a *national association* as an *industrial concern* the aim of which is to procure for every *member* of *society*, according to his stake in that society, the greatest comfort and well-being possible. One cannot but admire the wisdom these scholarly *economists* have displayed in this *work* and the perseverance with which they have opened up an entirely new road for us towards *happiness* and *freedom*.

*Smith*, having observed the processes used in the different *industrial concerns*, gathered his *observations* together; he formed them into a body of knowledge; he generalized from his ideas; he established principles and created a *science* based on the *art* of acquiring *wealth*; just as Aristotle wrote his *Poetics*, based on his observations on the work of the poets who had preceded him.

One piquant circumstance to be noted is that *Smith's book* was very favourably received by all *governments*. Happy blindness of governors who have always relied on the *strength of bayonets*! Admirable sagacity of those who try to escape the action of force and whose aim is to deprive *governments* of this *improper* custom!

*Smith's book* is the strongest, most direct and most complete critique ever made of *feudalism*: every page contains a demonstration of the fact that the *communes* or *industry* were preyed upon by this *régime* which was of no use to them whatever; that *governments*, such as were established, tended constantly to ruin the *people*, because they only *consumed*; whereas the only way to create wealth is to *produce*.

His work can perhaps be taken as a collection of detailed refutations of all the actions of *governments*, and, consequently, it can perhaps be seen, as a whole, as a demonstration of how necessary it was for the people to change the *principles* and the *nature* of their *governments*, if they wanted to put an end to their poverty-stricken existence and to enjoy peace and the fruits of their labour.

The book also contains the proof that a *nation*, if it is to acquire prosperity, must proceed in the same way as the *manufacturers*, the *merchants*, and everyone engaged in some *industry*, and that, consequently, the *budget* of a *nation* which wants to become free and rich, should be drawn up on the same principles as the particular *budget* of any *industrial enterprise*; that the only sensible goal that a *nation* should pursue was to *produce* as much as possible, with the least possible administrative expense.

M. *Say* rearranged *Smith's* ideas; he classified them more methodically; he made a *doctrine* out of the work, in a way not attempted by the author; he added new considerations to those which *Smith* had produced, and he entitled his book: *Traité d'economie politique*.

In this book, the critique of the conduct of existing *governments* is more pointed; the comparison between the *principles* of *military administration* and those of *industrial administration* is more directly established.

*Smith* advertised the science which he had created very modestly; he presented it as a means by which *governments* could enrich themselves; he announced it only as a secondary science, as an auxiliary and dependant of *politics*.

M. *Say* went one step further than *Smith* from the *philosophical* point of view: he established, as the main argument of his work, that *political economy* is distinct from and independent of *politics*; he stated that it has its own foundation, quite different from the one upon which the science which deals with the organization of *nations* is based.

The most despotic governments always exhibit the same blindness; they could not wait to have the work of M. *Say* translated and to establish *chairs of political economy*; chairs, that is, which taught that the *feudal* and *military form of government* (which is more or less that of all the *European peoples*) is a *form of government* which lags behind the enlightenment and is ruinous and completely useless for the people from every point of view; that a *budget* drawn up according to the views of and in the interests of this *form of government* is an absurdity; that the *budget* of a *nation* should be made up in the same way as that of an *industrial enterprise*; that a *nation* must of necessity be organized with one of two ends, either to *steal* or to *produce*, that is, that it must be either *military* or *industrial*; otherwise it will be nothing but a *bastard association*, if it does not declare itself openly for one of these two ends.[1]

1. This last idea, which is both subtle and useful, is due to M. COMTE. He was the first to say that a people finds itself in a false political situation, in which its efforts are to a great extent self-defeating, if they do not opt clearly for the *military type* (that is to say, for stealing) or for the *industrial* type (that is, for peace). It was M. COMTE who, in an excellent book, showed that the *Romans* were completely war-orientated, and that all their institutions worked together to give them the greatest possible military strength. It was he who revealed how the *Romans* acted consistently in the spirit and enlightenment of their epoch. It was he again who proved that *modern peoples* were lagging behind the enlightened spirit of their age, and that

At the point now reached in the work of providing *industry* with the *principles* by which it should govern its conduct, only one thing remains to be done: this is to spread the knowledge of *political economy* among the industrialists. It is difficult to believe, although it is only too true, that a science as useful and necessary to *industry* as *political economy*, a science which is peculiar to *industry* should be the least known by far of all the existing sciences.

### ON THE STEPS WHICH INDUSTRY SHOULD TAKE NOW

We have established that *industry* today possesses real strength and in addition that it also possesses principles which it lacked formerly—or, at least, it is now very easy for industry to acquire these principles, because they exist.

If this is, as we believe, the real point which *industry* has reached today in its political career, why is it that the direction of *society* has not fallen into its hands? How has it come about that the *industrial régime* has not been established, and the *feudal* and *military* system still exists? This is primarily because *industrial principles* are still not widely enough known and as a result have not acquired the credit which should give them confidence and strength; and, secondly, because real strength and principles are not enough, as one might at first think, to give *industry* the leading place in *society*; industry still requires a legal method for ensuring that *power* passes into its hands. It is through ignorance of this method that industry used, and could only use, the method of *insurrection* when it attempted to seize power. Now, *insurrection* is first of all the most inadequate of all methods; and second, it runs absolutely contrary to the interests of *industry*; for industry, any use of force is an evil, and it is *industry* that is most affected by popular uprisings, because of all types of property, *industrial property* is the most easily destroyed.

Thus, after the *problem*, solved by *Smith*, of how to create suitable *principles* to direct the *advance* of *industry*, the *problem* which naturally presents itself for solution, in the interests of *industrial progress*, is that of how to find a legal method by means of which high *political power* can be delegated to industry.

---

as a result showed themselves to be completely inconsistent in their conduct, in entrusting the main positions and the supreme direction of affairs to the *military class*, while at the same time they eagerly desire to enrich themselves through commerce and clearly intend to foster the prosperity of *industry*.

We are eager to take this opportunity to render justice to M. Comte's talent as this worthy *publicist* is at the moment facing grave difficulties.

It does not require either great intellectual ability or much study to think of the means of insurrection; but it is more difficult to find a *legal means*. We have devoted ourselves to the solution of this problem, as we are convinced that this solution is the only one which industry lacks today; the only step which remains to be taken to bring about the establishment of the *industrial régime*, the end to which all the efforts of the civilized *nations* have been directed for over *six hundred years* and the end of the great *European revolution* which has been in preparation for so long.

We firmly believe that we have found this *solution*, and we think that the measures we have proposed will enable us to reach this goal justly; for this measure ought to have the inevitable result that, in time, a *chamber of commons* as a whole, or at least an overwhelming majority of it, will be composed of *members of the communes*, that is, of *industry*; and, in addition, since such a *chamber of commons* will have high *political power*, because it alone has the right to vote the *taxes*, it follows that the measure proposed would cause high *political power* to pass to *industry* in a completely legal way, entirely in accordance with the existing *constitution*. Furthermore, this would take place without any abrupt change, since the measure by its very nature can only take effect gradually.

This is why we are firmly convinced that the adoption of this measure is the *step* which *industry* ought to take *today*, and that, consequently, it will sooner or later be adopted, in accordance with the universal law, confirmed by all historical observations, that nothing can permanently halt the *progress* of *civilization*.

## BEHAVIOUR OF THE JURISTS DURING THE FRENCH REVOLUTION COMPARED WITH THAT OF THE INDUSTRIALISTS

### *Behaviour of the Jurists*

Having, in the two previous *chapters*, enabled the *reader* to follow rapidly the *history* of the *tribunals* and of *industry*, it would seem that we would be failing to establish clearly the connections which must be made, if we did not end with a comparison between the behaviour of the *jurists* and the behaviour of the *industrialists* during the *French Revolution*.

How, then, did the *jurists* behave? In the first place, it was the *Girondins* who overthrew the old government; it was they who set up the *Republic*; it was they who prevented the restoration of the *monarchy*; and the same party, known as the

*Girondins*, was led by *Guadet*, *Vergniaud* and *Gensonne*, all three *jurists*, all three *advocates*.

Once the old *government* had been overthrown, it was *Robespierre* who seized *power*; and what was *Robespierre*? Again, a *jurist*: his most important lieutenants were also *jurists*. *Committees of public safety* and *general security* were set up everywhere, all composed of *jurists*. It is a fact that during the stormiest and most distressful years of the *Revolution*, France was governed by *jurists*.

They were jurists, also, who administered the *departmental assemblies*, those of the *districts*, and those of the cities, called *municipalities*; all of these were governed by jurists.

The jurists were not content merely with seizing the *legislative*, *administrative* and *executive* power; they also succeeded in directing popular feeling. They supplied the leaders of the *Jacobins*; they formed a club of *Cordeliers*;* lastly, they held, almost exclusively, all the *administrative offices* of the various *popular societies* in those unhappy days.

Thus, once it has been recognized that the *Reign of Terror* was invented by the *jurists*, who had become masters of all, and that the terror was founded by them upon the ruins of the old order, which they had destroyed; it must also be recognized that they were the instigators, the 'regulators' and even, to a certain extent, the executors of the many atrocities which marked their sinister creation.

Always inspired by the same *guiding spirit*, that of *domination*, they remained true to themselves in all our great political crises. They needed power, no matter what the cost; and in order to have as much power as possible, these new *Proteans* were able to assume any shape called for by circumstances. Let us follow their progress.

*Bonaparte* arrived and, in his turn, assumed supreme power. At once, this same body of *jurists*, who only yesterday had professed the most die-hard *republicanism*; who had just invented the never-to-be-forgotten phrase, written in huge letters on all the walls, on all the public buildings: *Unity, indivisibility of the Republic; liberty, equality, fraternity or death*, were among the first to bow to the new *idol*. They vied with each other as to which of them would show the most zeal, the greatest speed to serve and to consolidate the new power. *Cambacérès* created the role

* A society of 'Friends of the Rights of Man' formed in 1790; it played an active part in the movement against the monarchy in 1792 and in the establishment of the worship of Reason. The club disowned Danton and attacked Robespierre—its leaders were guillotined on March 24, 1794.

of *civilian lieutenant* to a *military despot*. At that time, the *speeches* in all the law courts, in all the tribunals, proved that *despotism* was perfectly in tune with the spirit of our legislature. Nothing was more curious among these manifestations than the little book which appeared at the time of *Napoleon*'s fall, entitled *Oraison funèbre d'un grand homme, by a society of men-of-letters*. It was composed of all the adulatory passages, of all the specious and erroneous maxims which had fallen from the mouths or pens of these versatile creatures, who never shrink from sacrificing everything to their own interests; and as every sentence carried the name of its author, it was easy to see that the greater part of the work was once again written by *jurists*.

However, *Bonaparte* was overthrown as a result of military action; the former *government* was restored, and the body of *jurists* changed its tune. But they were no less anxious to serve power, and to limit the freedom of the people. The way in which they interpret the Charter is invariably *anti-liberal*.

The *Revolution* gave the *jurists* an opportunity to reveal the spirit which motivates them: this is an unquenchable thirst for *power*, to the point where to possess it, even in a subordinate rôle, if they cannot be absolute masters, becomes the object of their desires and their efforts; this will not astonish us too much, if we remember that the *Roman emperors*, the greatest despots who ever lived, invented the *science* practised by the *jurists*, as well as the *legal principles* which they undertake to apply.

### *Behaviour of the industrialists*

The *industrialists* did not play an active part in the *Revolution*: they governed nothing; administered nothing of the public affairs; they made no attempt to seize *power*; none of the arbitrary actions which made those years so unforgettable were committed by them: on the contrary, it was they who suffered most from acts of this kind. The *industrialists*, during that time twice lost their capital: the law of the *maximum** took it from them once; then, later, under *Bonaparte*, there came the *law* that ordered the burning of all *English goods* and which ruined *industry* a second time.

The *industrialists*, who never sought to seize power when the old *government* fell, showed the same reluctance to become the tools of the various powers which have followed one after the other ever since.

The political spirit shown by the *industrialists* since the origin

* First law of the *maximum* May 1793, revised September 1793—abolished December 1794; established a maximum price for essential goods.

of their incorporation, that is since the *enfranchisement of the communes*, which they showed throughout the course of the *Revolution*, which they still profess today and according to which they act, is a combination of ideas which they constantly put forward as their goal: 1. to avoid any political upheaval and therefore never to change the form of the established *government*, no matter what it may be; 2. to limit the action of *power* and to restrain it as much as possible; 3. to diminish the cost of *government* and all misuse of *taxation*.

Today, by means of the *electoral law*, several important *industrialists* are to be found in the *Chamber of deputies*. If we look carefully at all the *opinions* they have expressed, we shall see that they have constantly tried to obtain, to reconcile and to combine the greatest peace, liberty and economy.

*Consequence of this comparison*

It clearly follows from this comparison that:

1. It is in the interests of *those who govern* and *those who are governed* to extend the *political importance* of the *industrialists*, since, on the one hand, they are always inclined to support the existing *government* and, on the other, they work ceaselessly to limit *power* and to decrease *taxation*.
2. It is equally in the interests of *those who govern* and of *those who are governed* to curtail the *political influence* of the *jurists*, because this body is, on the one hand, ambitious, revolutionary and always ready to overthrow or to seize power; and, on the other hand, when they cannot snatch power or are forced to give it up, they are invariably ready to serve those who do possess it against the interests of the *people*; lastly, we see that in both cases the jurists work to diminish the liberties of the *nation* and to increase the burdens which weigh upon it.

# VI

# *Le Politique*

## THE NATIONAL OR INDUSTRIAL PARTY COMPARED TO THE ANTI-NATIONAL PARTY

*Le Politique ou Essais sur la politique qui convient aux hommes du XIX^e^ siècle, par une société de gens de lettres,* 1819; II, 1, pp. 195–209.

*Le Politique* was published first in 1819 and was meant to consist of four parts divided into: *La politique pure, La politique littéraire, La politique scientifique,* and *Mélanges. Le Politique* was to be published in instalments, but some extracts were published afterwards as separate pamphlets. The *National Party, etc.* was a small pamphlet of fifteen pages, independently published in April 1819 (pp. 353–67).

### *Composition of the two parties*

The national party is composed of:

1. Those engaged in work which is of direct use to society;
2. Those who direct this work or whose capital is invested in industrial concerns;
3. Those who contribute to production by work useful to the producers.

The anti-national party is composed of:

1. Those who consume and produce nothing;
2. Those whose work is of no use to society or to the producers;
3. All those who profess political principles the application of which are harmful to production and tend to deprive the industrialists of first place in social esteem.

One very important thing to notice is that since all citizens have become equal before the law, it is by no means the accident of birth that they find themselves allied with one or other of these parties, but their occupations and opinions decide to which of the two they should belong.

Thus, M. de Lafayette, who farms, M. de Larochefoucault-Liancourt, who is a manufacturer, M. Le Voyer d'Argenson who is an iron master, clearly belong, through their occupations as well as through the liberal cast of their opinions to the industrial class, while MM. Barthélemy, Bellard and Pastoret, who are of humble origin, have deliberately aligned themselves with the anti-national party.

*On the morality of one of these parties.—on the immorality of the opposing party*

What is moral? What is immoral? This question must be answered before we compare the morality of the industrialists with that of the anti-industrialists.

In politics, as in religion, upright men, those who are devout and those who are not, recognize that all morality derives from the great principle which was proclaimed by Jesus Christ:

*Love your neighbour as yourself: do unto others as you would that they should do unto you.*

Thus the question is to know whether the conduct of the industrialists or the non-industrialists conforms best to the principle which is the basis of morality. Now, it is clear that the whole life of the industrialists is spent in a way which is useful to their neighbours, since they devote their time and their means to the production of things which can satisfy the primary needs of society and provide pleasures for it.

It is equally clear that the conduct of those who do not belong to the industrial party is immoral, since they consume without producing anything; since, in fact, they live on others; since they enjoy all the advantages provided for them by the work of the industrialists without giving anything in exchange which might be useful or agreeable to them; since, in short, they do not do unto their neighbour what their neighbour does unto them.

The reader will be forced to conclude with me that the industrial party acts morally, while the conduct of the anti-industrialist party is utterly immoral.

One can be equally convinced of the moral superiority of the industrialists by regarding the matter in another light.

It is a fact that the landed proprietors have little credit, while the shopkeepers, manufacturers and other industrialists have a great deal.

Why is this so? Because the industrial proprietors have long enjoyed the reputation of being more punctilious in meeting their obligations than the non-industrial proprietors.

Now morality lays down that it is a duty to pay debts, since this is to act towards one's neighbour as one would wish him to act towards oneself, and in this respect the conduct of the industrialists is more moral than that of the non-industrialists, as they pay their debts more promptly.

*On the wealth of the two parties*

A man who spends the whole of his income, no matter how large his fortune may be, cannot be considered wealthy; it is the man with savings who possesses true riches, because a man's wealth lies essentially in what is left over; it consists in the amount which he has at his disposal.

In 1815, the Chamber of deputies was almost entirely composed of landed proprietors. The state needed money. These 'rich' men in straitened circumstances were unable to find enough money to come to its aid, because they had no savings upon which they could draw. Furthermore, their income was not sufficient for the outlay they felt obliged to make in order to maintain the position required by their aristocratic origins. They were ingenuous enough to ask the nation to lend them capital, at a time when it was being crushed by the heavy burdens it had to shoulder.

The King wisely drove off the drones and called upon the worker bees; he asked industry for the amount he needed.

What happened?

The producers, whose capital is very small compared with that of the landed proprietors, hastened to supply the state with all the money it needed.

From all of which I conclude that real wealth is to be found in the hands of the industrialists, although the non-industrialists possess the greatest share of capital.

*On the political ability of both parties*

Before comparing the political ability of the two parties, I must reply clearly to this question:

What is the most important quality of political ability today?

My answer is simple and easy.

Since men became equal before the law, political rights have no longer been based upon the possession of money or of things which can only be procured with money. The greatest, the most important power entrusted to the government is the right to tax the citizens; it is from this right that all the others flow. Today, therefore, political science consists essentially of being able to draw up a good budget.

Now the ability to do this is administrative ability, from which it follows that administrative ability is the principal ability needed in politics.

Let us now see whether the industrial proprietors or those whose capital is not invested in industrial concerns have greater need of administrative ability in the running of their affairs.

It is obvious that without administrative ability the industrialists can neither grow rich nor even preserve their fortunes; while the landed proprietors need only keep their expenditure within their income and save their rents to grow wealthy.

It remains for us to examine whether the industrial proprietors or the landed proprietors have best managed their private affairs.[1]

As I have already said in the previous paragraph, we have proof that it is the industrial proprietors who have managed best, since it was they who came to the King's rescue and raised the sums he needed, while the landed proprietors left him in difficulties.

The reader will surely conclude with me that the industrial proprietors are superior in political ability to the landed proprietors, since they are superior to them in administrative ability. Thus, the question which has been posed in the paragraph has found its solution.

*On the strength of the two parties*

In the national or industrial party are to be found:

1. All those who till the soil, together with those who are in charge of agriculture;

2. The wheelwrights, the blacksmiths, the stonemasons, the locksmiths, the joiners, the weavers, the shoemakers, the tailors; in a word, all the artisans, the manufacturers, the merchants, all those who trade by land or sea as well as all those whose work is directly or indirectly useful to production or to the use of its products;

Consequently, all the scientists who have devoted themselves to the positive sciences belong to the industrial party, because their discoveries contribute greatly to the improvement of the processes used by the artisans and they often give rise to new products;

Artists should also be considered as industrialists, as they are producers in many respects and among them they contribute greatly to the prosperity of our manufactures by the designs and models with which they furnish the artisans;

1. The landed proprietors will hasten to tell us that they were despoiled; I would reply that this only happened once, while the industrial proprietors were despoiled several times; once by the law of the *maximum*, and a second time by the burning of the English merchandize, etc., etc.

Lawyers with liberal views who devote their talents to the defence of the industrialists against the pretensions of the former nobles and against the despotic action of state officials;

The small number of priests who preach sound morality—that is, the duty to employ one's time and means in useful work;

Lastly, all citizens (in whatever their positions by accident of birth or circumstances) who freely use their talents and their means to liberate the producers from the unjust supremacy exercised over them by idle consumers, are part of the great body of the industrialists.

In the anti-national party, one finds noblemen who work for the restoration of the *ancien régime*; those priests who preach that morality consists of blind faith in the decisions of the pope and of the clergy; landed proprietors living like nobles, that is to say, doing nothing;

Judges who uphold despotism, soldiers who support them, and, in a word, all those opposed to the establishment of the régime which is most advantageous to the economy and to freedom.

Here, briefly, are the basic forces and the way in which they are found to be grouped to form the two distinct, utterly opposed parties.

I do not know how to estimate accurately the strength of each of these parties, but I believe that it is no exaggeration to say that the industrialists are at least fifty times more numerous than the supporters of that system in which the bees are ruled by the drones.

*Summary*

The conduct of the industrialists is moral, that of the upholders of despotism is immoral; thus moral force, which is the most powerful, is on the side of the industrial party; this party also possesses physical force, since it is at least fifty times more numerous than the party of the idle rich.

This party is also supported by reason, since those who study the positive sciences (and who are the best reasoners) are on its side.

It has on its side also the force of imagination, since artists are part of the industrial party.

Again, the industrialists are superior in political ability to their adversaries.

Lastly, the industrialists have on their side financial strength, since they have more ready money than the landed proprietors who are not industrialists.

I pass on to a summary of the forces and means at the disposal of the anti-industrial party, that is of the party which tries to keep the producers under the domination of immoral men, who consider the nation to be a collection of men destined by God to procure their pleasures.

This party expends all its strength in the practice of bad habits contracted by the people under the *ancien régime*, in superstition, in the veniality of judges, in the corruption of public servants and in the lack of patriotism of army officers who dedicate themselves to the service of power, without examining how it is exercised.

I will not add anything to the comparison I have just made. For the time being, I will simply say that a struggle between two parties so disproportionate in strength and means is really astonishing.

## ON THE QUARREL BETWEEN THE BEES AND THE DRONES*

*Conclusion of what I said in the previous article*

In my first article, I established that the party of the producers was superior to that of its adversaries in numbers, in morality, in the capacity to reason and on imagination; I proved that it was equally superior in political ability.

I did not accompany these facts with any reflections, nor did I draw any conclusions from them; I thought that I should submit them for examination and to the reader's attention before drawing any conclusions.

I shall now present my conclusion which should be all the more appreciated because it has been delayed.

I conclude then that the party of the producers is in almost exclusive possession of all the basic, positive forces which can act on society; is in reality invested with the greatest political power; and, as a result, is in a position to give to the Charter whatever form it likes, whatever will most fully satisfy its needs and desires.

Before going further, I think that I should answer an objection which until now has produced an effect like that attributed to Medusa's head on all to whom it was presented.

It will be said: parliament is invested with the right of making

* '*Sur la querelle des abeilles et des frelons sur la situation respective des producteurs et des consommateurs non producteurs*', II, 1, pp. 211–19. This was another small pamphlet of twenty-three pages, independently published in 1819, but being an extract of the eleventh issue of *Le Politique*, pp. 405–27.

laws and it is composed, for the great part, of noblemen, of landowners living like noblemen, of public servants, etc., in a word, of people who have no connection with industry, whose interests are quite separate from those of industry and opposed to them, and who wish to preserve the political supremacy which they have hitherto exercised over the producers.

To attempt to draft the Charter in the national interest, that is, in the interest of the producers, would be the beginning of a revolution, and would call down all the vindictiveness of those laws, which until now have been designed to keep the producers under the yoke of the noblemen and of those who live like noblemen.

I reply to this: in all countries a force exists which is superior to that of governments, and this is the force of public opinion.

Anyone who takes the trouble to think about it, will be convinced that parliament will not attempt to oppose the political measures which are desired by a sizeable majority of the industrialists; he will be convinced that the measures which they desire will inevitably be adopted, no matter how contrary they may be to the wishes of parliament.

The main obstacle, then, does not lie in the corrupt composition of parliament but essentially, it is to be found in the political apathy of the producers, in their want of solidarity and the lack of clarity in their ideas.

*Object of the second article*

The aim of this second article is to explain why a struggle should exist between the producers and the non-producers, and how it is possible for this struggle to be prolonged when the producers have a decided superiority over the non-producers, in physical and moral force.

Here, in a few words, is the explanation for this extraordinary fact:

The noblemen, the proprietors, living like noblemen, the higher clergy, the magistrature, the high-ranking army officers are much concerned with public affairs, that is, with politics.

The working industrialists and the managerial industrialists, artists and scientists are very little concerned with politics.

The former have very little power, but a very strong will; the latter possess enormous political power, but they still have no idea how strong they are.

The former have a fixed goal and ideas which stop at and are confined to those measures which can ensure their own domination.

The latter have not yet seen clearly how they should act in order to free themselves from the domination of others.

Now, as I have just said, the noblemen and their supporters are very active in politics and form an organized party, while the industrialists are passive in this respect and lacking in organization; the result must be, and is in fact, that the workers, the producers of useful things, although absolutely superior in physical and moral strength to the party of the noblemen, continue to remain under its domination.

This is how I explain the extraordinary phenomenon of the struggle existing between two parties, one of which is a veritable giant, and the other, in reality, only a pigmy.

*Some observations on the political conduct of the industrialists since 1789*

Someone is bound to say to me:

'Most of the priests and aristocrats have emigrated; nearly all the public servants of the old government have been dismissed; the supporters of the *ancien régime* no longer administer public affairs, they have been pursued and persecuted for twenty years on end; so that the producers have found themselves inevitably invested with political powers; consequently, they have been able to organize society as they wanted.

'Now the disorders which occurred at that time, the public crimes which were committed, the anarchy which was created and the despotism which followed are proofs of the political incapacity of the industrialists, whom you put forward as the only men fit to administer the affairs of the nation properly.'

I reply:

From the early years of the Revolution up to the time of the departure of the last foreigners, France has never ceased to be at war, and the war which she had to undertake to win her independence was so terrible that it became the object to which everything else was sacrificed, and it devoured all the means of the producers.

In such circumstances, the government was inevitably given unlimited powers and the direction of affairs inevitably passed into the hands of the army.

To arm, to feed, to clothe the soldiers, to enrich the generals and the suppliers, this was how the products of the industrialists' labours were used; in short, during that long and terrible time the nation could only have a military government.

Now, military government being the form of government which is most strongly opposed to the needs and tastes of the producers, it is utterly unjust and false to regard them as having administered the affairs of the nation during the course of the Revolution. On the contrary, at no other time has despotism oppressed them so hard and so closely; they were never governed so much; never were their complaints less regarded by the government.

The law of the strongest (the only one recognized by the military class) governed France almost exclusively throughout the whole of the Revolution. The law of common interest was indeed evoked by the government with regard to the producers, but this was solely with the aim of robbing them. *The maximum, the requisitioning, the burning of the English merchandize, the government's monopoly of the trade in colonial produce* were all inventions which can be attributed to the genius of the revolutionary governments, and which were put into practice by Robespierre and Bonaparte.

It will be said to me that it was executive power which was in the hands of the military class; but legislative power was not without some influence and the military never formed a majority in the house of representatives.

To which I reply: Some farmers, some manufacturers, a few merchants as well as some artists and scientists were, it is true, appointed deputies during the Revolution, but they never formed more than an extremely weak minority in the chamber, in which the overwhelming majority was at all times formed by jurists.

Now, the political opinions of the legal experts were necessarily anti-industrial because for the most part they are inevitably taken from Roman law, from the ordinances of our kings and from feudal customs, in short, from all the legislation which preceded the Revolution and which is the object of their studies and reflections.

The result, then, was that during the Revolution political power was entrusted to the military class and to the jurists and the laws made during that time were based on two kinds of despotic principle, the first old, the other new; and, in consequence, these laws were contrary to the interests of the industrialists and unfavourable to production.

# VII

## *The Organizer*

### FIRST EXTRACT FROM THE ORGANIZER*

*L'Organisateur par Henri Saint-Simon, de Novembre 1819 à Février 1820*; II, 2, pp. 17–26. This text is also known as 'The Parable of Saint-Simon' (*Parable de Saint-Simon*, see editorial note, II, 2, pp. 25–6).

Like *Le Politique*, *L'Organisateur* was conceived as a periodical. Only one issue appeared, however, in 1819, and one issue in 1820, both in different editions, containing separate extracts. This extract is also 'The First Letter' in a series of Letters (see footnotes on pp. 142, 145 and 167) addressed to readers.

Let us suppose that France suddenly lost its fifty leading physicists, its fifty leading chemists, its fifty leading physiologists, its fifty leading mathematicians, its fifty leading poets, its fifty leading painters, its fifty leading sculptors, its fifty leading musicians, its fifty leading authors; its fifty leading mechanics, its fifty leading civil and military engineers, its fifty leading artillerymen, its fifty leading architects, its fifty leading doctors, its fifty leading surgeons, its fifty leading pharmacists, its fifty leading sailors, its fifty leading clockmakers; its fifty leading bankers, its two hundred leading merchants, its six hundred leading farmers, its fifty leading iron masters, its fifty leading armaments makers, its fifty leading tanners, its fifty leading dyers, its fifty leading miners, its fifty leading drapers, its fifty leading cotton manufacturers, its fifty leading silk manufacturers, its fifty leading linen manufacturers, its fifty leading manufacturers of hardware, its fifty leading manufacturers of china and porcelain, its fifty leading manufacturers of crystal and glass, its fifty leading ship chandlers, its fifty leading carriers, its fifty leading printers, its fifty leading engravers, its fifty leading goldsmiths and other workers in metals; its fifty leading stonemasons, its fifty leading carpenters, its fifty leading joiners, its fifty leading blacksmiths, its fifty leading locksmiths, its fifty leading cutlers, its fifty leading foundry workers, and the hundred other individuals of various unspecified professions who comprise the most able men in the sciences, in the fine arts, and in the arts and crafts, making in all the three thousand leading scholars, artists and artisans in France.[1]

* II, 2, pp. 17–26.

1. Usually the word artisan is used only for simple workers; to avoid circumlocution, we mean by this expression all those who work with material products, to

As these are essentially the most productive men in France and those who produce the most important products, those who direct the work which is of most use to the nation, and who are responsible for France's production in the sciences, the fine arts and in the arts and crafts, they are really the flower of French society; of all Frenchmen they are most useful to their country who win the most glory for it, who promote its civilization most as well as its prosperity; the nation would become a body without a soul, the moment it lost them; it would immediately fall into an inferior position in relation to the nations with which it competes today, and it would continue to be inferior to them as long as it failed to repair its loss, as long as it failed to replace its chief men. It would take France at least a generation to repair this misfortune, for men who are distinguished in work of practical use are rareties, and nature is not prodigal with rareties, above all with those of this kind.

Let us pass on to another supposition. Let us concede that France would preserve all the men of genius which she possesses in the sciences, in the fine arts and in the arts and crafts, but that she had the misfortune to lose, on the same day, Monsieur, the King's brother, Monseigneur le duc d'Angoulême, Monseigneur le duc de Berry, Monseigneur le duc d'Orléans, Monseigneur le duc de Bourbon, Madame la duchesse d'Angoulême, Madame la duchesse de Berry, Madame la duchesse d'Orléans, Madame la duchesse de Bourbon, and Mademoiselle de Condé.

Let us suppose that she lost at the same time all the great officers of the crown, all the ministers of state (with or without departments), all the counsellors of state, all the *maîtres de requêtes* (masters of the court of requests) all the marshals, all the cardinals, archbishops, bishops, grand-vicars and canons, all the prefects and sub-prefects, all the employees in the ministries, all the judges, as well as the ten thousand richest landowners who live like nobles.

This misfortune would certainly distress the French, because they are kind-hearted and because they could not view with indifference the sudden disappearance of such a large number of their compatriots. But the loss of these thirty thousand individuals, supposedly the most important in the state, would only grieve them from a sentimental point of view, for it would not result in any political damage to the state.

First of all, this is because it would be very easy to refill the

---

wit: the farmers, the manufacturers, the traders, the bankers and all the agents or workers whom they employ.

places which had become empty; there are a great many Frenchmen who are fit to carry out the functions of the King's brother just as well as Monsieur; many are capable of filling the position of prince quite as suitably as Monseigneur le duc d'Angoulême, as Monseigneur le duc de Berry, as Monseigneur le duc d'Orléans, as Monseigneur le duc de Bourbon; many Frenchwomen would make just as good princesses as Madame la duchesse d'Angoulême, Madame la duchesse de Berry, as Mesdames d'Orléans, de Bourbon and de Condé.

The antichambers of the palace are full of courtiers, ready to fill the places of the great officers of the crown; the army contains a great many soldiers who are quite as good captains as our present marshals. How many clerks are as gifted as our ministers of state? How many administrators are more fitted to direct the affairs of the departments than the prefects and the sub-prefects who do so at the moment? How many lawyers are as successful legal experts as our judges? How many parish priests as capable as our cardinals, our archbishops, our bishops, our grand-vicars and our canons? As for the ten thousand landowners living so magnificently, their heirs would need no apprenticeship to entertain as lavishly as they do.

France can only become prosperous through the effects of and as a result of the advance of the sciences, the fine arts and the arts and crafts; now the princes, the great officers of the crown, the bishops, the marshals of France, the prefects and the idle landowners do not work directly for the progress of the sciences, the fine arts, the arts and crafts; far from contributing to them, they can only harm them, since they try to maintain and extend that preponderance which conjectural theories have exercised over positive knowledge up to now; by depriving the scholars, artists, and artisans, as they do, of the first place which is theirs by right, they inevitably damage the prosperity of the nation; they harm it, since they use their wealth in a way which is not directly useful to the sciences, to the fine arts and to the arts and crafts; they harm it since they deduct in advance annually from the taxes paid by the nation a sum of three to four hundred million francs in the guise of appointments, pensions, gifts, compensation, etc., for the payment of work which is useless to the nation.

These suppositions highlight the most important fact in present-day politics; they present this fact from point of view from which it can be grasped at a single glance with all its implications; they prove clearly, although indirectly, that the social organization is imperfect; that men still allow themselves to be governed by violence and trickery and that the human species (politically speaking) is still plunged in immorality.

Since the scientists, the artists and the artisans, who are the only men whose work is of positive use to society and who cost it almost nothing, are subordinated to the princes and the other members of the governing class who are simply to a greater or lesser degree incompetent creatures of routine:

Since those who dispense the honours and the other national rewards, in general owe the preponderance which they enjoy to an accident of birth, to flattery, intrigue and other unworthy actions:

Since those who are in charge of public affairs every year share among themselves half the taxes and do not even use a third of the contributions (which they do not seize personally), in a way that is of use to those whom they administer.

These suppositions reveal that society as it exists now is indeed an upside-down world.

Since the nation has agreed as a fundamental principle that the poor should be generous to the rich and that, in consequence, the less well off deprive themselves daily of a part of the necessities of life to augment the surplus of the great land-owners:

Since the greatest culprits, the generous robbers, those who oppress the whole nation and who take from it three to four hundred million francs annually, are entrusted with punishing petty crimes against society:

Since ignorance, superstition, idleness and the taste for expensive pleasures are the appanage of the highest leaders of society, and capable, thrifty, hard-working people are only employed in a subordinate position and as tools:

Since, in a word, in all kinds of occupations it is those without ability who are in charge of the able; and since, from the moral point of view, it is the most immoral who are called to educate the citizens in virtue; and that from the point of view of distributive justice, it is the most guilty who are placed in the position of punishing the faults of petty delinquents.

Although this extract is very short, we believe that we have sufficiently proved that the body politic is ill; that its illness is serious and dangerous; that it is the most damaging illness it could have contracted, since its whole and its parts are affected at the same time. This diagnosis should come before all the others; for those who are well (or who think that they are well) are in no way disposed to listen to the doctors who prescribe the remedies or the special diet which will cure them.

In the second extract we shall examine what medicine should be given to the invalid.

### THE AUTHOR TO HIS COMPATRIOTS*

*Third letter*

I am going to reply to the two following questions:

What should we have done?

What have we done?

I hope that my replies to these two questions will completely reassure honest men about my intentions and that, once my aim has been made sufficiently clear to them, I can in the following issues of this publication develop my principles and draw conclusions from them, without causing anyone anxiety and without feeling any myself.

I shall divide the examination of what we should have done into four letters, because there are four things which we should have done and which we have not done, and each deserves to be looked into separately.

We should have started by clarifying our ideas about the political system which we wanted to rid ourselves of, and also about the social system which is demanded by our degree of civilization. We should, before doing anything else, have formed a very clear idea of both; this should not have been difficult, for both these conceptions can be outlined in a few words, as I am about to do.

The old political system (I wish to speak of the one which is still in force and which we want to be rid of) was created in the Middle Ages. Two very different, essential elements combined to form it; from its very beginning and throughout its existence, it was a combination of the ecclesiastical system and the feudal system. The combination of physical force (possessed preeminently by those who bear arms) with the wily and foxy methods invented by the priests, had invested the leaders of the clergy and the nobility with sovereign powers and had enabled them to subjugate all the rest of the population.

No better system could have been established at that time; for, on the one hand, all the knowledge that we then possessed was still superficial and vague, and general metaphysics contained the only principles which could serve as a guide to our medieval ancestors and, consequently, the general metaphysicians had to guide society in scientific matters.

* II, 2, pp. 36–44. The 'Second Letter' not included in this collection, deals with the question of the obsolescence of institutions.

On the other hand, the only way open for a great people to increase its wealth in these barbarous times was by conquest, so the military had to take charge of the national affairs of each state.

Thus, the fundamental basis of the old political system was, on the one hand, a state of ignorance: with the result that any reasoning about how to ensure the well-being of society was not supported by observations and rested only upon simple insight.

And, on the other hand, a state unskilled in the arts and crafts, by making the people incapable of producing wealth by improving raw materials through their work, left them no way open to enrich themselves other than by seizing the raw materials of other peoples.

As a result of industrial progress, the peoples acquired the means by which they could all prosper at the same time by enriching themselves through peaceful labours.

At the same time, positive knowledge was acquired; phenomena of every kind were observed; and philosophy based on experience today contains principles which can guide the peoples towards morality and well-being far more certainly than can metaphysics.

Out of this state of affairs there arose the means and consequently the necessity to found a new political system.

The fundamental bases of a new system are, then, on the one side, a state of civilization which gives men the means to use their powers in a way which can be useful to others and profitable to themselves.

And, on the other side, a state of knowledge in which society, aware of the methods it must employ to improve its lot, can take these principles as a guide and need no longer entrust despotic powers to those whom it has put in charge of the administration of its affairs.

It is not the difference in the division of power which constitutes the difference of system; it is the difference in the nature and the quantity of power wielded by those who govern over those whom they govern.

All forms of government are applicable to all political systems.[1]

So long as those who govern are seen as the most important, the most capable, and the most useful members of society; so long as the leaders are awarded enormous salaries to increase the esteem in which they are held and their power; so long as

1. By this I do not mean that the forms of government and the method of sharing power are immaterial; I only mean that they are of secondary importance.

the nation allows them to choose the methods they think proper to employ in improving its morals and ensuring its tranquillity and prosperity; so long as they are chosen, either from among the metaphysicians (that is from those who are still subservient to blind creeds, possess only superficial knowledge, and try to reason from general facts), or from the military (people whose noblest occupation consists in improving the methods of war between men), the national will remain tied to the old system. It will remain subjected to this system, regardless of the form of government it adopts, whether that form be republican, aristocratic, absolute monarchy or constitutional monarchy. And it will remain subjected to it regardless of whether it chooses its military leaders from among the heirs of great feudal families or from the class of descendants from the serfs; if its leaders in scientific affairs are chosen from the theologians or from those metaphysicians who have studied in the law schools.

The nation will not find itself ready for the new political existence which it must begin to lead, until it reaches a stage at which it becomes clearly aware of all the immorality and all the monstrousness of the social system which it has been subjected to until now; until its eyes having been opened to the combination of coercion and cunning which the nobility and the clergy have used to exploit it for their own profit, it decides entirely to demolish the old machine and to replace it with a new one which will be conceived and set up according to principles drawn from sound morality and true philosophy; until the nation has recognized that its government will inevitably be despotic, so long as the leaders are taken from among the military and the metaphysicians; or until it has realized that those who govern will inevitably be despotic so long as society regards them as the most important people in the state and the most useful and therefore deserving of the highest esteem; until, finally (having grasped the idea that its prosperity can only result from the advance of science, the fine arts and the arts and crafts) the nation regards the scientists, artists and craftsmen as the most useful members of society and therefore worthy of the highest degree of consideration; what a fortunate time this will be for the human race, for they will find that the functions of those who govern will be reduced to the level of ushers in schools: the ushers only have to keep order; it is the teachers who are in charge of the pupils' studies. The same should be true of the state: the scientists, artists and artisans should guide the work of the nation; the governors should only see that this work is not disturbed.

You can, if you want to, my dear countrymen, immediately appreciate the political value of the ideas which I have just laid before you.

Take the trouble to consider (from the point of view I have put to you) what has happened since 1789, and what is happening today; you will see that, if, from the beginning of the crisis, the nation had agreed in principle to adopt the system which was most favourable to the progress of the positive sciences, Robespierre would never have been able to govern France through his *sans-culottes*; because commonsense would have proved to the nation that the most ignorant class was unfit to direct the work of scientists, artists and artisans; for the same reason, Bonaparte would not have been able to establish a military government, because it would have been clear that the armed forces, who are consumers, are in no way fit to direct the work of industry; and today, finally, there would be no question as to whether it should be the idle landowners or the leaders of industry who should have the greatest influence over elections, and the composition of the government would not be regarded as being of any importance.

*Fifth letter**

*The second thing which we should have done* was to adopt the English constitution as a provisional system, as a transitional constitution, as a kind of scaffolding which was needed for the convenient construction of a new social edifice.

The third thing which we should have done was to discover a way to improve the constitution; and we should have been sure that we would find many important improvements to make, because over a century has gone by since this particular political combination was put into practice, and this century has been the one in which men have been the most concerned with politics.

*What is the most important improvement which should be made in the English constitution?* is thus the third question for which the answer must be found.

The English constitution is marred by a fundamental flaw which we would have perceived very easily and which we would have remedied very easily if we had taken the trouble to analyse it. This flaw is the bad composition of the House of Commons.

* II, 2, pp. 46–50. Editor's note: The 'Fourth Letter', very brief, introduces the idea that the nation should have adopted the parliamentary system which proved so successful in England.

It is the House of Commons which votes the taxes; thus it is in the nation's interest that this House should be made up of men with a personal interest in seeing that taxation is as light as possible, and yet the great majority of the English House of Commons is interested in increasing rather than in diminishing taxation.

A great many of its members are public servants and public servants are obliged to support the wishes of the government for fear of losing their jobs or at least of being denied promotion; regardless of the direct dependence on the government in which they find themselves, their common interest leads them to desire that the government should have large sums of money at its disposal, since the part of their revenue which goes in appointments is necessarily proportionate to the sum total of the taxes.

The members of the House of Commons who are not public servants are for the most part idle landowners who want posts in the government to increase their incomes and prestige; thus, they are, with some slight difference, in the same position as the former.

Once we had recognized that the English House of Commons was badly constituted, we should have looked for the way to give a better composition to our own, and we would have found it easily had we looked for it because it springs quite naturally to mind: the expression *House of Commons* points clearly to it.

The House of Commons should be composed of the leading members of the communes, that is, it should be made up of the leaders of the different kinds of industrial work, since the leaders of industry are the citizens with the greatest interest in economizing in public expenditure and are the most opposed to despotism, because taxation cannot profit them in any way and they do not exercise despotic power; the concern to conserve and increase their fortune through success gained by the work they direct, takes all their time and makes it impossible for them to accept places in the government.

So, in the third place, we would have improved the parliamentary system by filling the House of Commons with leaders from every branch of industry.[1]

1. At the time when the communes were enfranchised, artisans were to be found only in the towns; agriculture was still in its infancy and the great lords, together with the Church, in possession of almost all French soil, were also the owners of the stores of farming implements which were used to till their lands. Things have changed radically in this respect since then, above all in the departments north of

*Sixth letter**

Once we have done the three things I have spoken of, we find ourselves in a position to proceed to the establishment of the new political system, for the new composition of the lower chamber would have made it possible to establish the social organization required by the present state of civilization and the lower chamber is invested with supreme political power because it votes the taxes.[1]

I will describe the course which the chamber of deputies (composed as I said in the previous letter of the leaders of industry) should take. In order to explain more clearly and rapidly I shall let the chamber itself speak:

'There shall be a first chamber which will be called the Chamber of *Invention*.

'This chamber will have three hundred members; it will be divided into three sections, which can meet separately, but whose work will only be official when they have debated in common.

'Each section can call the assembly of the three sections together.

'The first section will be composed of two hundred civil engineers; the second of fifty poets or other literary creations, and the third of twenty-five painters, fifteen sculptors or architects and ten musicians.

'This chamber will concern itself with the following matters:

'It will present, at the end of its first year of existence, a plan

---

the Loire. A class of artisans has been formed who farm the land and work it with their own implements. This class of worker has become the most important of all and should play the most important part in the chamber of commons.

The landowner should not be confused, as hitherto in politics, with the agriculturalist. *A contract or a conquest can create a landowner; farming implements and skill are needed to create an agriculturalist.*

There is still a prejudice in favour of landowners which greatly retards the progress of civilization. Many people are kind enough to accept the claim of the landowners that they are the class in society which is most interested in maintaining order, which is completely untrue; it is the agriculturalists who suffer most from disorder. A barn is pillaged, the horses led out of the stables, the cows, pigs and sheep are eaten. In a few hours an agriculturalist can be ruined, but no one can either destroy or take away the soil. A landowner has only his income at risk, but an agriculturalist runs the risk of losing his capital.

* II, 2, pp. 50–61.

1. The result of the fact that the House of Commons has the sole right to vote the taxes is that this House is invested with supreme political power; for the government, being unable to act without money, the House can impose upon it any obligations it wants to, by only giving it money conditionally.

of public works to be undertaken for the enrichment of France and the improvement of the lot of its inhabitants, to cover every aspect of usefulness and amenity; it will thereafter give its advice annually on what should be added to the initial plan and on the improvements which can be made to it.

'Irrigation, the clearing of land, opening up new roads, digging out canals will be regarded as the most important parts of this plan; the road and canals should not be seen solely as means to facilitate transport; their construction should be conceived in such a way as to make them as pleasant as possible for travellers.[1]

'This chamber will undertake another task which will be to prepare a plan of public holidays.

'These holidays will be of two kinds; those of *expectation* and those of *commemoration*.

'They will be celebrated successively in the capital, in the capitals of the departments and districts, so that able orators, of whom there are never very many, can spread the benefits of their eloquence.

'In the feasts of *expectation*, the orators will explain to the people the plans for public works which parliament has in hand, and they will encourage the citizens to work eagerly by making them aware of how greatly their lot will be improved when they have put these plans into execution.

1. Fifty thousand acres of land (and more, if judged suitable) will be chosen from among the most picturesque sites crossed by the roads and canals. These will be set aside as places of rest for travellers and of lesisure and amusement for the local inhabitants.

Each of these gardens will contain a museum of natural produce as well as the industrial products of the surrounding countryside; they will also contain dwellings for artists who want to stay there, and they will always maintain a number of musicians whose task it will be to inspire the inhabitants of the district with feelings, appropriate to the moment, conducive to the greatest good of the nation.

The whole of France should become a superb park in the English style, embellished with everything that the fine arts can add to the beauties of nature. For too long, luxury has been concentrated in the palaces of kings, in the dwellings of princes, in the town-houses and castles of a few powerful men. This concentration is very harmful to the general interests of society because it tends to establish two distinct degrees of civilization, two different classes of men, those whose intelligence is developed by the habitual sight of beautiful objects, and those whose imaginative faculties are never developed, as the material work which occupies them exclusively does not stimulate their intelligence at all.

Present circumstances are favourable for the achievement of national luxury. Luxury will become useful and moral when the whole nation can enjoy it. To our century has fallen the honour and advantage of directly applying to political matters the advances made in the exact sciences and the fine arts since the brilliant epoch of their regeneration.

'In the feasts consecrated to *commemoration*, the orators will try to convince the people of how much better is their position than that of their ancestors.

The nucleus of the Chamber of Invention will be made up of:

'1. The eighty-six civil engineers in the departments;

'2. The forty members of the *Académie française*;

'3. Those painters, sculptors and musicians who are members of the *Institut*;

'Every member of this chamber will enjoy an annual salary of 10,000 francs.

'Every year a sum of twelve million francs will be put at the disposal of this chamber to be used to foster inventions which it deems to be useful. The first section will dispose of eight million francs and the two others of two million each.

'The nucleus of this chamber will proceed to make up its own numbers.

'The chamber will constitute itself, that is to say, it will itself lay down the conditions which must be fulfilled to become a voter, as well as those which are laid down for candidates. Its members will not be able to be nominated for more than five years, but they will be eligible for re-election indefinitely, and the chamber will be able to adopt any method of replacement they desire.

'This chamber can co-opt one hundred national members and fifty foreigners. The associates will have the right to sit in the chamber; they will have a consultative voice in it.

'A second chamber will be formed which will take the name Chamber of *Examination*.

'This chamber will be composed of three hundred members, one hundred of them will be physicians engaged in the science of living organisms, one hundred physicians engaged in the study of animals, and one hundred mathematicians.

'This chamber will be entrusted with three kinds of work.

'It will examine all the plans presented by the first chamber and it will give its detailed and reasoned opinion on each of them.

'It will draw up a plan of general public education. This plan will be divided into three degrees of education, corresponding to the three different degrees of affluence among the citizens. Its aim will be to make the young as capable as possible at thinking about, at directing and at carrying out useful work.

'Given that every citizen is free to profess his own religion and that, consequently, he can bring his children up according to whichever one he prefers, there should be no question of religion in the educational plan presented by this chamber.

'When the plan has been agreed by the two other chambers, the Chamber for Examination will be given the task of carrying it out and of supervising public education.

'The third task of this chamber should be to draw up a plan of public holidays of the following kind:

'Holidays for men, holidays for women, holidays for boys, holidays for girls, holidays for parents, holidays for children, holidays for the leaders of workshops, holidays for workers.

'On each of these holidays, speakers, nominated by the Chamber of Examination will speak on the social duties of those in whose honour the feast is celebrated.

'Every member of this chamber would have an annual salary of 10,000 francs.

'Every year a sum of twenty-five million francs would be put at the disposal of this chamber. The sum would be used by it to defray the costs of the public schools and to encourage the acceleration of progress in the physical sciences and mathematics.

'The Chamber of *Examination* will be constituted by fulfilling the same conditions as the Chamber of *Invention*.

'The class of physical sciences and mathematics of the Institute will supply the nucleus of this chamber.

'The Chamber of Examination will be able to co-opt one hundred national members and fifty foreigners with consultative votes.

'The Chamber of Commons will be reconstituted when the first two have been formed; it will then take the name of Chamber of *Implementation*. This chamber will see that, in its new composition, each branch of industry is represented and that it has a number of deputies proportionate to its importance.

'The members of the Chamber of Implementation will not receive any salary because they ought all to be rich, as they will be drawn from among the main leaders of industry.

'The Chamber of Implementation will be in charge of carrying out all the resolutions; it alone will be entrusted with setting the scale of taxation and of collecting the taxes.

'The three chambers together will make up the new parliament which will be invested with sovereign power, both constitutional and legislative.

'Each of the three chambers will have the right to convoke parliament.

'The Chamber of Implementation will be able to call the attention of the two others to those objects which it deems suitable.

'Thus, every project will be presented by the first chamber, examined by the second and will be definitvely adopted only by the third.

'If a project presented by the first chamber should ever be rejected by the second, in order not to waste time, it will be sent back to the first, without going to the third.'

Now, my dear compatriots, I will tell you the first three things that the new parliament should do: I will speak in its name, just as I have spoken in the name of the Chamber of Deputies.

'All Frenchmen (particularly the legal experts) shall be invited to put forward a new system of civil law and a new system of criminal law, which will be related to the new political system. Property will be redefined and founded on bases which will make it more advantageous to production.

'All the projects presented to parliament will be published at public expense.[1] Parliament will choose the plan for the civil law and that for the criminal law which it thinks the best; it will reward their authors generously and admit them to the chamber during the debate on the codes which they have presented, giving them a consultative vote in that debate.

'All Frenchmen (particularly the military engineers) will be invited to present a plan for the general defence of the country. This plan will be drawn up so as to require the smallest number of permanent troops possible. The authors of these endeavours should not lose sight of the fact that all the methods used to defend our territory will become useless and will be abandoned the moment the neighbouring peoples have adopted the same political system as the French.

'The author of the plan selected will be paid by the nation.

'A loan of two hundred million francs, with a sinking fund, will be made up to indemnify those with financial interests who have suffered by the establishment of the new political system.

'A national reward will be given to the author of the work which best fulfils the three following conditions:

'1. To demonstrate the superiority of the new political system over the old;

'2. To establish the best way to share out the indemnity of two hundred million francs to those whose interests have been damaged by the establishment of the new system;

1. The projects will not be published in full; only extracts will be published and these extracts will only be the length of one printed page.

'3. To prove that the sum of two hundred million francs accorded in indemnity to individuals opposed to the establishment of the new system is extremely small in comparison to the advantages the peaceful establishment of the liberal régime will procure for the nation.'

Here, my dear compatriots, is the first draft of what I consider we should have done, and what I think we ought to do.

S.S.

# VIII

# On the Industrial System

'God said: love and help one another'

## PREFACE*

*Du Système Industriel*; the first part, 311 pages, was published in Paris in February 1821; the second part, 220 pages, appeared later in the same year. But, as usual, Saint-Simon published several chapters in separate pamphlets.

The root cause of the crisis in which the body politic has been involved for the last thirty years is the complete change in the social system, which is taking place today in the most advanced countries as the final outcome of all the successive modifications undergone by the old political order up to now. More accurately, the crisis consists essentially in the passage from a feudal ecclesiastical system to an industrial and scientific one. Inevitably, it will last until the new system is fully operative.

These fundamental truths have been ignored to date, and still are being ignored by both the governors and the governed; or rather they have been and they still are felt only in a vague and incomplete way, which is utterly inadequate. The nineteenth century is still dominated by the critical spirit of the eighteenth; it still has not adopted the organizational character which really belongs to it. This is the real, primary cause of the frightening prolongation of the crisis, and of the terrible storms which have accompanied it up to now. But, of necessity, the crisis will come to an end, or at least will change into a simple moral movement, as soon as we can bring ourselves to fill the eminent rôle assigned to us by the march of civilization, as soon as the temporal and spiritual forces which must come into play have emerged from their inertia.

The general aim of the philosophical work, of which I am presenting a fragment to the public today, will be to develop and prove the important propositions which I have just stated briefly; it will be to fix the general attention as forcibly as possible on the true character of the great social re-organization reserved for the nineteenth century; to show that this re-organization, gradually prepared for by all the advances which

* III, 1, pp. 3–18. (Paris, 1821.)

civilization has made up to the present, has reached its full maturity today, and that it cannot be postponed without serious setbacks; to indicate clearly and accurately the way to bring this about, calmly, safely and quickly, in spite of the real difficulties; in a word, to co-operate, as far as lies in the power of philosophy, in the moulding of the industrial and scientific system, the establishment of which, alone, can bring to an end the present social turmoil.

I boldly put forward the idea that the industrial doctrine would spread without difficulty and would be accepted without much effort, if the majority of people were in a position to grasp it and to judge it. Unfortunately, this is not so. Bad and deeply ingrained attitudes of mind prevent most people from grasping how intelligent this doctrine is.[1] Bacon's *tabula rasa* is infinitely more necessary for political ideas than for any others and, for this reason if for no other, it must encounter many more difficulties as regards this area of ideas.

The problem faced by the scientists when they tried to instil the true meaning of astronomy and chemistry into minds which until then had been accustomed to look at these sciences in the manner of astrologers and alchemists, can be seen today in relation to politics, in which a similar kind of change must be made, i.e. the transition from the conjectural to the positive, from the metaphysical to the physical.

Forced to combat obstinate and widely held attitudes, I think that it will be useful to by-pass these and to anticipate a small part of my work, by explaining here in a general, brief way, the influence which vague and metaphysical doctrines have had and still retain on politics, the mistaken way in which they were taken for true politics, and lastly the necessity of abandoning them today.

The industrial and scientific system arose and developed under the domination of the feudal and ecclesiastical system. Now, this simple comparison is enough to show that between two systems so utterly opposed, there must have existed a kind of vague, intermediary system, uniquely destined to modify the old system in such a way that the new system could develop and, later, bring about the transition. This is the universal historical fact most easily predicted from the data I have put forward. Any change, temporal or spiritual, can only take place gradually. Here, the change was so great and, on the other hand,

1. This is why I consider people who are not ordinarily engaged in politics, all things being equal, to be more fit than others to understand and judge my work, and, in general, any positive political idea.

the feudal and ecclesiastical system was so totally opposed by its very nature to any modifications that, for these modifications to take place, it was necessary for special action to be carried on for several centuries by particular classes derived from, but also distinct from, the *ancien régime* and independent of it up to a point, and which, in consequence, must have constituted, by the sole fact of their political existence, what I call by abstraction an intermediary and transitional system in the heart of society. These classes were, in the temporal sphere, the jurists, and in the spiritual one, the metaphysicians, who are closely linked in their political action, like feudalism and theology, or industry and the observational sciences.

This universal truth is of the highest importance. It is one of the fundamental facts which should serve as a basis for the positive theory of politics. This is what it is most important to stress today because the vagueness and obscurity which have surrounded it up to now are what most complicate political ideas today and cause nearly all the digressions.

It would be completely unphilosophical not to recognize the useful and distinguished influence exercised by the jurists and metaphysicians in modifying the feudal and ecclesiastical system, and in preventing it from stifling the industrial and scientific system in its earliest stages. The abolition of the feudal courts, the establishment of a less oppressive and fairer system of justice were the efforts of the jurists. How often in France the action of the parliaments has served to safeguard industry against feudalism! To blame these bodies for their ambition is to blame the inevitable results of a cause which is useful, reasonable and necessary. It is to beg the question. As for the metaphysicians, it is to them that we owe the Reformation of the sixteenth century and the establishment of the principle of freedom of conscience, which undermined ecclesiastical power.

I should overstep the bounds of a preface, were I to insist further upon remarks which every unbiased mind can easily develop from the preceding points. As for myself, I declare that I cannot see how the old system could have been modified and the new developed, without the intervention of the jurists and metaphysicians.[1]

1. This intermediary stage was so ordered by the nature of things that it can be found even in the way purely scientific questions are treated. Which astronomer, physician, chemist or physiologist is not aware that, before passing from purely theoretical ideas to positive ones, in each branch of knowledge, the human mind used metaphysics for a long time? Every one of them who has thought about the advance of science must be convinced that this intermediary stage was useful, even absolutely indispensable, to bring about the transition.

On the other hand, if it is foolish to deny the particular usefulness of the part played by the jurists and metaphysicians in the advance of civilization, it is very dangerous to exaggerate this usefulness or to misconstrue its true nature. By the very fact of the end it had in view, the political influence of the jurists and metaphysicians was limited to an ephemeral existence, because it was of necessity modificatory and transitional and not in any way organizational. It had fulfilled its whole natural function at the moment when the old system had lost the greater part of its power, and the forces of the new had become really powerful in society, both temporally and spiritually. Up to that point, which was reached in the middle of the last century, the political career of the jurists and metaphysicians was still honourable and useful, whereas it has now in fact become positively harmful because it has outlived its natural limit.

When the French Revolution broke out, there was no longer any question of modifying the feudal and ecclesiastical system, which had already lost nearly all its real strength. It was a question of organizing the industrial and scientific system, which was called for in that phase of civilization to replace it. Consequently, the industrialists and scientists were the ones who should have taken the political stage, each in their natural rôles. Instead, the jurists put themselves at the head of the Revolution and conducted it according to the doctrines of the metaphysicians. It is superfluous to recall the strange twists and turns which followed and the evils which resulted from these digressions. But it must be carefully noted that, in spite of this terrible experience, the jurists and metaphysicians have remained consistently at the head of affairs and it is they alone who today direct all political discussions.

This experience, however costly it may have been and however decisive it really was, will not bear fruit because of its complexity, until a direct analysis has proved the absolute necessity of removing the universal political influence which is granted to the jurists and the metaphysicians which stems only from the assumption that their doctrines are pre-eminent. But it is very easy to prove that the doctrines of the jurists and metaphysicians are, today, by their very nature, quite unfitted to guide the political action of either the governors or the governed properly. This obstacle is so great that it outweighs the advantages which might be presented by individual abilities, no matter how brilliant they are.

Today, more enlightened minds recognize clearly the necessity for a complete recasting of the social system; this need has become so immediately pressing that it must be met. But the biggest mistake which is generally made in this respect is to believe that the new system should be built upon the doctrines of the jurists and metaphysicians. This mistake only persists because we do not climb high enough in the scale of political observations, because general theories are not examined carefully enough, or because political thinking is not yet based upon historical facts. Were this not so, the mistake would not be made of taking a modification of the social system—a modification which has exhausted its effect and which has no further part to play—for a genuine change in the system itself.

The jurists and metaphysicians are prone to take the form for the substance and words for things. Leading from that comes the generally accepted idea of political systems of almost infinite multiplicity. But, in fact, there are and can only be two really distinct systems of social organization, the feudal or military system and the industrial system; and in the spiritual realm, a system of beliefs and a system of positive demonstrations. The entire history of civilized mankind is inevitably divided between these two great systems of society. For a nation, as for an individual, there are in effect only two ends, conquest or work, to which correspond spiritually either blind faith or scientific demonstration, that is to say, demonstrations founded upon positive observations. Now, the end of universal activity must be changed, if the social system is genuinely to be changed. All other improvements, no matter how important they may be, are only modifications, that is to say, changes in the form and not in the system. Only metaphysics can make this seem otherwise, through its unfortunate talent for confounding what should be separate and separating what should be confounded.

Society was organized in a precise and characteristic manner so long as the feudal or military system was flourishing, because it then had a clear, predetermined objective, which was to wage war, an end to which all parts of the body politic were coordinated. Today, too, it tends to organize itself in a more perfect manner, a manner no less precise and characteristic, but directed towards an industrial objective, towards which all social forces will converge. But from the decline of the feudal or military system until the present, society has not really been organized because the two goals having been pursued simultaneously, the political order of necessity has showed nothing but a mixed character. Now what was useful and even necessary in a transitional and preparatory state of affairs, clearly becomes absurd as a permanent system today, when the transition has really taken place in all major respects. It is to this state, nevertheless, that the doctrines of the jurists and metaphysicians lead.

It cannot be too often repeated that a society needs an active goal, for without this there would be no political system.[1] Now to legislate is not an end in itself; it can only be a means. Would it not be odd if, as a result of all the progress of civilization, mankind today had succeeded in associating in societies merely to pass laws for each other?[2] This would surely be the

1. Bonaparte realized this fundamental truth, when he undertook to reform the feudal and ecclesiastical system. Only he applied it wrongly. This was due as much to his lack of ability as to his ambition, since his education should have made it possible for him to know how a leader of a civilized nation should direct its activity. In our age, an ambitious man, if he realizes that he lacks ability, becomes a soldier, and if he is able, an industrialist.

2. One would say, without doubt, that the purpose of the social contract in this case would be to guarantee the maintenance of freedom. This is merely to turn the same idea round and to mistake a transitional order of things for the system which is to be set up.

The maintenance of freedom had to be the first object of concern, so long as the feudal and ecclesiastical system still retained some power, because at that time freedom was exposed to heavy and continuous attack. But today there is no need for the same anxiety about the establishment of the industrial and scientific system, since this system must inevitably bring with it, without any direct help, the highest degree of social, temporal and spiritual freedom. In such an order of things, a great apparatus of political groupings, solely designed to preserve freedom from an attack to which it must no longer be seriously exposed, would be like Don Quixote's tilting at windmills.

Besides, the maintenance of individual freedom cannot be the goal of the social contract. Freedom, considered from the true point of view, is an outcome of civilization, progressive as it is, but it cannot be the object. People do not band together to be free. Savages join together to hunt, to wage war, but certainly not to win liberty, because from this point of view they would do better if they remained isolated. An active goal, I repeat, is necessary and freedom cannot be the goal because it presupposes it. For real freedom does not consist in staying with folded arms within an association; such an attitude should be severely reprimanded, wherever it exists; on the contrary, it consists in developing, unfettered and in the widest possible way, a temporal or spiritual capacity, useful for association.

Let us observe further that, successively, as civilization advances, the division of work, taken spiritually and temporally and from the most general point of view, increases in the same proportion. The inevitable result is that men depend less on each other individually, but that each man depends more on the mass, in exactly the same way. Now, the vague and metaphysical idea of freedom, as it is held today (if one continues to take it as the basis of political doctrine) will tend to hinder the action of the mass on individuals. From this point of view, it would act against the development of civilization and the organization of a well-regulated system, which demands that the parts should be firmly linked to the whole and dependent on it.

I am not speaking of political freedom, because it is only too clear that even less than individual freedom can it be seen as an end of association. Besides, I can state on this subject, as a pointer to the true state of affairs, that the right to take part in public affairs, without any requirement of competence, in theory, confers a kind

purest humbug. Would this not mean that men met solemnly in order to draw up new rules for the pawns, imagining them to be the players? Such an obvious absurdity is nevertheless natural and, as such, excusable among jurists whose judgement is usually vitiated by the habit of only looking at the forms. But among the industrialists accustomed, on the contrary, to consider only fundamentals, the prolongation of such an error is utterly inexcusable. . . .

## ON THE INDUSTRIAL SYSTEM (I)*

Because no efforts are being made to re-establish the influence of the concept of *King by the grace of God*, people may fear that it will be replaced by the idea of the sovereignty of the people. This is a natural fear, but completely unreal. A moment's reflection will show this to be true.

---

of *natural* right on every citizen and restrains only in practice, but always without the requirement of competence, is by itself the most complete and obvious proof of the vagueness and uncertainty in which political ideas are still plunged. Would anyone ever have thought, without this, of declaring, indirectly it is true, but in no uncertain terms, that to reason about politics does not require natural or acquired ability?

Why is it not proclaimed that Frenchmen who pay thousands of francs in direct taxation are fit to make discoveries in chemistry, when exactly the same principle has been established for politics which is, after all, just as difficult and as important as chemistry? Why? Because the requirements of the competence necessary to engage in chemistry are clear and those relating to politics are not. And in what does this difference lie? In that today chemistry is a positive science, while politics is still only a body of conjectural doctrine which has not earned the name of science.

It is a characteristic of metaphysics, precisely because it teaches nothing real, to persuade a man that he is fit for anything without any need of special study. The remarkable circumstance which I have just pointed out, only exists today for politics and philosophy, the mother of politics, because they alone, among all the branches of our knowledge, have remained metaphysical. But the same thing can be observed about those sciences which are the most positive today, for the period when they were still plunged in the shadowy realm of metaphysics. The requirements of the competence necessary to win the right to cultivate the sciences only became clear and precise and ceased to be the universal subject for debate when those sciences took on a positive character. It should be absolutely the same for politics. One can maintain today without exposing oneself to ridicule that political science is innate and that one only needs to have been born French to be able to reason: such language is even thought to be patriotic. But when politics has climbed up to the level of the observed sciences, a time which cannot be far off, the requirements of competence will become clear and fixed and the cultivation of politics will be exclusively entrusted to a special class of scientists who will put an end to the ill-informed gossip.

* III, 2, pp. 208–11. Most of *Du Système Industriel* is concerned directly with the problems of the restoration of the Bourbons. The passages selected here are those in which Saint-Simon raises these problems to a higher, theoretical, level.

Legitimacy, as it is understood, has not existed as a systematic and valid doctrine since the Reformation. In order to preserve a political existence which had been deeply shaken, the clergy agreed to become subordinate to the monarchy, and put forward this piece of dogma to ensure the good will of the monarchy for themselves. Before then, there had indeed been talk of *by the grace of God*; but it did not have this lofty religious character nor the importance which it later gained when the kings employed it indiscriminately together with *by the strength of my sword*. Now it is remarkable that the famous dogma of the sovereignty of the people, if it was not invented, at least began to gain credit in Holland at about the same time. If one looks at the progress of these two dogmas, one sees that they march continually abreast. Such a constant relationship points to a far closer connection between them than is commonly supposed. And, in fact, it is not difficult to see that they are closely bound together or, rather, that the one created the other by their opposing juxtaposition.

No matter how superficially one may reflect on this, one will see that these two dogmas only exist in opposition to each other. The popular meaning of the expression *sovereignty of the people*, in fact the only clear meaning which can be given to it, is sovereignty *by the will of the people*, since the people know very well that, except for a few moments of very brief delirium, the people have no time to be sovereign. Now, as it is agreed that this will is not decided by fixed conditions, derived from the interests of the people and that it is completely independent of the worth of the sovereign, it follows that the expression *sovereignty by the will of the people* is only significant when it is opposed by *sovereignty by the grace of God*. It merely signifies a simple formality which must be fulfilled towards the people or their representatives, beyond which there is nothing else, i.e. consent is no longer demanded; so, everything depends on this demand, and consequently the demand can only be seen as a criticism of the idea of *by the grace of God*, which really means only the independent consent of the people. These two opposing dogmas thus have nothing but a reciprocal existence. They are the last traces of the long metaphysical war against the political principles of feudalism which took place throughout western Europe after the Reformation. In time of war, one is forced to use the same weapons as one's enemy. An abstraction, therefore, gave rise to another abstraction. The metaphysics of the clergy were staked against the metaphysics of the jurists, who were destined to fight against them. But now this battle is over.

ON THE INDUSTRIAL SYSTEM (2)*

. . . You are continually told about the *interests of the revolution*; it is a much used and conventional expression: everywhere, and on every occasion, it is loudly proclaimed that the object of the so-called *liberal* cause, which you take as the industrial cause, is to ensure the triumph of *the interest of the revolution*, and it is cleverly insinuated that the Bourbons are an insurmountable obstacle to this triumph. Allow me to say, Gentlemen, that I think this is really humbug: I would use a weightier expression, if I could think of a more accurate one.

What a strange power words have to confuse ideas! You are, gentlemen, and rightly so, profoundly and deeply attached to the revolution, in the sense that you firmly and ardently desire the genuine change of system which was its true objective from the beginning, and at the same time, you feel vaguely that this end has not been achieved, without being able to point directly to what is required to achieve it. The party which has usurped your trust will teach you what is lacking! Thanks to this vagueness and uncertainty, by the clever use of a phrase, it has succeeded in making you believe that the interests of all those who have enriched themselves at your expense since 1789, and who have so firmly promoted your affairs, are one with those of the industrial cause for which the revolution was fought. In this way the party succeeded in making you desire, as the triumph of the cause, the success of the ambitious plans of the pupils of Robespierre and Bonaparte; no sooner did the latter possess power, than they found nothing more urgent to do than to oppose the establishment of the industrial system with all their might. This is, nevertheless, the true state of affairs, clear to anyone who has not been hypnotized.

It is no longer to the past, gentlemen, that you should look, but to the future. You should only remember the past in order to profit from the experiences which you bought so dearly. The only thing which should concern you is the success of the industrial cause, the real and true object of the revolution, which was vaguely heralded at the beginning, but for which there has never been less done than in this period.

As for the political interests which were created in this period, you need only defend those attached to the division of property, and put into practice by the sale of privileged goods, although you should regret, in principle, that this division was not carried out peaceably, in the industrial manner, instead of

* III, 2, pp. 12–15.

being torn up violently in the feudal way. But these interests are unassailable and you cannot seriously fear that they will be attacked in a way which will cause you any anxiety. With this single exception, you have nothing whatsoever in common with what are called *the interests of the revolution*; on the contrary, they are all strongly opposed to your own and your most ardent wish should be that their ambition should be curbed.

## LETTER TO THE INDUSTRIALISTS*

Gentlemen,

In the previous letters, I have only discussed from a national point of view the opinion on a change of dynasty. In order to complete the examination, it remains for me to present it to you from a higher point of view, that of Europe.

Gentlemen, the great movement of civilization in which the French people have been involved since 1789 should not be seen as purely national. It has a more universal character. All the peoples of western Europe are taking part in it in a manner more or less easy to discern. The three recent examples of Spain, Naples and Portugal have just given the clearest proof of this. You must view your cause in this important respect in order to get a complete idea of your true political situation. Let us develop this theme further.

Since the universal establishment of the Roman domination in western Europe, there has always existed among the different nations which compose it a sort of homogeneous political link which, in spite of very real national differences, stamps them with a communal character and, in this respect, separates them completely from the states of eastern Europe. Their civilization developed in an almost uniform way, at least in all the most essential respects, although it did not advance everywhere with the same speed. This similarity has become progressively more complete as the growth of enlightenment has facilitated and multiplied communications of every kind.

Hitherto, this analogy has appeared merely to be an inevitable result of the nature of things, which the peoples have obeyed involuntarily, without being aware of it. The formation of modern societies in the Middle Ages took place among the various nations, in the same way and at about the same time,

* III, 2, pp. 21–4. In *Du système Industriel*, Saint-Simon writes several open letters to the Industrialists, to the King on different subjects. The first letters to the industrialists were mostly on the main political problem in France at the time: the Restoration. This is the fifth letter.

when great political conformity already existed among them, by virtue of a common domination.

It was inevitable that their later advance should feel the effects of this communal origin, up to a point, and that, in effect, without any design, a certain similarity should be established, and their progress should be almost simultaneousness. But today, instead of this simple analogy, there can and there even ought to be a true combination of political effort established among these peoples, with the object of establishing the industrial régime, which has always been their final common destination and which today should be the goal of all, even though they are not all equally close to it. The possibility, or better, the necessity, of such a combination is one of the most important and fortunate results of the progress of enlightenment.[1]

Thus, Gentlemen, the cause which you ought to espouse is not simply French, it is European. In the action which you are called upon to take in France, you should see yourselves as collaborating with all the industrialists of western Europe. To your national duties are thus added, Gentlemen, duties of a more universal nature; European duties, based, like the others, upon your interests, upon the rôle which the progress of civilization has assigned to you today in order to establish the industrial régime. It is easy to determine your obligations in this respect: they are part of the general need to attune yourselves politically to the other peoples of western Europe; that is to adopt at once the improvements which they have adopted and, in your turn, to set an example in the part of the common work which has been allotted to you.

1. The statements I have just made will later be the object of a special and direct examination. The question with which I am dealing here obliges me to limit myself for the moment to general indications.

To demonstrate the whole importance of this great European combination, I propose to show: (1) that the complete establishment of the industrial régime would be impossible in each nation, in isolation, unless the peoples of western Europe establish it simultaneously; (2) that if, in truth, the progress of civilization has reserved for France the exclusive honour of beginning the organization of the industrial system, it is no less true that, once the first impulse has been given, some parts of this great enterprize should naturally be carried out by those among the other Western nations who are the most advanced, France playing only a secondary rôle in this part of the common task.

## TO THE KING*

*First Address*

'God said: love and help one another'

Sire, every association of men which has a well-defined character, from the simplest to the most complex, must be either military or industrial, because true association cannot exist without a common purpose, and there are only two such purposes possible for any collection of men, just as there are for a single individual: they are either conquest or work. Any nation which is not clearly organized for one or other of these two purposes is not a true political association; it is only an agglomeration of individuals of a very doubtful character.

There are, therefore, only two possible true constitutions, each answering to a different purpose, the military constitution and the industrial one. The choice between them is decided by the state of civilization of each people and of its neighbours—The Charter,† which is neither a military nor an industrial constitution, because it is trying to be both at once, is therefore not a real constitution.

Reason shows and the facts confirm that the military constitution belonged to the early history of mankind. It necessarily corresponded to that state of ignorance of the laws of nature which resulted in a failure to act upon nature in order to adapt it to man's advantage. But as these laws were revealed and as this activity developed, so society gradually advanced under the shadow of the military constitution, in the direction of the industrial constitution, the true and final destination of civilized mankind.

The moment when the industrial constitution is ripe can perhaps be determined with some accuracy by this twofold basic condition: 1. When the overwhelming majority of the nation, as individuals are joined in greater or lesser industrial associations and bound, two by two, three by three, etc., by industrial links which will enable a general system to be formed, directing them towards a great common industrial purpose, in which they will all be co-ordinated according to their respective functions; 2. when the observation of the laws of nature are fully active taking into account all the various natural phenomena; which will enable all the separate sciences to be unified in a universal system of the study of nature, corresponding to the universal

* III, 2, pp. 184–234.

† See note on selection of texts in Introduction, p. 59.

system by which nature acts. When a society has reached this point and is not surrounded by purely military nations, it can be said that it is approaching the industrial constitution.

This is the universal advance of mankind, reduced to its simplest expression, and taking into account only the main facts from among those which result from the very nature of things, from which, as Montesquieu so wisely said, in the last analysis, the laws of politics, just as much as the scientific laws, must derive.

Sire, when one compares with this model—the general outlines of which I have just sketched—the positive advance of society in France up to the present day, it can be seen that, since the enfranchisement of the communes and the introduction of the cultivation of the sciences of observation in Europe by the Arabs, France has made continual and ever-increasing progress towards the industrial system and, correspondingly, the military system has fallen into disarray. In fact, France has now reached the stage of being able to adopt the industrial constitution: for the basic preconditions set forth above have now been completely satisfied.

For, firstly, out of thirty million Frenchmen there are twenty-nine and a half million industrialists, making up between them various associations which are spread widely enough and adequately combined between them; secondly, the observation of nature is being carried out in all branches of science; astronomy, physics, chemistry and physiology, the latter being in our time at the summit of the scientific edifice. Lastly, although France's neighbours may not all have satisfied these two major conditions to the same extent as she has done, they are all nevertheless clearly working in the same direction; they are all at the same stage of civilization.

Sire, as a result of the considerations already mentioned, the only constitution possible in France today is the industrial one. The Charter, which is clearly not the industrial constitution, cannot therefore pass for a true constitution; or if one insists on giving it this title, it is a constitution which cannot acquire any solidity, since it is not the constitution which the state of civilization today demands of us.

Sire, a real constitution can never be invented; it can only be recognized. The true constituent power cannot be either a king or an assembly; it is philosophy[1] which studies the advance of

1. Objections will perhaps be made against the conclusions drawn from this assertion, that this philosophy can be found neither on the throne nor in a legislative assembly. I would reply, in the first case, that philosophical ability could, un-

civilization and which sums up all its observations in a universal law, from which the constitutional principle derives and which has been verified by the mass of enlightened men. In short, the search for the foundations of a constitution is, by its nature, a function of spiritual power, which cannot be carried out by the temporal power in any way.

It can be shown through history that things have always worked out in this way until the present time, although it has always been a question merely of more or less profound changes in the original order of things. How much more pressing it is that it should be so today, when a genuinely new constitution is in question.

It is, therefore, not surprising that the so-called constitutions drawn up by the legislative assemblies of France and the imitation of an assembly in Spain should have *constituted* nothing. Similarly, it is very natural that the Charter cannot constitute anything either—even though it was conceived in a far more experimental and, consequently, far wiser spirit. If things were otherwise it would be surprising, and rightly so, for this would be absolutely contrary to the nature of things.

What is the Charter then if it is not a true and definitive constitution? It is important to be precise about this now.

The Charter should be seen as a felicitous modification of the old political system, which established a provisional and preparatory order of things, under the shelter of which society can peaceably carry out its transformation into the industrial and scientific system.

When the royal power and the nation both realize that the establishment of this system is the only possible end of the revolution, without doubt the greatest difficulty will have been overcome, for the state of crisis will cease at that moment. But the organization of the system will take time, for such an undertaking is slow by its very nature, and because of the theoretical work it demands and the changes which it requires in the daily habits of nearly all classes—those who must rise and those

---

doubtedly, be found on the throne as elsewhere; but it would lack the education which would enable it to gather together the materials of its observations and a social position which would leave it free to co-ordinate them. As for the second case, I would add that it can certainly happen that a philosopher could be a member of a legislative assembly, as of any other society; but that this office, far from being favourable to his political investigations, on the contrary, would greatly hamper him unless he took no active part in the assembly, in which case the hypothesis would not apply. Condorcet who was, irrefutably, the most able philosopher of the last half of the eighteenth century, engaged in more true politics after he had been proscribed by the Convention than when he was an influential member of it.

who must fall. This is why it is absolutely necessary that the Charter, which allows work towards the formation of the new system to be undertaken with confidence, should be brought into operation gradually, following the natural course of events and, as a result, should profit little by little from the advantages which this system will engender, even before it has been completely constituted.

Such advantages are undoubtedly precious enough to earn the affection and gratitude of the French nation for the Charter and its august founder. These two sentiments would not lose any of their strength, by being based on a real and positive appraisal of the Charter. On the contrary, the more it is seen in its true colours, the more it will appear to be appropriate to the present time, which is truly a period of transition. The surest way of jettisoning these favourable interpretations lies precisely in regarding the Charter as a definitive constitution; for, in spite of the fact that the nation can only perceive very vaguely the true nature of the system towards which the progress of civilization is now leading it, it does nevertheless feel, in a very real, if obscure way, that the order established by the Charter in no way satisfies its fundamental desires.

The opinion which I have just set forward being of some importance, since it covers the great political question in general terms, must be strengthened by what I believe to be its most distinctive considerations.

I shall have the honour to indicate some of them briefly to Your Majesty. . . .

Sire, the first article of a constitution, the most important of all, is clearly the one which enunciates the goal towards which this contract proposes to direct society. If this goal is not fully developed, all the other articles, which are only legitimate in as far as they relate to the first, inevitably remain in limbo, and from that moment onwards the text loses its constitutional character. Has a notary ever forgotten to indicate the purpose of the association when drawing up a contract for a society?

Nevertheless, this is the great gap in the Charter. Nowhere is the purpose of the association even hinted at. It begins, as do all the constitutions dreamed up since 1789, by putting forward the rights of Frenchmen, which can only be clearly determined when the purpose of society is established in a positive way, since the rights of every associate can only be based upon the abilities which he possesses and which contribute towards the common goal—this is the case in all private associations. It is really strange that something which is universally regarded as absolutely necessary for associations of even thirty or a hundred individuals, should be missed by everybody when the number of the individuals is raised to some thirty million. All this first part of the Charter, which is the most important since it lays down the principles, is an all too faithful reflection both of the void in which political ideas still languish and of the unfortunate hold which metaphysics still has over men's minds.

We also see from this remarkable lack of definition in the Charter, which results in a failure to indicate, explicitly or implicitly, the purpose of society and government action, that the text can be used to direct society in the most contrary directions. For instance, it can be used to re-establish the feudal and ecclesiastical system in all its purity: it is enough merely to substitute for the word *Chamber* the word *State*. . . . In the second place, the Charter can be put into effect in a manner which paves the way for the coming of the industrial and scientific system; for nothing in its text formally contradicts this move: this, of course, should be its true destination, as I believe I have proved; this would be the only sound way to breathe life into it, the only one which accords with the interests of the House of Bourbon and of the French nation. But, nevertheless, it should be recognized that it is an odd constitution which can, at will, be seen either to be re-establishing the *ancien régime* or paving the way for the industrial system. The very fact that such flexibility is possible is enough to prove that the Charter is not a true constitution.

Sire, there is another way to convince oneself directly, and without reference to the above considerations that the Charter cannot be seen as a definitive and durable constitution; this is that the Charter, as a whole and in its most essential clauses is clearly simply the English constitution which was established in 1688. In this respect, it can be judged by experience.

I shall begin by observing that, in England as in France, and in general throughout western Europe, the parliamentary system cannot be the definitive one and can only serve as a transitional stage on the way to the setting up of the industrial system, which society is called upon to establish today. The reasons upon which I have based this opinion for the case of France are, in fact, applicable to all the nations which have reached the same stage of civilization, and principally to England.

England, for different reasons, which nearly all stem in the last analysis from the isolation of her geographical position, was able to arrive at this modification of the feudal and ecclesiastical system which is called the parliamentary régime, sooner than

France, although the degree of civilization which prevailed then in England was inferior to that which prevails in France today. The result was that this régime was able to last so long in England that it came to be taken for a definitive régime. But this circumstance changes nothing of the essential nature of the parliamentary régime, which is to be intermediary and transitional. The only result for England will be that the transition will as it should take longer than in France, as it began at a lower stage of civilization, at an epoch when the continuous tendency of civilized man towards the industrial constitution was not yet strongly enough pronounced.

For the rest, this conclusion is directly confirmed by observation; for today all those who have thought deeply about the political and civil state of England, considered in its most essential aspects and especially with reference to the distribution of property, are generally convinced that the English constitution is nearing the end of its existence. It would be odd if attempts were made to consolidate the English constitution in France, just when it is clearly about to collapse in England itself.

It now remains for me to show that the reasons for the maintenance of the parliamentary régime in England do not exist in France and that, consequently, this régime cannot even pretend to that minor permanence which it was able to attain among our neighbours, and which is still very inferior to that of a truly definitive system.

It cannot be too often repeated, for it is the principle underlying all healthy politics, that a constitution is only durable so long as it is, in its essential elements, the expression of the state of society at the time at which it was established. A political force is not created; either it is numbered among the leading powers of society when it has reached a certain stage of civil development, or it simply appears; that is all. This recognition or, if you wish, this legitimization of the most powerful forces which exist in a society at every important stage of civilization is what is called its constitution and, without this, it would be merely a metaphysical dream.

In the nature of things the English constitution was drawn up according to this principle, and this is why it could endure as long as the state of civilization to which it corresponded was not essentially changed. But it is for the same reason that the Charter could not acquire true stability, other than as a provisional constitution, because it treated as real political forces elements which were not rooted in social reality. This is easily seen when one considers the political elements which, together with the royal power and the communes, combine to form the English constitution. I shall confine myself here to pointing to two of the most important elements of this observation.

Sire, the preponderance of the Anglican Church over the other religious communions and its existence in the form of a corporation of which the head is the king is, without doubt, one of the main supports of the English constitution. This is not the place to explain how Henry VIII, seizing on Luther's reform at the very beginning and before it had come to maturity, succeeded in delaying at least, if he could not prevent, the overthrow of the old spiritual power by means of a device which would have been impracticable a little later on. It is sufficient to remark on the fact here and to recognize the importance it had for the stability of the English constitution. But does any similar prop exist in France?

The Charter laid down in principle that Catholicism is the State religion. This must be true in practice if it is to have any political validity; but this is clearly not so. There is no *State religion* in a country in which theological ideas have been subjected to criticism for a long time and have lost almost all their influence. Therefore, before attempting to make the old spiritual power a prop, it was necessary to have reconstituted it; but this, in an enlightened state, is an absurd and fanciful undertaking. Bonaparte intended to make himself pope in France, in imitation of Henry VIII, and thought thereby to strengthen his power greatly. This was clearly to set about the task the wrong way round and to start at the end, even to suppose that it was possible to restore to the power of the church its old supremacy.

Originally, the power of the clergy was based fundamentally upon the great superiority of its knowledge over that of the other classes; once that superiority disappeared—which happened, in fact, a long time ago—the foundations of the ecclesiastical power were undermined; for it is in the very nature of things that spiritual power should belong to the most enlightened class. The only spiritual power which can establish itself today is that of the scientists, who correspond to the industrial constitution and whose fundamental authority has been unshakeably established by the constant progress made in the observed sciences since the Arabs introduced them into Europe.

If, then, it is true that there is no real spiritual power in the régime established by the Charter and if it is clear that no true constitution can exist without spiritual power, how can it be thought that the Charter can be a true constitution? How can it even be hoped that it can have the stability of the English constitution, when it lacks one of the fundamental elements of the constitution?

Then, Sire, the House of Lords is still one of the main powers which help to maintain the English constitution. But the House of Lords is only a true force in the state because it is a force, and a very great one at that, in society. There are many reasons for this, above all, the concentration of the greatest estates in the hands of members of that House, estates which have been kept in the same families by the laws of feudalism which prevent them from being broken up. This intermediary power would clearly never have been a really effective aid to royalty, had it not possessed separate and independent power. It is not by virtue of any pre-established theory of political equilibrium that the House of Lords is counted among the essential elements of the English constitution; it is simply a matter of fact and the theories were only dreamed up after the event. The House of Lords quite naturally became a part of the English constitution because the class of the peers, at the time when the constitution was set up, was one of the most powerful civil forces in England, and could not therefore be refused admission to the number of political powers.

If the Charter is judged by these principles, which are only an expression of the facts, one recognizes from this aspect, as from the one which I have just considered, that it lacks any real foundations. What is a house of peers in a country in which feudalism no longer exists and in which land has long been divided among a small number of families? What kind of peers are they whose existence is only founded upon pensions or upon the positions which the royal power gives them? Theirs is only a sham force, which is taken for a genuine force. Neither the English peerage nor any of the elements capable of creating it exist in France. Our House of Peers can only pass for an extension of the council of state and augments the royal power no more than that institution does, in fact it produces rather a contrary effect since royalty, instead of receiving, is obliged to give. Also, the House of Peers plays only an absolutely insignificant, and almost ridiculous role; it has and can have no political importance.[1] Its existence scarcely makes itself felt. All the debates take place solely between the crown and the communes because in France today the only true forces are, in fact, the crown and the communes. Whether to keep or to suppress the House of

1. M. de Montlosier revealed this fact very clearly in his last book.

Peers is a matter of indifference from the political point of view and is only of limited interest from the financial one, because of the sum of five or six million francs which the nation is obliged to pay every year to support these hypothetical lords.

In order to complete this examination and at the same time to sum it up, let us suppose that any Englishman active in public life and particularly one of the members of the Cabinet is asked what would become of the English constitution if the following changes were made:

Take from the King the office of head of the Anglican Church and destroy the supremacy of that church;

Take from the two Houses the King's Bench, and no longer admit judges to it simply by virtue of their office, abolish feudal customs throughout England, abrogate all the old civil laws and draw up new codes for all the branches of the judiciary;

Remove from the old peerages the territorial fortunes which they have enjoyed since before the English Revolution;

Suppress the *rotten boroughs* and share out representation fairly in the House of Commons;

There is not a single Englishman active in public life who would not formally declare that such subtractions would remove all its strength and solidity from the English constitution.

How then can one imagine that the Charter, which is simply the English constitution without any of these supports could acquire solidity and become a lasting constitution?

Sire, according to the various considerations which I have had the honour to submit to Your Majesty in this article, it seems to me proven that the Charter can in no way be seen as a durable and definitive constitution. The order of things which it establishes should only be seen as a provisional order, its object being to facilitate the transition of society towards the industrial constitution, which is the only one which can establish itself today.

This view of the Charter, far from alarming Your Majesty is, on the contrary, the only one which could lead the people in a healthy and conciliatory direction, for the people feel instinctively that the Charter is not that new political system, which they feel that they need so much even without clearly understanding its nature. They are carried along by this ignorance to look for even greater modifications of the old political system which can only really be found in the organization of the industrial and scientific system. Their minds are thus hostile to a greater or less degree, towards the Charter. If, on the other hand, the opinion which interprets the Charter as a necessary means of transition towards the industrial constitution were to become dominant, the people would immediately feel that if the Charter did not fulfil the conditions they demand in the definitive régime, the object of their desires, it conforms in every way with all they could ask of a provisional order of things, destined to pave the way for this régime.

[Sire, you also said:] 'We should not ask of nascent institutions what can only be attained by their complete development and the habits which they are destined to form.

'Until this has come about, let us know how to recognize that, in public affairs, patience and moderation are also forces, and forces which are the least deceiving of all.'

The thought contained in this passage naturally evokes an important observation, which I have the honour to submit in a few words for the enlightened criticism of Your Majesty.

Sire, the object of this passage, no doubt, was to ask the French nation to bear patiently the unhealthy political system which oppresses her and to wait with moderation until the complete development of the Charter has fulfilled its promises.

The merchant who has sent out a ship to trade with India does not expect to receive at once the benefits which his undertaking should bring to him. However eager he may be to enjoy them, he knows that such an expedition needs time and he waits patiently until the natural term has been reached. But if the vessel, loaded up for a long time, were to remain in harbour for months on end, in spite of a favourable wind or, what, is an even more apt analogy, if the ship's officers, after putting out to sea, took a course which led in absolutely the opposite direction to India, would it be suitable to exhort the merchant to bear this misfortune patiently and to wait placidly until this ill-led undertaking had been successful? And, if his whole existence was bound up in it, surely such words be not only ridiculous but cruelly derisive?

Nevertheless, it is in this ridiculous light which the absurd behaviour of the present government is putting the exhortation addressed by Your Majesty to the French nation, in the passage which I have just quoted, an exhortation which, by itself is very sensible.

Let the monarchy place itself at the head of the general movement which is pushing society towards the establishment of the industrial and scientific system today and then a vast course of extensive improvements, clear and assured, many of them imminent, will open the eyes of the French nation. The nation will distinguish perfectly well for itself those which are immediately practicable from those which only the complete development of this system can bring about. But if the government persists in its mad attempts to re-establish the feudal and ecclesiastical system, the nation will have the undoubted right to show its impatience and even its indignation. In this respect, far from the French people having shown any blameworthy attitudes.

I would go so far as to say that they have earned the praise and gratitude of the king for the really admirable patience and moderation with which they have borne the annoying consequences of governmental incompetence for six years. The people were upheld by the single hope that the royal power would at last open its eyes to the incompetence of its advisers. Your Majesty, I do not hesitate to say, did not do justice to this wise and generous frame of mind in your speech. The French nation has been patient, moderate and trusting, to a far greater extent than the monarchy had any right to demand, given the conduct of the government. But the government will perhaps remember that all patience has its limits and will stop before patience is exhausted.

The passage quoted above can perhaps be looked at from a second, still more important, point of view.

Your Majesty appears to be persuaded, according to this passage, that patience and moderation are the political forces upon which most reliance should be placed. I have no fear in stating that this seems to me to be an erroneous opinion because these forces are, of their nature, purely passive and, because of this, quite inadequate to the present state of things, which demands that the most essentially active powers should be called into play as much in the king's interests as in those of the people.

When a society ceases to be active in one direction, it must become active in another; for the first need of any nation, and above all of the French nation, is activity. The French were highly exalted in the military sense, under Bonaparte's domination; today they must be even more highly exalted in the industrial sense. Nothing, indeed, is easier. It is the only way to destroy the memories of glory which are still attached to this degenerate period, upon which is founded a large part of the influence which the faction hostile to your dynasty still exercises over many people.

Prudent and moderate men did much evil during the Revolution, because they allowed ambitious and intransigent men to gain an ascendency which they could have prevented by exerting themselves as much as the malcontents did. This sad experience fully confirmed the truth, which has already been superabundantly proved both by the knowledge of man and by the history of all ages, that to resist with complete efficacy, action must be balanced with action. Thus, in public affairs even more than in private ones, patience and moderation far from being 'the forces which deceive the least' are, on the contrary the most deceiving, because they are normally supposed to be open to very great powers of resistance, which they do not have and will never have.

Today, it is certain that the political apathy of the industrialists and of the scientists is precisely the greatest obstacle to the establishment of lasting peace, which must be most urgently overcome. The result is, in fact, that the direction of national opinion is inevitably left to incompetent men, to the ambitious and to the intriguers who are still the only people prepared to act. The industrialists and the scientists only reserve for themselves the right to criticize the plan which the others have laid down. This can clearly have no effect so long as they do not themselves take over the leadership of the national cause, and make it their own cause.

Thus, far from Your Majesty being able to count on patience and moderation as political powers, Your Majesty should, on the contrary, regard the political inaction of the mass of the nation as a veritable plague. The most efficacious measure which could be adopted in favour of your august dynasty is to persuade the scientists and industrialists, by placing yourself at their head, to become active in the political sphere, for they alone can thwart the plans of the troublemakers.

Between the downfall of one system and the establishment of another, there necessarily intervenes a period, longer or shorter, of political inactivity. But to represent this state of transition as a permanent one, to imagine that the French nation can rest peacefully in political stagnation, is clearly an error, and a very serious one. The French nation feels the need to play a leading role in Europe, and it is in the industrial and scientific direction that she is likely to play it. So long as the political order does not conform to this national tendency, society will necessarily be in a state of crisis.

. . . Your Majesty ended your speech by announcing that according to your wish, 'this session will finish the work successfully begun by the last one.'

The government has only too accurately fulfilled this part of Your Majesty's promises.

In the last session, the intention of the government to become the Don Quixote of the noblemen and of the clergy was clearly shown. The government had arranged for them to have the majority in the so-called chamber of commons and they were assured, over and above this, of the monopoly of debate which is so much a part of the weakness and unpopularity of that faction. In the present session, the government issued simply preparatory measures; it began to make direct attempts to organize the political machine in a feudal and clerical sense.

It was with this in view that the government had drawn up an ordinance on public education whose clear intention was to give to the clergy the direction of national education and to propose a law on the municipalities with the manifest object of putting the noblemen, the public officials, the jurists, the idle landowners, in a word the whole flock of non-producers, at the head of the commons of France. It remains for me for an instant to draw Your Majesty's attention to these two great acts of folly.

Sire, national education is the special function of the spiritual power. But it is not by virtue of an ordinance, or a law, or a charter of any kind that a class of men can become the spiritual power. It is solely through the superiority of their enlightenment. Effectively, this was originally the basis of the power of the clergy. But for a long time this superiority has been completely dissipated and passed over entirely to the scientists, who alone today have all the real existing knowledge. This is a fact that all the ordinances and even all the possible constitutions cannot change. Thus, the spiritual power is really in the hands of the scientists. This is clearly verified by observation since they alone today have the power to command universal credence. A reasonable ordinance on this question should have as its object only the solemn recognition of this fact, instead of struggling against it, and should adopt or rather regularize its inevitable consequence by entrusting the supreme direction of national education to the scientists.

Some men whose biased minds are continually occupied in combining elements which are incompatible because they belong to different systems, think that everything could be reconciled by giving to the scientists that part of education relating to positive knowledge and leaving the teaching of morals to the clergy. It was inevitable that such a state of affairs should exist transitionally between the period of the crumbling of the old spiritual power and that of the maturity of the new. Indeed, it is one of the great characteristics of the profound anarchy in which society has found itself between the decadence of the old political system and the final constitution of the new. But that such a fundamental disorder should be seen as a permanent and normal state of society is extraordinary. As a general thesis, it is monstrous that the teaching of morals and of the positive subjects should be entrusted to different bodies, for it is monstrous[1] that the ignorant should be in charge of enlightened men. The first condition to command belief in precepts is the perception in those who receive them of the superiority of the intellect of the enlightened men who pronounce them. A second condition, the necessity of which is even more obvious, is the established morality of the teaching body. But the clergy have long since lost any influence in this second respect, as in the first, because they have cast off the Christian character in order to assume a retrogressive one.

Sire, national education should be reconstituted today in the hands of the scientists according to an entirely new plan. The government could cover itself with glory by putting this beautiful and noble undertaking into force, the only one of its kind which is not ephemeral. Instead, it has preferred to cover itself with ridicule by trying to re-establish, for the advantage of the clergy, educational plans which belong to the fourteenth century.

The bill on the municipalities gives rise to essentially similar remarks as those above. It can be said that, with this measure, the government is putting itself in a false position with reference to a great temporal fact, just as it did by the one above, with reference to a great spiritual fact.

Fired with superficial zeal, dazzled by ephemeral power—indeed never having measured the true strength of power, never having risen to the idea that this strength is durable only when it is linked with the internal order of society, which, in turn, results from the state of civilization—the government imagined that all it had to do was to decree by an ordinance that such a class of men would be the *notables* of the nation, for this to be true in fact. Thenceforward, starting from this principle, in itself a just one, that the municipal administration shall be entrusted to the *notables*, it conceived the idea of putting it into the hands

1. In order to see this enormity in all its clarity, one can imagine the case of a young pupil in a school who is more learned than the chaplain whose task it is to teach morals. If this does not happen in our schools, given the poor education which our youth receives, it does happen frequently in the higher establishments of education, such as the *Polytechnique*, the *École Normale*, etc. Besides, exactly the same thing takes place every day in the churches when a sermon is preached.

of the gentlemen, the public officials, the jurists and the idle landowners, by proclaiming them, by its own authority, the *notables* of the French nation. The government has substituted this expression of its feeble will for the reality of observed facts.

If such an extravagant project could be realized for a time, the municipal administration which, by its nature, should be the most popular of all, would find itself given over to men who exert over the people no real and permanent influence and who have no way of winning their confidence. This administration would be far worse organized than it has been since the enfranchisement of the communes, six hundred years ago. Fortunately the monstrous consequences will open the eyes of royalty to the absurdity of the line adopted by the government.

Sire, in a nation composed of twenty-nine and a half million producers against five hundred thousand non-producers, it is easy to decide from which of these two categories the municipal administrations should be chosen, because it is easy to determine where are the true *notables*. The gentlemen, the public officials, the jurists and the idle landowners, in spite of all the importance which they believe they have and which is conventionally given to them, are not *notables* in any way, no matter how they may be considered today. These classes do not possess any of the true social superiority, not that of physical strength nor even that of wealth, nor that of intelligence, nor of enlightenment. They have no influence upon the people who see them, with natural intuition, as a swarm of drones united against the bees. In what respect would they then be *notables*? The only *notables* today in France, with the exception of the scientists and the artists, are the leaders[1] of agriculture, of manufacturing and commerce. It is in them that the power is exclusively to be found to influence the people, because it is to them that the people are accustomed to defer in their daily relationships.

The immediate result of this indisputable fact is the need to choose the municipal administration from among those latter classes. The nature of things does not allow, in this respect, any freedom of choice because it sets very precisely the condition which it must satisfy if it is not to be null and void. This clear condition is that an administration, which is essentially designed to work upon the people in a direct way, should be entrusted to the men who have most influence with the people.

1. I mean here by *leaders* of different works, all the industrialists who are not simply *workers*, that is to say the actual executants, and who take a lesser or greater part in the direction of the work.

To act otherwise is to set the political order in opposition to the social or civil order, a state of affairs which cannot be maintained for any length of time. The whole argument then can only bear upon the question of knowing which men have most influence upon the people. Reduced to these terms, the solution is self-evident, unless of course one introduces shadowy metaphysics into a study which reduces itself naturally to the simple observation of a fact.

It remains for me, Sire, to present briefly to Your Majesty the conclusion of the different considerations examined in this address.

The general plan of policy adopted by the government and even by the cabinets of all the kings of Europe, united to follow it together, is radically absurd from all points of view, because it leads the governments in a direction which is contrary to that of European civilization.

This plan is even more harmful to the interests of your august dynasty, whose fate it immediately threatens, than it is to the interests of the French nation whose cause is in itself robust enough to face all the consequences of ministerial incompetence, however harmful they may be.

It feeds continually the influence of the faction led by the nobility created by Bonaparte, whose ascendancy over national opinion increases day by day, following a deplorable course linked to the extent to which the government makes new efforts in favour of the gentlemen and of the clergy.

Lastly (and this aspect of it alone would be enough by which to judge such a senseless plan) it is even contrary to the true interests of the handful of rebels for whom it is devised, and for whom the wisest plan would be to withdraw into their natural incompetence. In allowing them to indulge their feeble fury in pursuing their fantastic projects, the government is involuntarily preparing for them the sort of future that can be expected by a foolish insect which has dared to irritate a lion.

The fundamental defect of this plan is that it offers to royalty, as a support, declining classes who no longer have any real strength who lend to the royal power all their fictitious power and who, in consequence, instead of being its support are, on the contrary, a liability; a liability which is difficult to bear, given the unpopularity of these classes, or rather the extreme aversion they inspire in the body of the nation. The result is, necessarily, as a general consequence, that this plan, far from bringing to an end the profound social crisis into which society has fallen, tends to prolong it and to aggravate it more and more, to increase its anarchic character, by separating the people and the kings more and more the one from the other.

The only line of conduct which could end this crisis, the only one which is in accord with the true interests of kings as well as peoples, consists in having royalty backed by the immediate political action of the social forces who have become all powerful today; in a word, to place royalty at the head of the irresistible movement which is impelling the existing society towards the system of organization which will establish a new spiritual power in the hands of the scientists and a new temporal one in the hands of the heads of industrial enterprises.

Civilized mankind has always inclined towards this system since its infancy, but especially since the enfranchisement of the communes and the introduction of the positive sciences into Europe by the Arabs. Starting from this memorable period, to which should be attributed the direct origin of the industrial and scientific system, the internal order of society has been established upon that basis by imperceptible degrees. This civil or elementary organization is today fully effected in the most civilized countries, and especially in France. The moment has at last arrived to work directly for the constitution, political or general, of the new system. Prudence advises kings to put themselves at the head of this enterprise so that it will not operate without and in spite of them.

It has needed, I am not ashamed to say, lengthy meditations over a long period on the advance of civilization to reach this general view which links and dominates all the facts. But, once it has been found, it needs only common sense to recognize the truth, so much does it correspond to the real state of affairs. The judgement to be made reduces itself, as it were, to a simple question of statistics.

A glance at the statistical table of France shows, in fact with perfect clarity, that the masses of men organized among themselves in the industrial and scientific system possess to a high degree all the real superiority over their adversaries; superiority in numbers, in physical strength, in wealth, in administrative capacity, in morality and finally in the one thing which is so decisive: in intelligence and acquired positive knowledge. Such a striking result shows how absurd it is that the immense majority should be held back in its progress by the other classes of the population, how contrary it is to the nature of things that this weak and parasitical residue should any longer keep the leadership of a society with which it has nothing in common.

Sire, the general conclusion of this address is that Your

Majesty should take upon yourself the character of the founding king of the industrial and scientific system, and put in force as quickly as possible the theoretical and practical work necessary for the development of the political constitution of this system, by regarding the Charter as a provisional control, destined solely to govern the society for the time this transition will take, as I think I proved in the part of this address relating to the Charter.

# IX

## The Catechism of the Industrialists

*Catéchisme des Industriels*, Paris, 1823–6; IV, 1, pp. 3–13/73–112, 40–9, 73, 94, 178–83, 195–200.

FIRST INSTALMENT

Q. What is an industrialist?
A. An industrialist is a man who works to produce, or who puts within the reach of different members of society, one or more material means of satisfying their needs or their physical tastes; thus, an agriculturalist who sows wheat or who raises poultry or cattle is an industrialist; a cartwright, a blacksmith, a locksmith, a joiner is an industrialist; a shoemaker, a hat-maker, a linen-maker, a maker of cloth, a maker of cashmere are also industrialists; merchants, hauliers, merchant-seamen, are industrialists. All these industrialists together work to produce and place within the reach of all the members of society all the material means for satisfying their needs or their physical tastes, and they form three great classes which are called agriculturalists, manufacturers and merchants.
Q. What place should the industrialists hold in society?
A. The industrial class should have the first place because it is the most important of all; because it can do without the others, whereas the others cannot do without it; because it exists by its own efforts and it personal labours. The other classes should work for the industrial class because they are its creatures and it supports them. In a word, as industry does everything, everything should be done for it.
Q. What rank do the industrialists hold in society?
A. In the present social system, the industrial class occupies the lowest rank of all. The social order gives more respect and power to work of a secondary nature, even to idleness, than to the most important work, to work which is directly useful.
Q. Why does the industrial class, which should occupy the first rank, find itself occupying the lowest? Why are those who, in effect, are first, ranked last?
A. We shall explain this in the course of this catechism.
Q. How can the industrialists pass from the inferior position in

which they find themselves to the higher one which they have the right to occupy?

A. This catechism will explain how they should improve their social condition.

Q. What is the nature of the work which you undertake? In a word, what is your object in preparing this catechism?

A. We propose to show the industrialists how to increase their well-being as much as possible; we propose to reveal to them the general methods which they ought to use to increase their social importance.

Q. How will you achieve this aim?

A. On the one hand, we shall give the industrialists a picture of their true social situation; we shall show them that it is a completely subordinate one, and thus far below what it should be, since they are the most able and useful class in society.

On the other hand, we shall trace the route they should follow to reach the first rank in esteem and power.

Q. Therefore, in this catechism you are preaching insurrection and revolt? For those particular classes which possess power and esteem will certainly not be disposed to renounce the advantages they enjoy.

A. Far from advocating insurrection and revolt, we are putting forward the only way to prevent the acts of violence which threaten society and which will only be averted with difficulty if the industrial power remains passive amid the factions struggling for power.

There will never be permanent public peace until the most important industrialists are in charge of the administration of public wealth.

Q. Explain this to us and tell us how public order will be threatened unless the most important industrialists are put in charge of the administration of the national wealth?

A. The explanation is very simple; the general political inclination of the great majority of society is to be governed as cheaply as possible; to be governed as little as possible; to be governed by the most able men and in a way which completely guarantees public order. Now the only way to satisfy the desires of the majority in these various respects lies in putting the most important industrialists in charge of public wealth; for the leading industrialists are the people most interested in the maintenance of peace; they are those most interested in economy in public expenditure; they are also most interested in limiting despotism. Lastly, they are, of all the members of society, the ones who give proof of the greatest ability in positive administration, their success in their own businesses having established their ability in this field.

In the present state of affairs, public order is threatened because the behaviour of the government runs directly counter to the most positive wishes of the nation. What the nation wants principally is to be governed as cheaply as possible, and never has a government been so expensive; it costs far more than it did before the Revolution. Before the Revolution, the nation was divided into three classes: the nobles, the bourgeois and the industrialists. The nobles governed; the bourgeois and the industrialists paid them.

Today the nation is divided into only two classes; the bourgeois, who made the Revolution and conducted it in their own interest, have destroyed the exclusive privilege of the nobility to exploit the public wealth; they have admitted themselves into the governing class, so that today the industrialists must pay both the aristocrats and the bourgeois. Before the Revolution, the nation paid five hundred million francs in taxes; today it pays twice that sum and it is still not enough; the government frequently calls for large loans.

Public order will be increasingly threatened because costs will inevitably go on rising. The only way to prevent possible insurrections lies in charging the most important industrialists with the task of administrating public wealth, that is, entrusting them with the budget.

Q. What you have just said is very good, very interesting and of the utmost importance; but it does not tell us exactly what we want to know. The point which we ask you to elucidate is this: is it possible to take the direction of the national finances of society out of the hands of the nobles, the army and the lawyers and the landowners; in a word, out of the hands of the non-industrial classes, and put it into the hands of the industrialists, without resorting to violence?

A. Violent methods are good for overturning, for destroying, but that is all they are good for. Peaceful methods are the only ones which can be used to build, to construct, in a word, to establish solid constitutions. Now, the action of investing the most important industrialists with the supreme direction of the financial interests of the nation is a constructive action; it is the most important political measure which can be taken; this measure will serve as the foundation of the whole new social edifice; it will put a stop to revolution, it will protect the nation from any new shock. The most important industrialists will undertake to draw up the budget, without payment, and the result will be that this function will be very little coveted. The industrialists who draw up the budget will base it upon economy in the administration of public affairs. Thus, they will only pay very modest salaries to the civil servants. As these posts will be very little sought after, they will be comfortably reduced in number, so that the number of claimants will diminish, too, and, inevitably, an order will be established in which a great many places will be filled without payment, because the idle rich will have no other way of procuring esteem.

When one studies the character of the industrialists and the way they conducted themselves during the Revolution, one recognizes that they are essentially peaceful. It was certainly not the industrialists who made the revolution; it was the bourgeois, that is, it was the soldiers who were not of noble blood, the jurists who were commoners, the landowners who were not privileged. Even today, the industrialists only play a secondary role in the existing political parties and they have no opinion or political party of their own. They lean towards the Left rather than towards the Right because the claims of the bourgeois do less violence to their ideas of equality than do those of the nobility; but they have not succumbed to the ideas of the Liberals; it is peace that they desire above all. The Liberal ring-leaders, inside and outside the Chamber are generals, jurists and landowners. The nobles and the bourgeois want to be in charge of the administration of public wealth primarily in order to exploit it for their own profit. The leading industrialists, on the contrary, want to be in charge of it to run it as economically as possible.

The industrialists are well aware that they are the most fit to take charge of the financial interests of the nation, but they never put forward this idea, for fear of causing an immediate disturbance of the peace; they wait patiently for public opinion to come round to this idea and for a genuinely social doctrine to summon them to take the helm.

From this, we conclude that peaceful means, that is, debate, demonstration and persuasion, are the only means which the industrialists should use or support to take the administration of public wealth out of the hands of the nobility, the military class, the jurists, the landowners and the public officials, in order to pass it on to the most important of their own number.

Q. We agree provisionally that the industrialists will not seek to use violence to cause the supreme direction of the financial interests of society to pass from the hands of the nobles and the bourgeois into those of the most important of their own number;

but the peaceful intentions of the industrialists cannot be used to prove that this class is fit to lead. We ask you, therefore, to tell us what are the means the industrialists should employ to bring about the radical change in society which we are discussing.

A. The industrialists make up more than twenty-four of the twenty-five parts of the nation; thus they possess superiority in the sphere of physical force.

They produce all the wealth; thus, they also possess financial strength.

They are superior in intelligence, for it is their work which contributes most directly to the national prosperity.

Lastly, since they are the most fit to administer the financial interests of the nation, human as well as divine morality call upon their leaders to assume direction of the finance.

The industrialists are therefore invested with all the necessary means; they are invested with the irresistible means to bring about the transition in the social organization which would transform them from the class of the ruled into the class of rulers.

[pp. 40–49]

Q. You are too trenchant, too absolute, too exclusive; you want there to be only one class, that of the industrialists; this is absolutely impractical since the industrialists themselves need soldiers, lawyers, etc. Can you justify yourself in the face of this reproach?

A. To produce a system is to produce an opinion which is, by its very nature trenchant, absolute and exclusive: this is our reply to the first part of your objection. You go on to say that we wish there to be only one class in society, that of the industrialists; you are wrong: what we want, or rather what the advance of civilization requires, is that the industrial class should be established as the first of all the classes; that the other classes should be subordinate to it.

In the Dark Ages, the leadership of the nation was in the first place military and in the second industrial. At that time, all social classes had to be subordinate to the military class. This was, effectively, the social organization of that epoch and it would have been wrong had it not had this trenchant, exclusive and absolute character. The progress of civilization has led to a state of affairs in which the leadership of the French people is essentially industrial; therefore the industrial class should be placed above all the others; therefore, the other classes should be subordinate to it. Of course, the industrialists need an army; of course, they need law courts; of course, proprietors should not be forced to invest their capital in industry; but it is monstrous that the military class, the jurists, and the idle rich should be the main directors of the public wealth in the present stage of civilization.

Q. Stop! You are going far too far for the moment; you are going to the root of the question and you are losing sight of the point which is occupying us at the moment, which is that of specifying the nature of the present state of affairs in politics. Tell us briefly what you mean.

A. Here in a few words is the résumé for which you ask: THE PRESENT TIME IS ONE OF TRANSITION.

Q. Let us go on to consider the future and tell us clearly and briefly what the political fate of the industrialists will be?

A. The industrialists will form the leading class in society; the most important of them will take on the administration of the public finances without payment; they will be the ones to make laws and decide the positions that the other classes shall occupy; they will give importance to each of them according to the services that they render to industry; this will be the inevitable result of the present revolution; and when this result has been obtained, peace will be guaranteed absolutely, national prosperity will advance with all possible speed, and society will enjoy all the individual and collective happiness for which human nature could wish.

This is our opinion on the future of the industrialists and of society. Here are the considerations upon which this opinion is based:

1. The recapitulation of society's past has proved to us that the industrial class has constantly grown in importance while the others have always diminished; and from this, we conclude that the industrial class must end by becoming the most important of all.

2. Pure commonsense has led everyone to the following reasoning: as men have constantly tried to improve their lot, the goal to which they have always striven has been that of establishing a social order in which the class employed in useful work is the most highly esteemed. This is the goal which society will inevitably attain in the end.

3. Work is the source of all virtues; the most useful work should be the most highly esteemed; thus divine and human morality both call on the industrial class to enjoy the first place in society.

4. Society is composed of individuals; the development of social intelligence must be the same as that of individual intelligence on a larger scale; if we look at the progress made in the education of individuals, we see, in the primary schools, that control of the children is the strongest factor; and in schools on a higher level, we see that the function of controlling the children constantly lessens in importance, while instruction plays a more important role. The same holds good for the education of society; military action, that is feudal action, had to be very strong in the beginning; it had to diminish progressively while administrative action had always to grow in importance, and inevitably, the administrative power came to dominate the military power in the end. In the end soldiers and jurists must take orders from those most capable of administration; for an enlightened society only needs to be administered; because, in an enlightened society, the power of the law, and the power of the armed forces to enforce obedience to the law, should only be used against those who disrupt the functioning of the administration. The guiding principles of social force should be supplied by the men who are most able to administer; now, as the most important industrialists are those who have given proof of the greatest administrative ability, since it is to their competence in this sphere that they owe what importance they have acquired, in short, it is they who should necessarily be given the direction of the social interests.

Q. We accept your explanation; we accept your opinion on the political future of the industrialists, and we are going to embark at once upon the examination of the great question, in relation to which all we have previously said has been only an introduction, a preparation; a question after which we shall only have to deal with secondary ones, for it is of the most direct interest to the industrialists.

Tell us how this radical change, which you have shown us must take place, should be brought about; tell us what the industrialists should do to raise themselves to the first rank in society; tell us what to do to bring this about; tell us how this undertaking should be conducted; tell us, above all, who will be daring enough to undertake such a thing.

A. Our reply to your question will be the most obvious and the most positive; we are the daring mortals who will undertake it: WE WILL UNDERTAKE TO RAISE THE INDUSTRIALISTS TO THE FIRST RANK OF ESTEEM AND POWER.

We say more: we tell you that this undertaking has already

begun by the publication of the first instalment of this FIRST INSTALMENT OF THE CATECHISM OF THE INDUSTRIALISTS.

Q. Your reply is very positive in that it is you who undertake to bring about this change which must place the industrialists at the head of society; but that is all that is positive about it. It remains for us now to see if your undertaking is well planned, if you are capable of directing such a vast enterprise; it remains for you to make known your plan and the course you mean to follow, and, above all, what financial means you possess to defray the expense of this undertaking, for the industrialists are not likely to show any interest in an enterprise, the financial aspect of which has been badly conceived and badly planned.

Moreover, we confess that we are very satisfied, that you will make this undertaking your personal concern.

It is certain that things which are everyone's business often end up by being no one's business; it is certain that personal interest is the only agent which can direct public interest. The difficulty is to find the device which combines personal with public interest. We do not think that we need to expand further on the subject of principle, since the examination has been reduced to that of a particular fact, of the fact of your undertaking. We beg you, then, to reply to the questions which we asked you at the beginning of this enquiry.

A. We shall begin by making ourselves known, for the public likes to know exactly who it is who takes the liberty of drawing attention to their own thought. We, therefore, make the following declarations to you—declarations which bear first upon our political conduct and then upon our work.

1. We played the part of an onlooker only throughout the Revolution; we held no public office; we were not even a village notable and we were not connected with any of the political parties which have divided France since 1789; in short, the opinion which we put forward is *virgin*.

2. We have not undertaken this enterprise lightly; it has taken forty-five years to think about it and to prepare it.

As a result of our reflections and study we have realized that in order to pass from the régime in which the industrialists are subject to the military class, the jurists and the landowners, to the social order which must place the direction of the general interest in the hands of the industrialists, one indispensable condition must be fulfilled, which is to have a very clear idea of the nature of the industrial régime, and to make it known to the most important industrialists; that is to say, we have realized that it is necessary to make the most important industrialists understand how they can and should use all their abilities in the service of industry and the interests of the producers; finally, we have recognized that this enterprise, which society needs, and which we are determined to undertake, presents only one difficulty, which is precisely that of obtaining a clear conception of the industrial system; and that the difficulty consists in finding the means to reconcile the scientific system, the system of public education, the religious system, the system of the fine arts and the legal system with the system of the industrialists; the difficulty lies in finding the way to unite the most able scientists, theologians, artists, jurists, soldiers and proprietors in the establishment of the social system which is most beneficial to production and most satisfying to the producers.

We declare to you, finally, that we have overcome this difficulty; we declare to you that, in this catechism, we shall demonstrate to the industrialists in a clear, well-developed way, the means which they should use to rally all useful abilities to the establishment of the social organization which can give them the greatest satisfaction.

### SECOND INSTALMENT*

Q. Let us pass on to the third objection: to the one which is designed to prove to you that it is the English political system which should be adopted by the French nation rather than the system which you propose.

We ask you first if you recognize, if you accept that experience is the best guide for nations as for individuals?

A. Yes, we recognize this without any doubt, without any reservation.

Q. Once you have accepted this principle, it will not be difficult to convince you that your system is worthless, since it is in opposition to the principle which you have just accepted. We will establish our reasoning on this point; refute it afterwards if you can.

The English are the richest and most powerful people; it is they who above all have the greatest influence on mankind and yet they are far from being in the first rank as far as size of the territory of the mother country and population are concerned. It is in England that the numerically largest class are the best-housed, the best-fed and the best-clad; it is in England that the rich are able to procure the greatest comfort throughout the

* IV, 1, pp. 73–94.

whole country; lastly, the English people enjoy practically all the advantages which other nations desire.

To what do the English mainly owe the benefits which they enjoy? Undoubtedly, it is to their form of government, that is to the superiority of their social organization over all the political systems which have been put into practice by other nations up to now.

Let us now compare the political arrangement which is the basis of the English constitution, with the principle which you have given as the foundation of your system, and you will see that there is a radical difference between the two.

You say: The administration of public wealth should be undertaken by the leading industrialists, because the industrial class is the most competent in administration.

The English say: The main aim of those who administer the public finances should be to encourage the industrial class as much as possible, because industrial production is the real source of national prosperity; but the industrialists should certainly not be entrusted with the administration of the national finances, because they have not enough knowledge to direct this administration and the attention which administration demands would distract them from their work.

And, in fact, in England it is the peers of the realm, the bishops and the judges in the Upper House, and the lawyers, men of private means and the military in the House of Commons, who have the greatest say in the administration of public wealth, since they compose the Upper House exclusively and have an overwhelming majority in the House of Commons and the Privy Council.

We conclude from what you have just said that your system is in opposition to the English constitution; that it is in opposition therefore to the constitution which experience has shown to be the best and that, consequently, it is worthless. What is your answer?

A. Our answer, just as your question was, will be based on observation, that is, on experience.

We say to you, then: the series of observations on the advance and progress of civilization within French society, as it has existed from its origins up to the present, which we presented in the first instalment, has proved that the industrial class has constantly gained in importance and that the other classes have constantly diminished in this respect. From this accumulation of fourteen hundred years of experience, we come to the conclusion that the industrial class must in the end reach the first rank, that the industrialists must win, as the final result of the progress of civilization, the first degree of esteem and of power; lastly, that a time must come when the most important industrialists will find themselves charged with the administration of public wealth, etc.

We go on to reason from this conclusion, which has been rigorously deduced from experience, and we say: since the French Revolution took place more than a century after the English one, its results should be much more favourable to the industrial class and, in consequence, much more disadvantageous to the nobility and to the bourgeois; we say: the English revolution gave to the peers, the jurists, the military, the men of private means and the public officials the task of conducting the affairs of the nation in the interests of industry; the French revolution will in the end abolish the institution of nobility and then subject the jurists, the military, the men of private means and the public officials to the orders of the industrialists.

We have both argued from experience; thus, we have acted according to the principle which you put forward and which we accepted; but there is this primary difference between our opinions, that yours is only based upon partial experience, on the experience of what has taken place in Europe since the English Revolution, while ours is based upon the widest possible series of observations of the history of the modern nations; there is, further, this second difference, that you considered the revolution in England to be the final stage in the development of the progress of civilization from a political point of view; while we see that revolution and the social organization to which it led, as the penultimate stage only in a series of improvements to which the social régime of the European peoples was open.

As a result of the considerations which we have just laid before you, we claim that our system is good and that your reasoning is bad.

Have you anything more to say on this subject? Can you think of any other way to sustain your third objection?

Q. Yes, certainly, we can uphold our objection; yes, we are sure that we shall emerge victorious from this argument. We do not attach too much importance to words, we do not give primary importance to forms, we occupy ourselves mainly with the examination of basic questions.

You claim that the members of society who are most capable of administering the public wealth well, are the most important industrialists. You maintain that if the most important industrialists were put in charge of the direction of the interests of society, society would enjoy all the benefits to which it can lay claim, that it would be governed in the cheapest way possible, by those men who are most competent to administer its affairs well and in the way most likely to maintain public order. To accept your proposition, your principle, your system (it does not matter much what your plan is called) and we say to you: your system is accepted in England, the English have put it into practice; therefore, you should think that the French nation can do no better than to adopt the English constitution; that the French should try to adopt this constitution. A few words will suffice to prove the justice of this statement, that is to say, to ascertain that the industrial system has been established in England.

The administration of public wealth in England is controlled by the peers because they dominate the royal power and are masters of the House of Commons; for all the peers have greater or lesser interests in manufacturing or commercial enterprises; thus, the peers are industrialists and thus the industrial system has been established in England.

A. The English government is in no way an industrial government; it is a feudal government, modified as far as possible in favour of industry. A transitional régime has been established in England which has prepared the way and made it possible for the French nation, and the rest of European society, to pass from the feudal system to the industrial system, from the system of government to the administrative system.

This is how we should look at these things; looked at in any other way, they leave the mind unsatisfied and run counter to commonsense. For many years the French have regarded the English constitution as a masterpiece; it is talked of as the pinnacle of the perfection which the human mind can attain in politics; this proves that political science is still in its infancy; this proves that the men in public life are still routine-bound; this proves that their consciousness has still not been developed to the point where it can assimilate universal conceptions about the advance of civilization; and this is all it proves. In reality, England does not yet have a constitution; the order of things which has been established there has no solidity, no fixity nor is it capable of acquiring these qualities. The English social organization has activated the feudal principle and the industrial principle at the same time; now, these two principles, being different and even opposed in nature, direct the nation simultaneously towards two ends which are very far removed from each other, with the inevitable result that the English are engaged in a tug-of-war. The political state of England is a state of illness, of crisis, or rather, the régime under which she lives is a transitional one; her constitution, if you insist that the English people have one, is a bastard constitution.

Q. The illness which you tell us attacks the English people presents an entirely new pathological case which you must explain to us. This illness is very extraordinary; first, from the point of view of its duration, because more than a hundred and fifty years have passed since it began and it has still not come to an end. This illness is even more extraordinary from another point of view namely that the social prosperity of the English began at the same time as their political malady, and that advantages which they won over the other peoples have always increased as their so-called malady progressed.

Frankly speaking, Gentlemen, you who catechize, need yourselves to be catechized. You want to give us lessons in politics, while it is you yourselves who should take them; you undertake our education before you have taken pains to educate yourselves. You claim that England has not got a constitution; that the social organization in that country is a bastard one, that it is an order of things to which the English find themselves led by routine and which can only be maintained through gradually contracted habits; an order of things of which no clear and satisfactory account can be made; an order of things which cannot be established in any other nation; an order of things, finally, which cannot become the model for the re-organization of European society.

We answer to this; then have you not read either Montesquieu or Blackstone; do you not know the work of Delholme; have you not studied the fine debates which have taken place, on many different occasions in the English Parliament on the balance of powers?

Read *l'Esprit des Lois* and you will see that men have only invented three forms of government, to wit: despotic, aristocratic and democratic; if you think about it, you will recognize that these were the only three forms of government that could be invented; finally, you will find in a great many of the books by English and French publicists the proof that these three forms of government have been admirably combined in the English constitution and that from this combination the best possible government results.

Now that we have crushed and destroyed your argument, we hasten to tell you that you have made only one mistake, that of exaggerating the importance of your ideas. All the materials which you have used to construct your system are good; it is only the use you have made of these materials, the general conception which underlies your ideas that we would quarrel with. To be sure, all abilities should work for the development of industry; to be sure, governments should protect industry because it is the source of all wealth; to be sure, the theologians should encourage industry because useful work is the source of all virtues, just as idleness is the mother of all vice; to be sure, the legislators should make laws more favourable to production because the most hard-working nations are those in which public order is most easily maintained; but you should not conclude from this that industrial ability should govern all the other abilities. In a word, the English have found, they have fixed, the true point at which we must stop; you have lost sight in your work of a very old proverb which applies perfectly to the present situation: THE BEST IS OFTEN THE ENEMY OF THE GOOD.

A. Do not 'crow' with victory before it is yours; we have not yet come to the end of the discussion. It is only now that it becomes serious. We are very grateful for the indulgence you have been good enough to show us, at the end of the lively attack you have just made on our system; but we do not feel any need to profit from it; we feel we are able to repel all the darts which you have launched against us.

First of all, we shall reply to the jokes you made about the political malady which we said attacked the English nation; for we can only regard as jokes the considerations which you have put forward on this subject. As for us, we have no intention of treating lightly the most novel and important question which can concern the human mind at this moment; we say to you:

The idea of illness only played a very secondary role in the picture which we drew for you of the political situation of the English people; the main idea, which should mainly have engaged your attention, was that of the state of crisis which has existed in England since the revolution at the end of the seventeenth century. We shall explain this idea to you, since a simple statement of it has not been enough to make you understand it.

Mankind was destined, by the nature of its organization, to live in society;

First of all, it was called to live under a *governmental* régime;

It was destined to pass from the governmental or military régime to the *administrative* or *industrial* régime, once it had made sufficient progress in the positive sciences and industry.

Then, it had to undergo, because of the way it was organized, a long and violent crisis during its transition from the military to the peaceful system.

Relative to the progress of civilization these are the most general levels of achievement which the human spirit can attain at present.

We shall now apply this general observation on the advance of civilization to the circumstances prevailing in England. But to make this application exact and easy to grasp it is necessary to begin by describing the present social condition of the English nation, from the point of view of its internal politics and from that of its foreign policy.

When we take a bird's-eye view of England's domestic policy, we are struck from the outset by the existence of the most extraordinary phenomenon imaginable; we see that the English have allowed two fundamental principles to converge in order to form the basis of their social organization; we see that these two principles, being in their natures different and even opposed, the result had to be and still is that the English have simultaneously been subjected to two very different types of social organization that they have double institutions in all directions or, rather, that they have everywhere established the counter-institutions of all the institutions which were in force before their revolution and that they have for the most part preserved them.

Thus, we see that in England the *press-gang* co-exists with the law of *habeas corpus*; a shepherd is seen taking his wife and his ewe together to market, both with ropes around their necks. He sells his wife for a shilling without incurring any punishment for having degraded her by treating her like an animal, and he is sentenced to a fine of five pounds sterling if he ill-treats his ewe. The wealthy, populous and essentially industrial manufacturing town of Manchester has no representative in parliament, while a peer who owns land on which there are utterly deserted boroughs can himself nominate up to nine members, which he uses to support his feudal interests, to increase his political importance as much as possible, and to make the government pay him at the nation's expense.

A hundred folio volumes of small print would not be enough to describe all the organic inconsistencies which exist in England.

If we pass from the examination of the domestic policy of England to its foreign policy, we find the consequences of the imperfections in the organization which we have just pointed out; we see on the one hand that the English government declares that the sovereignty of the seas belongs to it and therefore demands that all flags should be dipped to the Royal Navy while, through another measure, it works at the same time to establish equality between the black and white races, by putting an end to the slave trade.

We see the English government supporting the governmental régime in Europe, while in America it protects the system of industrial organization against the governmental system.

In short, the English nation has for a long time been in a state of crisis as regards its internal as well as its external policy and this crisis, in which all the inhabitants of Europe and America, too, share today, is clearly the crisis which mankind was destined by virtue of its organization to undergo during its transition from the governmental to the industrial social system.

These are the most general considerations which we can lay before you in support of the opinion which you have argued since the beginning of this second conversation; now we ask you to agree that we are right or to recognize that you have been wrong. We ask you, in the name of commonsense, to recognize the accuracy of the facts we have thus laid before you; we will repeat them in order to clarify our argument.

1. England has no constitution, since a constitution is a plan of social organization by means of which all the political institutions of a nation derive from the same principle and direct the national forces towards the same goal; whereas English social institutions are of two different kinds and they direct the national forces of that people towards two opposite goals.

2. The English social organization, being radically imperfect should not be presented to the French people as a model which it should try to imitate as closely as possible; and a revolutionary state of affairs will inevitably continue to exist in France until the governors and the governed have acquired clearer ideas about the means which should be employed to establish a fixed and stable social order.

3. Lastly, the crisis in which England and France find themselves involved will inevitably end in the complete abandonment of the feudal system and the exclusive establishment of the industrial system. The nations which today have the reputation of being the most civilized will never really emerge from barbarism until the time when the most hard-working and peaceful class has been given the direction of public power, and when the military class is completely subordinate.

Q. Do not go to so much trouble to answer our objections; that is not the most important point in your argument; you must combat the views of the father of science. You must prove that Montesquieu was mistaken; this is the only way you can ensure your system is adopted.

A. Science makes continual progress. Today, there is not a pupil of the Polytechnic who cannot solve, with the utmost ease, problems of geometry which taxed the genius of Archimedes; there is not one of these pupils who does not know more about geometry than that prodigious genius ever knew.

More than fifty years have passed since the publication of *l'Esprit des Lois*. Since then the most memorable political event in history has taken place: the French Revolution. Thus we can reason from facts which were entirely unknown to Montesquieu.

Montesquieu was a great admirer of the social régime which had been established in England and he was right, for it was undoubtedly very superior to anything which had gone before; but we must not conclude from this that, had Montesquieu been alive today, he would not have found a way of improving it considerably.

The English have accepted, as we have already said several times, they have invented political institutions with an industrial character and they have set them against the old feudal institutions which existed there; the result has been that the feudal government was far more constrained in England than in the other European countries.

The French Revolution did not take place till nearly a century after the English one; it inevitably resulted in an improvement on the English constitution; for, when we reflect on how the English constitution can be improved, the first thing which strikes us is that industrial power, which was introduced into the English social organization as a power to counterbalance feudal power, should become the leading power in France.

## ON LIBERALISM AND INDUSTRIALISM*

We invite all industrialists who are dedicated to the public good and who are aware of the connections between the general interests of society and those of industry no longer to allow themselves to be called *liberals*: we invite them to hoist a new flag and to inscribe upon their banner the device: *Industrialism.*

We address the same invitation to anyone, regardless of rank and profession, if he is profoundly convinced, as we are, that the only way to establish a calm and stable order of things lies in entrusting with the supreme administration of public wealth

* IV, 1, pp. 178–83; the second instalment, or volume, of the *Catéchisme* contained two Appendices, only the second of these is included here.

those who pour the greatest amount of money into the public treasury and who draw out the least; we invite them to call themselves *industrialists*.

It is mainly to the true royalists that we address this invitation, that is to say, we address it especially to those who desire that national prosperity should be the basis upon which the tranquillity and well-being of the House of Bourbon rests.

Q. What benefit do you think can result from this change of name? What advantage do you think the substitution of the word *industrialism* for that of *liberalism* would bring? What are the drawbacks attached to the word liberalism, that make you think it is so important to abandon it.

A. You put too many questions at once; which would you like us to answer first?

Q. Tell us what are the drawbacks attached to the word *liberalism*; what good can come of its abandonment by the party which wants to improve the social organization, using only loyal, legal and peaceful methods to attain this goal?

A. The denomination *liberalism* seems to us to have three great drawbacks for well-meaning men who march under this banner.

Q. What is the first of these drawbacks?

A. The word *liberalism* has a normative connotation* (signifies an order of sentiments); it does not indicate a class of interests; the result is that the expression is vague and therefore bad.

Q. What is the second drawback?

A. Most of those who allow themselves to be called *liberals* are peace-loving men, men who are animated by the desire to bring the revolution to an end, by establishing through loyal, legal and peaceful means a calm and stable order of things; an order of things which is in tune with the state of enlightenment and civilization. But the leaders of this party are men who have preserved the critical approach, that is they are eighteenth-century revolutionaries. All those who have played a part in the revolution, first as *patriots*, then as *Bonapartists*, today call themselves *liberals*; thus, the party which is called *liberal* is composed today of two kinds of men with different and even opposing opinions. The founders of this party are men whose main aim is to overturn any possible government in order to put themselves in its place; whereas the great majority of this same party wishes to give the government the greatest possible stability and strength, provided that it takes openly the direction called for by the national interests.

Once the designation *liberalism* has been adopted and pro-

* Literally: '*désigne un ordre de sentiments*'.

claimed by the remnants of the *patriotic* and *Bonapartist* party, the name has very great drawbacks for those whose essential purpose is the establishment of a stable order of things by peaceful means.

We do not claim that the patriots and Bonapartists have not rendered services to society; their energy was useful, because it was necessary to demolish before it was possible to build. But, today, the revolutionary spirit which animated them runs directly counter to the public interest; today a denomination which does not indicate a spirit directly opposed to the revolutionary spirit cannot be acceptable to enlightened and well-intentioned men.

Q. What is the third drawback attached to the denomination of *liberalism*?

A. The party which called itself *liberal* has been defeated, not only in France, but in Naples, in Spain, in England; the members of the extreme Left in France carry no more weight there than do Mr. Brougham and Robert Wilson in England. The many defeats of the *liberals* have proved that nations, as well as governments, do not want to adopt their political opinions: now, when it has been pointed out to sensible men that they have taken the wrong course and chosen bad guides, they quickly change direction.

We conclude from these three reasons that we have just given you that peaceful men whose opinion tends towards the setting up of a calm and stable order of things should make haste to proclaim that they no longer want to be called *liberals* and that they should inscribe a new device on their banner.

Q. Has this not been done already? Has not M. Ternaux remedied the drawback of which you speak, by publishing his profession of faith?

A. In France, there are three denominations of political parties; we call *ultras* those who want to retard civilization, by re-establishing the political influence of the nobility and of the clergy as it was before the Revolution.

We call *ministerials* those who support the intentions of the ministers, either because they are animated by the appetite for reward, or by the fear of falling back into revolution, or by both reasons at the same time.

We call *liberals* those who want to force the government to change course, either because they intend to overset the government in order to take its place themselves, or because they are determined to use only loyal, legal and pacific means to reach their goal.

We declare, and this is the object of this second appendix, that: 1. the time has come for the two classes who make up the party known as *liberal* to divide; 2. that the *liberals* who have the firm determination to use only peaceful means to direct the march of the government towards the national interests, have only one means of forming a group separate from those who have preserved the old political prescription of 'move over, so that I can take your place', and that this means lies in adopting a new name for this party.

[pp. 195–200]

Q. Let us now return to the question which concerns us in this second appendix. You have proved to us that the name *liberal* is no longer suitable for those who have decided only to employ loyal, legal and pacific means to persuade the government to act openly in the interests of the majority of the nation, that is to say, in the direction of the interests of the industrial class; you must now tell us what name these men should adopt in order to form a political party which will be quite separate from all those which have existed between 1789 and now.
A. The name *industrialism* for the policy of this new political party and that of *industrialist* for those who join this party seem best to us.
Q. What are the advantages of these names?
A. It seems to us that there are three great and quite separate advantages attaching to the name *industrialism*.
Q. What is the first of these advantages?
A. The name *industrialism* concentrates attention on interests, and it is consequently preferable to that of *liberalism* or to any designation which indicates only attitudes; because interests are far less variable than attitudes.

For example, today someone who is nobly born cannot truly be *liberal*, unless he works openly to abolish all the advantages which the nobility still enjoys in respect of esteem, power or the ability to obtain preferment; for, experience has shown us that a very small number of noblemen have enough tenacity to succeed in such an undertaking. Experience has proved to us that it is, in general, very easy for the government to influence reputedly *liberal* noblemen to take the government's part; the truth is that the number of nobles reputed to be *liberals* is very great but the number who really are *liberals* is extremely small. In the whole of the new nobility there is not one to be found; for it is obvious that every man who has allowed political privilege to be created in favour of himself and his descendants is an *anti-liberal*.

Q. What is the second advantage attached to the name *industrialist*?

A. The industrial class is the most numerous: thus anyone who declares himself to be an *industrialist*, in a single word, makes a profession of faith that he intends to support the interests of the majority of the nation against all individual interests.

Q. Tell us, lastly, what is your third reason for advising those who want to use only loyal, legal and peaceful methods to abandon the name *liberals* and to adopt that of *industrialists*?

A. In this instalment we have established:

First, that primitive men being ignorant and subject to violent passions, the law of survival of the fittest had to serve as the foundation of the first social organizations, and the nations had to live under the military system alone, and then under the feudal system, for many centuries; concentration of arbitrary powers in the hands of a few was a lesser evil than anarchy.

We then established that the human race was destined to become enlightened, to refine itself by trade, to acquire the taste for work and production and then to propose the common interest as the basis for its organization.

Lastly, we have shown that the transition from the first to the second political system gave rise to a long and violent crisis.

We now add to these thoughts, the idea that the crisis of transition was started by the preaching of Luther, and that the object of our catechism of the industrialists is to bring it to an end.

I add that, from the time of Luther until today, the human spirit has been cast in a critical and revolutionary mould because the feudal government had to be overthrown before it was possible to work towards the establishment of the industrial organization of society; but that today, when the industrial class has become the strongest, the critical and revolutionary spirit must be extinguished and be replaced by a peaceful drive towards organization.

It is with the purpose of marking the formation of the party of peace and organization that we invite those persons who want to set up a calm, stable order of things to adopt the name of *industrialists*, because this name indicates both the end and the means: the end is to base the organization of society upon the interests of the majority; the means are to entrust the most important industrialists with the administration of public wealth.

Q. We regret deeply that the name of *patriot* should have been degraded and completely debased by the *sans-culottes*; for this name signifies an interest common to all the members of the nation: the national interest; and it was by this means, that not only one class in society but all classes were indiscriminately called upon to form this party.

A. The denomination of *patriotism*, even had it not been debased by *sans-culottism*, does not have the same value as that of *industrialism*. This is our opinion, and we shall justify it.

Let us first analyse the idea of *patriotism*; we find as follows: A *patriot* is a man whose sentiments are dominated by his affection for the national society of which he is a member; he is a man who is always ready to sacrifice all of his fortune and all his credit in the interests of his nation. Brutus immolating his son and thus sacrificing his paternal feeling to his affection for the Romans was a true model of *patriotism*.

We ask you now to tell us if, in the present state of enlightenment and civilization, men can or should be *patriots*?

We are convinced that having thought about it, you will agree that philanthropic sentiments, those new family sentiments of *Europeanism*, take precedence today among all Europeans over their national sentiments. You will recognize that what we have just said is true even of the English.

The best code of moral sentiments which we possess is that of Christian morality. Now, in this code much is said about the reciprocal duties of the members of the same family; the code tells all men to regard themselves as brothers, but it never urges men to subordinate their philanthropic and family feelings to *patriotism*.

# X

# New Christianity*

He who loves his neighbour has fulfilled the law.
The whole of the law is contained in these words:
You shall love your neighbour as yourself.
Saint Paul's *Epistle to the Romans*

### PREFACE

The extract which the reader is about to read was intended to form part of the second volume of *Opinions littéraires, philosophiques et industrielles*; but the subject with which it deals is so important in itself, and so much part of existing political conditions that it has been thought better to publish it separately and immediately.

To recall peoples and kings to the true spirit of Christianity, at a time when they have become most alienated from it, when laws on *sacrilege* are passed, and Catholics and Protestants in England are looking for ways to bring this long and painful struggle to an end; at the same time, to try to specify the action of religious feeling in society, when all men to a greater or lesser degree are aware of it or at least recognize the need to respect it in others; when the most distinguished writers are trying to discover its origin, forms and progress and when, on the other hand, theology is trying to stifle it under the weight of superstition: this is the principal aim that is pursued in the following dialogues.

The ministers of the different Christian sects who regard each other as heretics and who, in the true and moral sense of Christianity are all heretics in varying degrees, these ministers, we say, will certainly object to such an accusation and to the work in which it is put forward; but it is not mainly to them that this work is addressed, it is addressed to all who, whether they are classed as Catholics, or Lutheran Protestants, or Reformed Protestants, or Anglicans, or even Jews, see the primary end of religion as morality; to all who accept the greatest freedom of worship and dogma and yet are far from being in-

* *Nouveau Christianisme; Dialogues entre un conservateur et un novateur*, III, pp. 101–18, 172–92, Paris, 1825.

different towards morality, and who feel the constant need to purify and to perfect it and to extend its sway over all classes in society, while preserving its religious character; it is addressed, in a word, to all who are convinced that there was something truly sublime, something divine, in primitive Christianity, which was the predominance of morality over all the rest of the law, that is, over forms of worship and dogma, and who realize at the same time that the object of worship and dogma is to fix the attention of the faithful upon divine morality. From this point of view, criticism of Catholicism, of Protestantism and of the other Christian sects becomes inevitable as it has been proved that none of the sects has fulfilled the views of the founder of Christianity.

The desire to purify morality, to simplify worship and dogma impels many to set up a particular Protestant sect, for example, the so-called *reformed* religion, as the inevitable means of transition to a new religious order, or a even as definitive choice. They base their opinion upon what it is in that particular religion which brings it nearer to the spirit of Christianity than all the others, and they will certainly resent any attacks which they think are being made on Protestantism.

This is only one answer to the argument: mankind is not condemned merely to imitate; and it often happens that, while we fully appreciate the benefit that a former age gained from adopting a particular opinion or institution, this approval of what was done should go hand-in-hand with the establishment of an even better opinion or institution, and mistakes made in this respect are both harmful and ephemeral.

As for those who see ideas about God and revelation merely as formulae which had some use in the Dark Ages, and who regard the use of such formulae in the nineteenth century as anti-philosophical; these people who think that they can refute the author of this work with a *Voltairian sneer*, will probably look to their allegedly philosophical systems for a more general formula for morality, simpler and more popular than the Christian one; and if they only find as a substitute for it pure reason and the natural law, revealed in the hearts of all men, they should abandon the battle of words; besides, they would soon see how vague and uncertain is their use of words. If they can continue to doubt the supernatural excellence of the Christian principle, they should at least respect it as the most universal principle which men have ever used, as the highest theory which has been produced in eighteen hundred years.

### FIRST DIALOGUE*

*Conservative*. Do you believe in God?
*Reformer*. Yes, I believe in God.
*C*. Do you believe that the Christian religion has a divine origin?
*R*. Yes.
*C*. If the Christian religion is divine in origin, it cannot be improved; yet in your writings you urge the artists, industrialists and scientists to improve upon this religion: you thus become involved in a contradiction of yourself, since your opinion and your belief are opposed.
*R*. The contradiction which you think that you see between my opinion and my belief is only an apparent one; what God Himself has said must be distinguished from what the clergy have said in His name.

What God has said can certainly not be improved upon, but what the clergy have said in His name makes up a whole science which can be improved, as can all the other human sciences. Theological theory needs to be renovated at various times, in the same way as physics, chemistry and physiology.
*C*. What part of religion do you think is divine and what part do you consider to be human?
*R*. God has said: *Men should treat each other like brothers*; this sublime principle encompasses all that is divine in the Christian religion.
*C*. What! You reduce to a single principle all that is divine in the Christian religion!
*R*. God has of necessity related everything to a single principle; He has inevitably deduced everything from a single principle; without this, His will towards men would not have been systematic. It would be blasphemy to claim that the All-Powerful founded His religion upon many principles.

Now, according to this principle which God gave to men to guide their conduct, they should organize their society in the way which can be most advantageous to the greatest number; they should have as their goal in all their work, in all their actions the speediest and most complete improvement possible of the moral and physical existence of the most numerous class.

I say that it is in this and in this alone that the divine part of Christianity resides.
*C*. I agree that God has given men a single principle; I admit

* The subtitle of *Nouveau Christianisme* is *Dialogues entre un conservateur et un novateur*—'Dialogues between a conservative and a reformer'.

that He ordered them to organize their society in such a way as to guarantee the speediest and most complete improvement of the moral and physical condition of the poorest class: but I would like to point out to you that God left guides for the human race. Before He ascended into Heaven again, Jesus Christ entrusted His apostles and their successors with the direction of the conduct of men, by showing them how they should apply the basic principle of divine morality, and by making it easy for them to draw the most just conclusions from this principle.

Do you acknowledge that the Church is a divine institution?

*R.* I believe that the Christian church was founded by God Himself; I am imbued with the most profound respect and the greatest admiration for the behaviour of the Fathers of the Church.

These leaders of the early Church openly preached the unity of all peoples; they tried to make them live together in peace; they declared positively and energetically to the powerful that their first duty was to employ all their resources towards the most rapid improvement of the moral and physical condition of the poor.

These leaders of the early Church wrote the best book that has ever been published, *The Primitive Catechism*, in which they divided men's actions into two categories, good and bad, that is to say, actions which conform to the basic principle of divine morality and those which are opposed to it.

*C.* Explain your ideas more fully and tell me if you consider that the Christian Church is infallible.

*R.* If the leaders of the Church were those who were most capable of directing the energies of society towards the divine goal, I believe that the Church might be regarded as infallible and that society would do well to let itself be guided by them.

I consider that the Fathers of the Church were infallible for the times in which they lived, whereas the clergy of today seem to me, of all the institutionalized bodies, to make the greatest mistakes, mistakes which are most damaging to society; and their behaviour is the most directly opposed to the basic principle of divine morality.

*C.* The Christian religion is then, according to you in a very parlous condition.

*R.* On the contrary; never have there existed such a great number of good Christians; but today they are almost all to be found among the laity. Since the fifteenth century the Christian religion has lost its unity of action. Since that time there have been no more Christian clergy; all the clergy who today try to graft their own opinions, morality, forms of worship and dogma on to the moral principle which men received from God are heretics, since their opinions, their morality, their dogma and their forms of worship are to a greater or lesser extent in opposition to the divine morality; the most powerful Church of old is the one in which heresy is the strongest.

*C.* What will become of the Christian religion if, as you say, those who are responsible for teaching it have become heretics?

*R.* Christianity will become the universal and only religion; the Asians and the Africans will be converted; the members of the European clergy will become good Christians and will abandon the different heresies which they profess today. The true doctrine of Christianity, that is, the most universal doctrine which can be deduced from the fundamental principle of divine morality will manifest itself and at once the differences which exist between religious opinions will disappear.

Primitive Christian doctrine only gave society a partial and incomplete organization. The dues of Caesar remained independent of the dues granted to the Church. *Render unto Caesar the things which are Caesar's*, is the famous maxim which separated the two powers. The temporal power has continued to base its authority upon the law of force, while the Church has preached that society should only recognize as legitimate those institutions which aim at improving the condition of the poorest class.

The new Christian organization will derive temporal as well as spiritual institutions from the principle that *all men should act as brothers towards one another*. It will direct all institutions no matter what they may be towards the increased well-being of the poorest class.

*C.* On what facts do you base this opinion? What authorizes you to believe that a single moral principle will become the universal rule for all human societies?

*R.* The most universal morality, divine morality must become the only morality; this is the direct consequence of its nature and origin.

The people of God, those who received revelations before the coming of Jesus, a people which is the most widely scattered over the earth, has always felt that the Christian religion, founded by the Fathers of the Church was incomplete; it has always proclaimed that a great age would come, to which it has given the name of *Messianic*, an age when religious doctrine will be presented in the most universal way possible; when it will rule the actions of the temporal power as well as the spiritual power; and when all mankind will have only one religion and one organization.

So I see the new Christian doctrine clearly, and I shall set it forth; then I shall go on to review all the spiritual and temporal institutions which exist in England, France, Northern and Southern Germany, Italy, Spain and Russia, in North and South America. I shall compare the doctrines of these different institutions with that which is derived directly from the fundamental principle of divine morality, and I shall easily convince all men of good faith and good will that if all institutions were directed towards the goal of improving the moral and physical well-being of the poorest class, they would achieve the prosperity of all classes in society, all nations, with the greatest possible speed.

I am a reformer because I draw the most direct consequences ever made to date from the fundamental principle of divine morality. You who are as zealous as I am for the public good and who are animated by a conservative spirit, limit your task to that of preventing men from losing sight of the very principle which I wish to develop. Well, let us combine our efforts; I shall present my ideas to you, and you should fight them when it seems to you that I am straying from the path decreed to man by the Almighty.

It is with complete confidence that I undertake this task. The best theologian is the one who applies the fundamental principle of divine morality in the most universal ways; the best theologian is the real Pope, he is the Vicar of God upon earth. If my deductions are correct, if the doctrine which I am about to develop is good, I shall have spoken in the name of God.

I shall come to the point. I shall begin by examining the different religions which exist today; I shall compare their doctrines with that which is derived directly from the fundamental principle of divine morality.

*On Religions*

The New Christianity will be composed of sects very similar to those which today compose the various heretical associations in Europe and America.

The New Christianity, like the heretical associations, will have its own morality, its own form of worship and its own dogma; it will have its own clergy with its own leaders. But, despite this similarity of organization, the New Christianity will be purged of all the present heresies; morality will be the most important thing for the new Christians; the form of worship and dogma will be seen only as accessories, whose purpose is to fix the attention of the faithful of all classes upon morality.

In the New Christianity, all morality will be derived directly from this principle: *men should treat one another as brothers*; and this principle which is part of primitive Christianity, will undergo a *transfiguration* after which it will be presented as being the necessary end of all religious works today.

This principle, regenerated, will be presented in the following way: *Religion should guide society towards the great goal of the most rapid improvement possible in the lot of the poorest class.*

Those who must found the New Christianity and make themselves the leaders of the new church should be the men who are most capable of contributing by their work to the increased well-being of the poorest class. The functions of the clergy will be confined to teaching the new Christian doctrine, which the leaders of the church will work unceasingly to perfect.

Here, briefly, is the character which true Christianity should develop in present circumstances. We shall compare this conception of religious institutions with the religions which exist today in Europe and America; from that comparison we shall easily prove that all the allegedly Christian religions of today are simply heresies, that is, that they do not aim directly at the most rapid improvement possible in the well-being of the poorest class, which is the sole end of Christianity. . . .

*

*C.* I have followed your discourse attentively; while you were speaking my own ideas became clearer, my doubts disappeared and I felt my love and admiration for the Christian religion increasing; my attachment to the religious system which has civilized Europe has not prevented me from seeing that it is possible to improve it and, on this point, you have entirely convinced me.

It is clear that the moral principle: *All men should treat each other like brothers*, given by God to His Church, encompasses all the ideas which you express in this precept: *The whole of society should work to improve the moral and physical existence of the poorest class; it should organize itself in the way most suited to allow it to achieve this great end.*

It is equally certain that in the beginnings of Christianity this principle had to be expressed in the words of the first formula and that today it is the second formula which should be used.

At the time of the foundation of Christianity, as you have

said, society was divided into two classes of a completely different political nature: those of the masters and the slaves, constituting two distinct species of humanity, which were, nevertheless, intertwined the one with the other. It was then absolutely impossible to establish completely reciprocal moral relations between the two species: and so the divine founder of the Christian religion was confined to stating His moral principle in a manner which made it obligatory for every individual in both species of humanity, without being able to establish it a link which could unite masters and slaves.

We live now at a time in which slavery has been destroyed; only men of the same political species exist; classes are only separated by slight differences: you conclude from this state of affairs that the fundamental principle of Christianity should be presented in a form most likely to make it obligatory for the masses among themselves, without it, as a result of this, ceasing to be obligatory for individuals in their individual relations. I consider your conclusion legitimate and of the greatest importance; and from this moment, as a new Christian, I unite my efforts with yours in spreading the New Christianity.

But, in this respect, I have some remarks to make on the general direction of your work. The new form in which you present the principle of Christianity embraces your entire thinking on the system of social organization; a system which is supported at the same time by philosophical arguments from the realm of the sciences, the fine arts and industry, and by the religious sentiment which is most widely spread in the civilized world, the Christian sentiment.

Well, why did you not present this system, the object of all your thinking, from the religious point of view from the highest and the most popular point of view first of all? Why did you address the industrialists, the scientists and the artists instead of going straight to the people by way of religion? And at this very moment, why did you waste precious time criticizing the Catholics and the Protestants, instead of establishing your religious doctrine at once? Do you want it to be said of you, as it was said of Luther: *He was a good critic, but his doctrine was poor?*

The intellectual forces of man are very small; it is only by forcing them to unite towards a single end, it is only by directing them towards the same point, that one can successfully produce a great effect and obtain an important result. Why do you begin by using your critical powers, instead of starting with a doctrine? Why do you not immediately attack openly the question of the new Christianity?

You have discovered the way to stop religious indifference in the most numerous class; for the poor cannot be indifferent to a religion which has the overt aim of improving their physical and moral condition as quickly as possible.

Since you have succeeded in restating this fundamental principle of Christianity in a completely new way, should not your first concern be to spread knowledge of this regenerated principle among the class which is most interested in having it accepted? And as this class by itself is infinitely more numerous than all the others put together, your undertaking would be bound to succeed.

You should have begun by attracting a great many followers who would support you in your attack on the Catholics and Protestants.

Finally, when once you were clearly aware of the power, the fertility and the irresistible nature of your idea, you should at once have made it into a doctrine, without taking any precaution and without feeling any anxiety that its spread would be hindered by any political obstacle or any major refutation.

You say: 'Society should be organized in accordance with the principle of Christian morality; all classes should contribute with all their might to the moral and physical improvement of the existence of the members of the most numerous class; every social institution should contribute as actively and as directly as possible to the achievement of this great religious objective.

'In the present state of enlightenment and civilization, no political right should be put forward because it derives from the law of what is most powerful for individuals or from the law of the right of conquest for the masses; monarchy is no longer legitimate unless the kings use their power to force the rich to contribute towards the improvement of the moral and physical condition of the poor.'

What obstacles can such a doctrine encounter? Are not those who have an interest in upholding it infinitely more numerous than those who have an interest in hindering its acceptance? The supporters of this doctrine take their stand on the principle of divine morality, while their opponents have no weapons with which to oppose them other than the habits formed in the age of ignorance and barbarism, supported by the principles of Jesuitical egoism.

In short, I think that you should immediately spread your new doctrine and set up missions in all the civilized nations to persuade them to adopt it.

*R.* The new Christians should develop the same character and follow the course of the Christians of the early Church; they should use only their intelligence to persuade men to accept their doctrine. It is only through persuasion and demonstration that they should work for the conversion of Catholics and Protestants; it is by means of persuasion and demonstration that they will succeed in convincing these misguided Christians to renounce the heresies with which the papist and Lutheran religions are tainted, so that they can adopt the New Christianity wholeheartedly.

The New Christianity, like primitive Christianity, will be supported, aided and protected by the force of morality and by the omnipotence of public opinion; and if unfortunately, its acceptance should give rise to acts of violence and unjust condemnations, it would be the new Christians who would suffer these acts of violence and unjust condemnations; but in no circumstances would they themselves use physical force against their opponents; in no circumstances would they appear either as judges or as executioners.

Having found the way to rejuvenate Christianity through a transformation of its fundamental principle, my first concern, as it had to be, was to take all the precautions necessary to prevent the new doctrine influencing the poor to commit acts of violence against the rich and the governments.

I had first to address myself to the rich and powerful to win their approval for the new doctrine, by convincing them that it was not opposed to their interests, because it would clearly be impossible to improve the moral and physical existence of the poor by any means other than those which would tend to increase the enjoyment of the rich.

I had to convince the artists, scientists and industrial leaders that their interests were essentially the same as those of the mass of the people; that they belong to the class of workers, while at the same time they are its natural leaders; that the approval of the mass of the people for the services they rendered to them was the only reward worthy of their glorious endeavours. I had to stress this point, given that it is of the greatest importance, since it is the only way to provide the nations with leaders who truly deserve their confidence, leaders who are capable of directing their opinions and of bringing them to the state where they can form sound judgements on the political measures which are favourable or opposed to the interests of the greatest number. Finally, I had to show the Catholics and Protestants when exactly it was that they took the wrong turning, in order to make it easier for them to return to the right course. I must insist on this point, because the conversion of the Catholic and Protestant clergy would provide powerful support for the New Christianity.

After this explanation, I take up again the thread of my ideas: I shall not stop to examine all the religious sects which have sprung from Protestantism; the most important of them, Anglicanism, is so closely linked with the national institutions of England that it can only be properly seen in relation to all these institutions, and this examination will take place when I have reviewed, as I said I would, all the spiritual and temporal institutions in Europe and America. The Greek schism has remained up to the present outside the European system and I shall not deal with it; and besides, all the elements of the criticism of these different heresies are to be found in the criticism of Protestantism.

But my aim is not only to prove the heresy of Catholics and Protestants; in order to rejuvenate Christianity completely, it is not enough for me to ensure that it triumphs over all the old religious philosophies; I must also establish its scientific superiority over all the philosophical doctrines which have placed themselves outside religion. I must reserve the development of this idea for a further conversation, but, in the meanwhile, I shall give you a brief outline of the whole of my work.

Mankind has never ceased to progress, but it has not always proceeded in the same way nor used the same methods to increase the sum of knowledge and to perfect its civilization: on the contrary, observation shows that from the fifteenth century until the present, humanity has proceeded in a manner quite different from that which it followed from the establishment of Christianity up to the fifteenth century.

From the establishment of Christianity up to the fifteenth century, the human race was mainly concerned with the coordination of its general ideas, with the establishment of a universal and single principle and with the foundation of a general institution designed to superimpose the aristocracy of talent on the aristocracy of birth, and thus to subject all particular interests to the general one. Throughout this whole period, direct observation of private interests, of particular facts and secondary principles was neglected and despised by most of the enlightened men, and the opinion prevailed that secondary principles should be deduced from general facts and from a universal principle: this was a purely speculative opinion, given that human intelligence has not the means to establish generalizations accurate enough for particular facts to be drawn from them as direct consequences.

The observations which I have made in this dialogue, in examining Catholicism and Protestantism, are linked to this important fact.

Since the dissolution of the spiritual power in Europe as a result of Luther's revolt, that is, since the fifteenth century, the human spirit has detached itself from universal ideas: it has indulged itself in specialization; it has been engaged in the analysis of particular facts, and the private interests of the different social classes; it has striven to define the secondary principles which might serve as a basis for the different branches of knowledge; and, during this second period, the opinion has become established that considerations of general facts, of general principles and of the general interests of the human race were only vague and metaphysical, and could usefully contribute nothing to the progress of enlightenment and to the improvement of civilization.

Thus the human spirit has, since the fifteenth century, followed a course opposed to that which it followed up to that time; and certainly the important and positive progress which resulted in every branch of knowledge proved irrevocably how mistaken our medieval ancestors were in underestimating the study of particular facts, secondary principles and the analysis of private interests.

But it is equally true that great harm was done to society by the state of neglect in which, since the fifteenth century, work on the study of general facts, general principles and general interests was left. This neglect gave rise to the egoism which came to dominate all classes and individuals. This sentiment, once dominant in all classes and individuals, gave to Caesar the means to recover much of the political force which he had lost before the fifteenth century. It is to this egoism that we must attribute the political sickness of our age; a sickness which affects all those who do useful work in society; a sickness which enables kings to absorb a great part of the wages of the poor for their personal expenditure, and for that of their courtiers and soldiers; a sickness which gives royalty and the hereditary aristocracy the opportunity to steal that esteem which is due to the scientists, artists and industrial leaders for their direct and positive service to society.

It is therefore desirable that studies aimed at the improvement of our knowledge of universal facts, principles and interests should be resumed promptly and should be protected by society from now on, to the same extent as those studies concerned with particular facts, secondary principles and individual interests.

These, briefly, are the ideas which will be developed in our second conversation, the object of which will be to describe Christianity from the theoretical and scientific point of view, and to establish the superiority of the Christian theory over all particular philosophies, religious or scientific.

Finally, in the third dialogue, I shall deal directly with the New Christianity, or definitive Christianity. I shall describe its morality, its form of worship and its dogma; I shall put forward a creed for the new Christians.

I shall show that this doctrine is the only social doctrine suitable for the Europeans in their present state of enlightenment and civilization. I shall prove that the adoption of this doctrine offers the best and most peaceful means of remedying the great evils which have resulted from the encroachment of physical force on the spiritual power, which occurred in the fifteenth century, and of stopping this encroachment by reorganizing the spiritual power upon new foundations and giving it the necessary strength to curb the unlimited claims of the temporal power.

I shall further prove that the adoption of the New Christianity, by combining the study of the general principles of knowledge with those which aim at the improvement of specialized knowledge, do far more to accelerate the progress of civilization than any other general measure.

I conclude this first dialogue by declaring openly to you what I think about Christian revelation.

We are certainly far superior to our ancestors in the positive and specialized, useful sciences; it is only since the fifteenth century, and mainly since the beginning of the last century, that we have made great advances in mathematics, physics, chemistry and physiology. But there is a science much more important for society than physics and mathematics: it is the science which forms society; the science on which it is founded; it is morality; now, morality has followed a course diametrically opposed to that of the physical and mathematical sciences. Its fundamental principle was produced more than eighteen hundred years ago and since that time all the researches of men of the greatest genius have not been able to discover a principle superior in its universality or precision to the one produced in that age by the founder of Christianity; I shall go further: when society lost sight of this principle, when it ceased to take it as the general guide to its conduct, it at once fell again under Caesar's yoke; that is, under the sway of physical force which this principle had subordinated to intellectual force.

I now ask whether the intelligence which produced the governing principle of the human race eighteen hundred years ago—fifteen hundred years before we had made any significant progress in the physical and mathematical sciences—is not clearly of a supernatural nature, and whether a greater proof of the revelation of Christianity exists?

Yes, I believe that Christianity is a divine institution and I am convinced that God extends a special protection to those who direct their efforts to subordinating all human institutions to the fundamental principle of this sublime doctrine; I am convinced that I myself am fulfilling a divine mission in recalling peoples and kings to the true spirit of Christianity. And, full of confidence in the divine protection accorded to my work in a special way, I am bold enough to criticize the conduct of the kings of Europe, who have formed a coalition, and who have given to their union the sacred name of the *Holy Alliance*; I speak directly to them; I dare to say to them:

PRINCES,

What is the nature, what is the character in the eyes of God and of Christians, of the power which you wield?

What is the basis of the system of social organization which you work to establish? What measures have you taken to improve the moral and physical existence of the poor?

You call yourselves Christians, and yet you base your power on physical force, and you are still nothing more than the successors of Caesar; and you forget that the true Christians put before themselves as the final goal of their endeavours the complete abolition of the power of the sword, the power of Caesar, which is, by its very nature, essentially transitory.

And yet it is this power which you have undertaken to make the basis of the social system! To it alone, according to you, belongs the initiative in all the general improvements demanded by the progress of enlightenment. In order to support this monstrous system, you keep two million men under arms, you force the tribunals to adopt your principle and you have forced the Catholic, Protestant and Greek clergy to preach the heresy that the power of Caesar is the governing power of Christian society.

In recalling the peoples to the Christian religion by the symbol of your union, in giving them the peace which is the greatest good for them, you still have not won any gratitude from them; your personal interest is only too obvious in the devices which you present as being for the general interest. The supreme European power which rests in your hands is far from being a Christian power as it ought to be. The moment you act, you display the character and insignia of physical power, of the anti-Christian force.

All the measures of any importance which you have taken since you united in the Holy Alliance, have made the lot of the poor worse, not only for this generation but even for future generations. You have increased taxes, you increase them every year, in order to defray the larger costs of your armed soldiers and the luxury of your courtiers. The class among your subjects to which you extend a special protection is the nobility which, like yourselves, bases all its rights upon the sword.

However, your culpable conduct can be excused on several counts: one thing has led you into error and that is the approval given to your common efforts to overthrow the power of the modern Caesar. In fighting against him, you acted in a truly Christian way; but it is only because in the hands of Napoleon the authority of Caesar, which he won, had far more power than in yours, where it came only through inheritance. Your conduct can also be excused on another score: because it was the clergy who should have stopped you on the edge of the precipice, but who threw themselves over it with you.

PRINCES,

Hearken to the voice of God which speaks to you through me, and become a good Christian once more; cease to think of the armed forces, the nobility, the heretical priests and the perverted judges as your main supports; united in the name of Christianity, learn how to accomplish all the duties which Christianity imposes upon the powerful; remember that Christianity commands you to use all your power to increase the social well-being of the poor as rapidly as possible!

# XI
# On the Social Organization

## FIRST FRAGMENT

### *Comparison of the development of the individual intelligence and the general intelligence*

*De l'organisation sociale, fragments d'un ouvrage inédit* (V, 1, pp. 107–55), although written early in Saint-Simon's life, was published only after his death; but the subsequent text—*La classe des prolétaires*—is one of his latest writings, left in an unfinished draft.

If we observe the way in which members of the human race develop morally and physically from their birth until they reach manhood, we see that they develop in two different ways which, nevertheless, point to a common end: the most complete development of the moral and physical strength of which their organism is capable.

From the birth of individuals until they reach manhood, a moral and physical growth takes place in them which is gradual and continuous, but very slow. They also go through various crises which regulate their general, very rapid progress.

At the age of seven they go through a teething crisis, after which their emotional faculties and their ability to memorize suddenly increase.

Towards the age of fourteen, passions tend to break free from parental authority and the individual chooses the friends which he himself desires, and at the same time he acquires the ability to reproduce.

At twenty-one, a man having developed his moral and physical strength to the full, acquires his own character; his faculties are co-ordinated and directed towards his own particular bent.

If we go on to observe the laws and customs which society has established in order to regulate its conduct towards children from their birth until they have attained their majority, we see that legislators have recognized the existence and effects of the three crises we have just mentioned, and that they have apportioned the rights which they grant to the rising generation according to their view of its intellectual development at seven, fourteen and twenty-one years of age.

And it is a fact that they have declared children under seven to be incapable of sin, that is to say, incapable of governing their own conduct and hence of committing faults for which they could be held responsible and which are punishable in divine or human law; consequently, they devised the law in such a way that the dispositions dealing with children under seven were only intended to set up a general surveillance of the conduct of the children's natural protectors by society and to establish ways of replacing these when they were lacking.

The legislators only meted out correctional punishment to children up to fourteen, no matter how serious were the crimes they had committed, and they only accepted their emancipation if they had lost their parents.

They set the age of majority at twenty-one, considering this to be the time when individuals have generally acquired enough intelligence and a broad enough capacity for foresight for it to be unnecessary for them to remain under special surveillance any longer in the general interests of society.

If at the end of this series of observations, one examines the practices of the university in public education and instruction one sees that they fit in exactly with the legislative dispositions which we have just mentioned.

The public instruction of children does not begin before the age of seven.

From seven to fourteen, education plays a more important role than instruction, that is to say, the supervisors of the children's conduct during this time, in the schools and colleges, have a far greater influence over them than the teachers from whom they receive instruction.

From fourteen to twenty-one, the influence of the professors over the pupils is far greater than that exerted over them by their supervisors.

And at twenty-one, those who continue to follow the courses at the *Collège de France*, or in other establishments of public instruction, often find themselves free from any kind of supervision.

Lastly, if one observes the degree of intellectual development reached today by the French nation (whose revolution has placed it at the head of the human species as far as civilization is concerned), one sees that the country has passed the state of the third crisis and that its present social age corresponds to that of twenty-one in individuals; one also recognizes that the French nation proclaimed its majority on 4 August 1789 by abolishing all the institutions spawned by that state of slavery which was the primitive state of the industrial class, the body of the nation.

And after that, if one wants to draw a conclusion, one combines the various observations we have put forward, considers them, and draws from them the following inevitable conclusion:

Now that the French people has reached its majority as a nation, through the development of its intelligence, a radical change must follow in its social organization.

Having reached the highest possible vantage point on the road to civilization—which we have just traced—the philosopher will discern, on the one hand, the remotest past and, on the other, the most distant future; he will see in the background of the picture the establishment of slavery—a philanthropic institution when it was set up, for it saved the lives of millions of men; to it we owe the immense size of the population of the human race today, because it favoured the progress of enlightenment by supplying the ruling class with the means of developing their intelligence; they could not have done this without the establishment of slavery, since their time and their energy would have been taken up with work essential to the satisfaction of their basic needs. The philosopher will go on to consider, with lively satisfaction, and looking at that part of the road leading to the place where he is now standing, the diminution of slavery, the progress of enlightenment, the gradual improvement in the lot of the human race and, lastly, in the state of the French nation, which today forms its *avant-garde*, the complete abolition of slavery and a readiness to accept a social organization which has the good of the majority as its primary object.

From this point of view, the philosopher, as he glances now to the past, now to the future, will perceive more and more striking differences between the social condition of our ancestors and that of our descendants; he will recognize that among our ancestors the greatest degree of social importance was given to birth, to favour, and to the ability to govern; and then, turning to the future, he will see that social importance has been acquired by the greatest moral ability in science and industry.

Looking at the people in the mass in the past, he will see them engaged in armed struggle; considering them in the future, he will see them competing among themselves under the three great aspects of morality, science and industry.

Hitherto, men have walked backwards on the path of civilization, turning their backs on the future; they have usually had their gaze fixed on the past and they have glanced only very seldom and cursorily at the future. Now that slavery has been destroyed, it is upon the future that men should mainly concentrate.

Until slavery was abolished, governing had to be the principal activity; today, more and more, it need only be a subordinate activity.

## SECOND FRAGMENT

*Proofs that the French proletariat is capable of administering property well*

It must be proved here that the most numerous class, that is, the people, is today made up of men who no longer need to be supervised, whose intelligence is sufficiently mature and whose foresight is developed[1] enough for it to be possible to establish a system of social organization of which they will become full members.

The people can be considered to be divided into two classes: that of the workers occupied in agricultural labour, and that of men employed by manufacturers and by merchants.

Let us examine first the question of the agricultural workers.

With the sale of the national domains many thousands of proletarians, profiting from the unlimited opportunities which were offered to those who had enough character to declare themselves before the whole European aristocracy to be purchasers of such properties, passed suddenly into the class of landowners. Now, the way in which this mass of proletarians, who had suddenly become proprietors, has administered its property, has proved and established a major political fact, which is, that the lowest class in the nation is today composed of men whose intelligence is sufficiently developed and whose capacity for foresight is sufficiently strong for the law to be able to give up the tutelage it has exercised over them, without any disruption of public order; and that, from now on, since the nation should be considered as being composed of individuals who are all capable of administering property, the law should establish a political system in which the direction of the common interests will be entrusted to the men who are most distinguished by their positive and useful capacities, and government activity should deal only with those men whose conduct tends to be a threat to public order.

We shall quote an instance of which we were personally an eye-witness and which proves how far the capacity to administer

1. See the note at the end of this fragment.

property today is generally possessed by men whom the accident of birth has placed in the proletarian class.

A little province called the Cateau-Cambrésis belonged entirely to the archdiocese of Cambrai and to other ecclesiastical establishments; the inhabitants of this little province were so completely proletarian in relation to landed property that there was not one of them who could not be dispossessed of the land he occupied.

What happened when the land of this province was put up for sale?

All the inhabitants, with one accord, joined together; they made themselves the adjudicators of the territory of their communes; they then shared it out in such a way that the whole mass of the population, passed all at once from the class of the proletariat into the class of the proprietors.

Well! This change did not cause the slightest upset in the working of the land; the new owners showed that they were far more capable than the former ones, since the next year the land produced larger crops than ever before.

From what happened after the sale of the national domains, and from the local instance which we have just quoted to support the general fact, the consequence can clearly be drawn that the French people (given the present state of the development of its intelligence) can be governed far better and far more cheaply than it is at present; and that it will only achieve a stable society when governmental activity is transcended by the authority of men possessing to the highest degree abilities of the most widespread and positive utility.

Let us pass on now to the examination of the proofs of ability which have been given by the workers in the enterprises of the manufacturers and merchants.

At the beginning of the Revolution, a great number of manufacturers and merchants were ruined by the looting which took place during the insurrections; those entrepreneurs who escaped the looting were crushed by the law of the *maximum*, and those who were fortunate enough to escape both these industrial calamities, or to survive them financially, had their wealth seized by requisition and by the burning of English merchandize.

What would have happened after such widespread misfortunes if a great many workers who had been employed by the manufacturers and merchants, who were ruined and morally crushed by these misfortunes, if, as we say, a great many of these workers had not had the ability to replace them?

What would have happened is that the factories and the trade of France would have lost much of their importance for a long time, and that France today would have to pay to foreigners an industrial tribute far greater than the one she paid before the Revolution; in short, production would have decreased in France.

What has actually happened, on the contrary, is that production of every kind has infinitely increased since then, even during the evils of the Revolution; what has happened is that, in all the workshops and shops, the men who were employed as simple workers have become managers and directors of these works and have proved themselves to be more intelligent and more dynamic than their predecessors; so that France today is infinitely more prosperous, more productive and more important in agriculture, manufacturing and commerce than she was before the Revolution, although the greatest number among the present directors of all these kinds of work have emerged from the class of the people.

Can there be a stronger and more complete proof that the class of the people, that is, the vast majority of the population, has reached a level of intelligence, sufficient for the establishment in France of a social organization of society with the public good as its direct object, without any disturbance of the public order and, on the contrary, with great advantages for all classes of society?

## NOTE ON THE SECOND FRAGMENT

The education of men of all classes is divided into two parts, thus: education proper, and instruction.

The improvement of education proper is more important for the increase of the social well-being than that of instruction.

It is education proper which forms the habits, which develops the feelings, which broadens the capacity to take a general view of things; it is education which teaches all men to apply principles and to use them as sure guides to direct their conduct. Education can be seen as the continuous teaching of branches of knowledge which are indispensably necessary to the maintenance of the relations established between the members of society.

Let us imagine children, who have received the fullest instruction and have been utterly deprived of education; let us admit for a moment the existence of an establishment in which the children attend the lessons of the best teachers in every subject and are shut away separately during the interval between classes to avoid any kind of distraction. These children would be completely deprived of education as a result: what would happen to them when their studies ended? What would become of them when they went out into the world?

These children would not know the one thing which is most useful if they are to live successfully in society; they would have no experience of relationships; they would have to serve a very long apprenticeship before they were able to fulfil any sort of social function; and if a population thus raised were left to itself it would hardly be superior in terms of civilization to the first primitive societies of the human race.

We would add, in support of what we have just said, that in every generation some of the knowledge acquired by the preceding generations becomes so common that the fathers or the governors of the children inevitably possess it, and this enables them to be their teachers in this respect. Now straightforward teaching of these common notions develops the intelligence of the children and makes it far easier for them to grasp the more abstract knowledge which they receive from their true teachers.

It is among the proletariat, above all, for this class that education is infinitely more important than instruction.

The consequences of this truth being various and many, we shall enlarge upon it.

Let us suppose that a rich Russian boyar took it into his head to teach all his peasants to read and write. A few western Europeans, using the method of mutual teaching, will easily succeed in a few years in satisfying his desires completely, without it costing him very much.

Supposing this has been done, let us compare these Russian peasants, who know how to read and write, with the same number of French proletarians who do not know how to read and write, and let us see which do work that is most useful to society, which are most fit to be admitted by the law into the ranks of the full members of society.

It would undoubtedly be the French, for the French, although illiterate, would have acquired, by means of the education they received from their parents, far greater ability than that which can be produced by the mere ability to read and write; they are able to administer their property; those who work on the land are able to direct labours of this kind; the same is true of those who are engaged in the arts and crafts: while the Russians, who have been taught to read and write, will only have received from their parents an education similar to that which their parents themselves received, that is to say, a very bad education; and if you try to entrust the administration of any property to those Russians who know how to read and write, you will see the property deteriorate in their hands. The farm implements, the tools, the seed or the raw materials will be sold for spirits.

The high degree of civilization attained by the lowest class in France has not yet been sufficiently recognized; the positive improvement in the intelligence of the proletariat has not yet been appreciated at its true value. They have acquired great foresight; they have so mastered their passions and their most natural desires that almost all of them are capable of going hungry, while the seed corn is there.

It is above all in the superior degree of civilization of the most numerous class, in relation to the most numerous classes of other nations, that the French nation surpasses all the others and this superiority is undoubtedly the most positive factor of all.

When one compares the French proletariat to the English proletariat, one finds that the latter are moved by feelings which compel them to seize the first opportunity they can to begin the war of the poor against the rich, while the French proletariat generally show attachment and goodwill towards the rich industrialists.

To sum up what we have said both in this note, and in the chapter to which it is attached, we find:

1. That for the proletarian class, education is infinitely more essential than instruction;

2. That the education of the proletarian class in France is good; that it is better than the education received by the same class in the other European nations;

3. That the general superiority of the French nation over the other peoples lies mainly in the superiority of the French proletariat over the proletariat of other nations, from the point of view of its good disposition and the extent of its knowledge.

And we conclude that to increase the superiority of the French nation, it would be best to extend suitable instruction in the proletarian class, which is very easy by the method of mutual instruction.

The cost of one-tenth of the useless places in the offices of all the branches of administration would be enough to teach all the proletarians in France to read, to write and to count for ten years.

They could also be taught a little drawing, a little music and the use of the fine arts to inspire them with a feeling for the public good.

### THIRD FRAGMENT

*The class of the proletariat being as advanced in fundamental civilization as that of the proprietors, the law should classify them as full members of society*

The machinery of social organization was inevitably very complicated so long as the individuals who made up the majority were in such a state of ignorance and fecklessness that they were unable to manage their own affairs. In this state of underdeveloped intelligence, they were still dominated by brute passions which drove them to insurrections and, consequently, to every kind of disorder.

It was necessary in this state of affairs which inevitably preceded an improved social situation, that the minority should organize itself in a military fashion, that it should give itself exclusive powers of legislation, and that it should lay down the law in a way that would give it total power, in order to keep the majority in a state of dependence, and to hold the nation under repression. Thus, until today, society's principal efforts have been directed towards the maintenance of society itself, and since the object of these endeavours was the improvement of the moral and physical well-being of nations, they could not and should not have been considered as anything other than secondary measures.

Today, this state of affairs can and should change completely, and the object of the most important endeavours should be the improvement of our moral and physical well-being, since little effort is needed to maintain public order, the majority has acquired the taste for work (which precludes any tendency towards disorder) and today is composed of men who have recently proved that they were capable of administering every kind of property.

Since the minority no longer needs to use force to keep the proletarian class in subjection, the plans which it should support are: 1. those by means of which the proletariat will feel that their interests are most strongly attached to the idea of public order; 2. those whose object will be to make the transfer of property as smooth as possible; 3. those whose aim will be to give the highest degree of political consideration to the workers.

These plans are very simple and very easy to find, when we

take the trouble to judge things according to their own lights, and break free completely from the restrictions imposed upon our minds by the political principles accepted by our ancestors —principles which were good and useful in their day, but which no longer apply to existing circumstances.

Since the whole population today is composed of men who (with a few exceptions to be found equally in all classes) are fit to administer every kind of property, one can and one should work directly for the improvement of the moral and physical well-being of the social body.

Now, the most direct way of achieving the moral and physical improvement of the majority of the population lies in classing as priorities of state expenditure: first, the provision of whatever is necessary to provide work for all healthy men in order to guarantee their physical existence; second, expenditure whose objective is to spread positive acquired knowledge as quickly as possible among the proletarian class; and lastly, expenditure which can guarantee to the individuals who make up this class, the pleasures and enjoyments which will expand their intelligence.

To these should be added measures designed to ensure that public wealth is administered by the most gifted administrators, those with the greatest interest in good administration, namely, the most important industrialists.

And society, as a result of these basic arrangements, will be organized in a way which will completely satisfy reasonable men in all classes.[1] Then it will no longer be necessary to fear insurrection, and it will no longer be necessary, either, to support large permanent armies to oppose them; then it will no longer be necessary to spend enormous sums of money on the police; then there will no longer be anything to fear from abroad, since thirty million men who are content with their lot would repel the attack of all who should join in taking up arms against them.

To this we can add that neither princes nor peoples would ever be foolish enough to attack a nation of thirty million men who show no aggressive intention towards their neighbours and who are united among themselves by an excellent scheme based on their interests.

We can add further that there is no need to spy upon a society in which the vast majority is interested in maintaining the existing order of things.

Those who caused the Revolution, those who directed it and all those who, from 1789 until today, have guided the nation,

1. See the note at the end of this fragment.

have committed an enormous political error: they have all tried to improve the action of government when they should have subordinated it and set up administrative action as the supreme activity.

They should have begun by asking a question whose answer is very simple and very easy to find.

They should have asked who, in the present state of manners and enlightenment, are the men most capable of directing the national interests?

They would of necessity have had to recognize that scientists, artists and industrialists are those who possess the highest and broadest abilities, the most positively useful in the light of the present direction of the human mind. They would have had to recognize that the work of scientists, artists and industrialists is that which, from the point of view of invention and of execution, contributes most to the nation's prosperity.

They would have concluded from this that it was to the scientists, artists and the leading industrialists that administrative power should be given, that is to say, the direction of the national interests; and that the functions of government should be reduced to the maintenance of public order.[1]

The reformers of '89 should also have said:

The kings of England set royalty a good example by agreeing that they should not issue any order which had not been approved and countersigned by a minister; it is worthy of the magnanimity of the kings of France to show even more generosity towards their people, and to agree not to hinder any project concerning the general interests of the nation, without the approval of the men most capable of judging these projects, that is, without the approval of the most capable scientists and artists, and of the most important industrialists.

Society has often been compared to a pyramid. We agree that the nation should be arranged in pyramidal form; we are deeply convinced that the national pyramid should be crowned by royalty; but we argue that, starting at the base of the pyramid and going up to the top, each level should be composed of ever more precious materials, and when we look at the existing pyramid, it seems that its base is made of granite, that up to a certain point its levels are composed of very precious materials, but that its upper part, which holds a magnificent diamond, is nothing but gilded plaster.

The base of the national pyramid today is formed by the workers; the first levels raised up on this basis are formed by

1. See note 2 at the end of this fragment.

the heads of the industrial enterprises; the scientists who improve manufacturing processes and extend the sphere of manufacturing; the artists who put the imprint of good taste on all that is produced. The higher levels, which we declare to be made of plaster, which can be spotted quite clearly in spite of the gilt which covers it, consist of the courtiers, the nobility in general, old and new, the idle rich and, finally, those who govern, from the prime minister down to the lowliest clerk. Royalty is the magnificent diamond which crowns the pyramid.

## NOTES ON THE THIRD FRAGMENT

*Note 1*

Men are not so bad as they imagine they are. They judge themselves more harshly than they deserve. It is true that in theory they tend in general towards despotism; but in practice they show a preference for equality.

An Englishman gets a job in India; he takes it up eagerly and in his imagination he sees the despotic power he can wield in it and the pleasures he will thus enjoy; there, he can, if he likes, keep a harem; there, he will be surrounded by hundreds of servants: some will have the job of swatting the flies which might annoy him, while others are always ready to carry him in a litter; the whole population grovels at his feet; he is free to order the whipping of any Indian who has not carried out his wishes quickly or intelligently enough.

And yet, the moment he has made his fortune, this Englishman, who in India wallows in the pleasures of despotic power, is eager to return to England to rediscover the pleasures offered by equality. The moment he arrives at an English port, he is rudely jostled by the common men and yet this does not inspire him with any desire to return to the country in which everyone drew back to make way for him.

Very rich Russians leave their country to come to live in western Europe, while western Europeans only go to Russia to make their fortunes and are eager to return home with the riches they have acquired there.

There are powerful reasons why the rich prefer to live in countries in which equality between members of that society is carried to its furthest extent, because at the same time there are countries in which the rich can most easily and completely satisfy their every wish.

In French cities of any size, a man with money can, whenever he wishes and without having made any previous provision, eat well at a moderate price; in Russia it is only in the houses of the great lords that a luxurious table can be found.

A carriage breaks down somewhere in England; the traveller can choose between having it mended or procuring a carriage as good as his own on the spot: while in Russia a traveller whose carriage breaks down on one of the roads between the largest cities has no other recourse than to climb into a peasant's cart in order to finish his journey.

Thus, in fact, the richest and most powerful men have an interest in the spread of equality, since the means to satisfy their desires increase in the same proportion as the levelling of individuals making up that society.

One imagines that those who profit from abuses set great store by them: but this is not so; what they set most store by is that they should not be deprived by the advantages which they enjoy falling into the hands of others.

It was the nobility in France who brought about the suppression of the privileges which they had enjoyed, and they only regretted this sacrifice when they saw all the former commoners acting towards them as though they were now the privileged, and when they saw that a new nobility had been created to which they, the former nobility, were not admitted except as inferiors.

In finishing this note, we shall say what should perhaps have been said in the beginning, namely that by improving the lot of the masses, the well-being of men of all classes will be assured, and that in order to improve the lot of the masses it is not enough simply to oust the privileged; they must be destroyed; it is not enough that corruption should merely change hands; it must be abolished.

*Note 2*

We are about to show, in a few words, the many drawbacks which the superimposition of governmental action upon that of the administration entails today, when the mass of the nation is made up of men who no longer need to be under special supervision, because they have shown that they are capable of administering property of every kind; today, when the proletariat can pose no threat to public order, except when those who administer the national interests are so completely inept and selfish as to leave them without work.

It is very easy to convince oneself, and others, that one has the ability to govern, because the ability or inability to govern can only be proved by experience, and everyone can imagine and make others believe that he could govern well, as long as he has not actually done so.

The same is not true of mathematics, physics, chemistry, physiology, mechanical engineering, poetry, painting, sculpture, music, architecture, farming, manufacturing, trade and banking.

It is easy for any man to calculate for himself whether he possesses great gifts in the sciences or in the fine arts; it is easy for him to convince himself that he has obtained a position of great importance in one of the branches of industry; besides, mistakes of this kind are not very likely, since his neighbours would soon open the eyes of anyone who was blinded by conceit.

It follows from what we have just said that ambition in scientists, artists and industrialists to become members of the high administration of the national interests is not dangerous for society, and can even be useful, since they can only achieve such a position by worth-while work; but when ambition tries to obtain a place in the government, it results in great disadvantages for society, since the most incompetent men can cherish this passion, and in order to satisfy it, may labour to overturn the whole social edifice.

One of the most important results of this ambition, which seized almost all Frenchmen when the government of the unfortunate Louis XVI was overthrown, is very curious. The nation precipitated a revolution because it wanted less government and cheaper government, and yet today it has only succeeded in producing more government, and more expensive government than ever existed before the Revolution.

The industrialists produce far more than they did before the Revolution, but a great part of the increase in production is used to pay for useless military staffs and droves of clerks who spend most of their time reading the newspaper and mending their pens, which is not very satisfactory either for the needs or self-respect of the producers.

## FOURTH FRAGMENT

### *On the administration and the government of public affairs*

It could be said to us:

'Your most important opinion on politics, the one to which all your ideas relate, is that the best way to establish a tranquil and stable state of affairs in Europe is to superimpose the administrative power upon the governmental power; hence your first concern would be to draw a definite line of demarcation between administrative ability and governmental ability; you should say very positively in what each consists. By means of this explanation, you will be able to show clearly why the administrative ability should be superimposed upon the governmental ability.'

The high administration of society encompasses the invention, examination and execution of projects which are useful to the mass of mankind.

High administration, therefore, involves three abilities; that of the artists, that of the scientists and that of the industrialists, and the combination of all three fulfils all the necessary conditions satisfying the moral and physical needs of society.

When work has been begun which is specifically designed to establish a system of public good, the artists, the men of imagination, will lead the way in that great undertaking; they will proclaim the future of mankind; they will bring back the golden age from the past to enrich future generations; they will inspire society with enthusiasm for the increase of its well-being by laying before it a tempting picture of a new prosperity, by making it feel that all members of society will soon share in enjoyments which, up to now, have been the prerogative of a very small class; they will hymn the benefits of civilization and they will employ all the resources of the fine arts, eloquence, poetry, painting, music, to attain their goal; in short, they will develop the poetic aspects of the new system.

Scientists, men whose main occupation it is to observe and to reason, will demonstrate that a great increase in the well-being of all classes of society is possible—for the class which works hardest, the proletariat, as well as for those who have great wealth. They will put forward the surest, quickest means to ensure continuity in the work of the mass of producers; they will lay the foundations of public instruction; they will establish the hygienic laws of the social body and, in their hands, the science of politics will become complementary to the science of man.

The most important industrialists, relating all these ideas to production will decide which projects of public utility, conceived and expounded by the scientists and the artists together, are immediately practicable; they will devise the means of carrying them out and will entrust their direction to bankers, who are always at the head of financial affairs.

This is the course administration will take, firm, open and loyal; the one which scholars, artists and industrialists will follow, once the direction of the general interests has been entrusted to them.

Let us compare this course of action with that followed by the present government; let us see to what miserable devices governmental capacity has been reduced by the progress of enlightenment and of civilization.

Enclosed within the circle of the outdated doctrines of the feudal system, the rulers who, in general, have the best intentions towards the public good, try in vain to establish a calm and stable state of affairs.

Believing that they can only maintain their power by keeping a large staff in all the branches of the administration, as well as a great apparatus of governmental power, they are reduced, in the end, to extracting as much money as possible from the nation, either through taxes or loans, without arousing open discontent. They thus exhaust themselves in over-subtle schemes for the imposition and collection of taxes.

They are reduced to devoting the largest amount of the nation's money to the costs of administration, which are for the most part useless to society, and a very small portion to expenditure which is really useful to the producers.

They are reduced to preserving the great political importance of the nobility and courtiers and using all their ingenuity to obtain the money these people need to support themselves in a luxury which is thought to be indispensable.

Let us look at the conduct of the minister-president who, nevertheless, is the man who has best understood the importance of industry and the state of the society; let us examine the use he has made of the government's power.

We have seen him use all the government's influence, which he has in his power, to introduce a great many nobles and idle rich to the Chamber of Deputies, and has kept out, with the greatest care, the most successful industrialists, the most competent scholars and artists.

He has introduced a septennial parliament, without changing the rule which laid down that a man must be forty years old to be admitted to the Chamber; he has thus considerably sapped its energies, made it dependent upon the government, and at the same time subjected it to the influence of the high nobility.

He has concentrated the supreme direction of the national interests in the hands of the nobles, the bishops, the military, the jurists and the *administrators*, all of whom, no doubt, are very honourable as regards their private characters or because of the services which they or their ancestors have rendered to the nation, but who, nevertheless, have learnt administration at the expense of the public—who have always paid for their mistakes—and never at their own expense, as the industrialists do every day.

He keeps, at the ministry of the interior, out of respect for ministerial dignity, a distinguished lawyer, who is supremely ignorant about anything concerning industry, the sciences and the fine arts; who, unaware both of their importance and of the respect due to them, forgets himself to the extent that he allows his clerks to illtreat the men whose work has brought most honour to France.

The same minister-president also believes, through deference to the old doctrines, that the Jesuits should be allowed a great influence on public education—the Jesuits whose ultimate aim is to inculcate in youth the idea that mediocre abilities should take precedence over and direct abilities of the first order, and that vague knowledge should be placed above positive and useful knowledge.

Lastly, wishing to protect industry, M. de Villèle has set up a supreme council for trade; but he has staffed it mainly with men who have never been engaged in any branch of industry, and it is apparently out of humane deference that he has been kind enough to admit two or three retired industrialists.

These are the mournful remains of governmental capacity; dragged along by the torrent of civilization, it tries vainly, by holding on to the past, to continue to play the dominant role which social custom allowed to it in the past.

Let us now compare the fundamental links which exist between the administrators and the administered, with those which exist between the rulers and the ruled.

The basic principle of administrative management is that the interests of the administered should be directed in such a way as to allow the society's capital to prosper as much as possible and to win the approval and support of the majority of members of the society.

In order to be supported by the majority, that is in order to form a majority which approves of their administration, administrators can use only persuasion and the demonstration of the fact that their actions are the most beneficial possible for the society.

The administrators know that economy in the costs of administration is always desired by the members of the society and consequently they work constantly to diminish these costs.

For example, the costs of administration of a bank are very

low; its governing board costs nothing; the expenses of the royal exchequer are enormous.

The relations between the rulers and the ruled are of quite a different nature; the nobles say, and they can do so in all good faith, that they were born to rule and that the plebeians were destined by providence to obey.

The first need of society in the eyes of the nobles is that the nobility should shine with all the brilliance that luxury and power can give it; it seems to them that royalty should make common cause with the nobility. They recognize the king's right to entrust the direction of public affairs to whomsoever he wishes, but in their heart of hearts and their consciences they are convinced that it is his duty to entrust it only to the nobility.

The art of government consists, in their eyes, in the ability to preserve the preponderance of government actions over administrative activity: it consists in prolonging the existence of the feudal and ecclesiastical régime, although its main arteries have been cut, although criticism and the advance of enlightenment have completely destroyed its basic principles.

In short, the rulers believe that the best way to maintain the subjection of the ruled lies in increasing the number of public officials and in conferring dignity of office on the most important of them, in other words, giving them a great deal of money; physical force and trickery, the paid army and the police are the main means they employ to carry out their operations; to them, persuasion and demonstration are only secondary means; while they are the only means employed by the administrators.

When the king will be pleased to entrust the high administration of public affairs to an industrial administration, the costs will at once be enormously reduced, for the scientists and artists who have proved by their own efforts that they have ability of the highest order, will have no need to spend on appearances and make a great show in order to gain esteem for themselves. As for the important industrialists, they will think it a great honour to receive no salary for the care which they take of the administration of the nation's wealth.

The four demonstrations which follow appear to us to provide the most solid foundations for our opinion that in present circumstances administrative action can, without any major drawback and with very great advantages, be superimposed upon governmental action. We shall therefore prove first that the mass of the nation is sufficiently enlightened and civilized, that is possesses a profound enough knowledge of its true interests to remain at peace under the direction of a good administration and to oppose all the attempts of ambitious men to disturb the public order.

Next, that the artists, scientists and the industrialists have acquired ability on a broad enough base to enable them to deal with all the questions relating to the public interest and to direct the general interests of society properly.

After that, we must prove that many people are sufficiently accustomed to seeing their interests directed by the administrative powers, for them not to be astonished when they see the administrative mode introduced into the direction of the general interests of society.

Lastly, we must prove that the superimposition of administrative action upon governmental action will not harm France's relations with foreign powers, since this superimposition will assure her of allies with the help of whom she will be stronger than the whole of feudal Europe.

We shall deal separately with each of these questions:

1. We have proved, in a previous chapter, that the French proletarians have shown in concrete ways that they were civilized enough and that their ability to look ahead was developed enough for them to be fit to administer every kind of property. Now it is clear that men who can take charge of property are capable of behaving well under a good administration.

A great many artists, scientists and industrialists concern themselves today with questions of general interest; since the beginning of the Revolution, they have all made a profound study of these questions, and these studies have given them the ability to set up a good administration for public affairs.

The question of public education has been discussed and clarified by many writers and several scholars.

All the questions relating to the economies which could be made in the public expenditure have been examined by industrialists whose great ability for financial administration has been proved by the successful way in which they have conducted their own businesses.

2. The establishment of the Bank of France, insurance companies, savings banks, companies for building canals, and the formation of a host of other associations concerned with the management of very important affairs, have accustomed the French to the administrative method of managing great interests; hence this method can be applied to the administration of general interests without this innovation in the highest

administration of public affairs causing astonishment or surprise, or upsetting the habits already acquired by the present generation.

3. The Revolution, whose great moral effects are beginning to develop, stimulated the French politically; thus, we should not be astonished if today they are superior to the English in organic ideas. But it is equally true that the English who preceded the French in this intellectual field, who were, in a way, the creators of this branch of our knowledge and who until now have surpassed all the other peoples in political skill, will quickly imitate the French and adopt the system in which administrative action will be superimposed upon governmental action; by the very nature of the new system, a frank and indissoluble alliance between the two most industrialized peoples in the world will follow; and it is well-known that the union of France and England will constitute the greatest social force in the civilized world.

# XII
# The Class of the Proletarians

*La Classe des Prolétaires (brouillon inachevé de la main de* SAINT-SIMON), VI, pp. 455–7.

The men who compose this class feel that their lot has not improved to the extent which should result naturally from the advance made by positive ideas; they are only conscious of their rights, it is true, in a vague way; if they are questioned, they are not able to explain clearly how the evils of their situation can be lessened, but they certainly have a very positive awareness that parliament could make their physical and political condition infinitely happier than it has been hitherto.

They are discontented on two very distinct counts; they feel the direct discontent, which we have just mentioned and they feel another which is indirect and which we shall now describe.

There is a feeling of unity, of companionship, if you will, which binds together all the members of the industrial class, so that the lowliest workers in the factories of Messrs. Perrin, Ternaux or Gros d'Avilliers see themselves as the colleagues of their chiefs, just as the soldiers in the armies of Turenne and Condé called themselves the brothers-in-arms of their generals. But the condition of the leaders of the industrial class is now much improved; they have acquired more prestige than they enjoyed before the Revolution. Their property, that is, their personal property, has been in a way ennobled by the electoral law and their colleagues in the industrial class who have not yet acquired anything, are inevitably vexed when they see their leaders becoming counts or barons and thus passing into the feudal class. Before the Revolution, the manual workers, who form the mass of the industrial class, had some support because they made common cause with the bankers, merchants and manufacturers. Today, when they see themselves abandoned by all the powerful elements in their class, they are inevitably angry with the present political scene.

To sum up, we say that the workers are angry on several counts and in particular, at this moment, over a matter of the greatest urgency: because they have no work and are dying of hunger.

What means can be found to calm the anger of the workers,

who make up the mass of the French people? How can their just claims be satisfied? The answer is to take steps to ensure that they have employment; such a measure demands first of all a considerable sinking fund and the only way to procure the money needed for this is to cut other expenditure. Above all, the heaviest expense must be cut: and the upkeep of the army is undeniably the greatest expense. The disbanding of the army is then, the first measure to take to appease the people, to make them happy and to avoid being exposed to the effects of their discontent.[1]

It is by the use of force that the proletarians have been contained until now, and prevented from disrupting the social order. Half the money which this use of force has required would be enough to secure their devotion to the government. As for the renewal of the domestic troubles caused by the political ones, we have seen how easily the government dealt with them. Work to make the French people happier and you will be working in the way most likely to ensure their continued peace.

1. The entire amount of money spent by the ministry of war is utterly lost to the nation, while that used to provide work for the impoverished class would augment the national income, if the choice of work were made intelligently and, above all, if it were known how to direct this work so that it could be supervised by those who have a personal interest in it.

# Index